ARCHWAYS
TO THE
INFINITE

PETER MURNANE

ARCHWAYS TO THE INFINITE

My journey towards
the transcendent

Published in Australia by
Garratt Publishing
32 Glenvale Crescent
Mulgrave, VIC 3170
www.garrattpublishing.com.au

Copyright in this work remains the property of the contributing authors.

Copyright © 2018 Peter Murnane

All rights reserved. Except as provided by the Australian copyright law, no part of this book may be reproduced in any way without permission in writing from the publisher.

Design and author photo by Lynne Muir
Cover image © Jennifer Valmadre, *Embarking #5* 2004, encaustic and mixed media on board 900x900mm
Typesetting by Mike Kuszla
Edited by Greg Hill

Printed by Tingleman Printers

Scripture quotations are drawn from the New Revised Standard Version of the Bible, copyright © 1989 by the Division of Christian Education of the National Council of the Churches of Christ in the USA.
Used by permission.
All rights reserved.

ISBN 9781925009477

 A catalogue record for this book is available from the National Library of Australia

Cataloguing in Publication information for this title is available from the National Library of Australia.
www.nla.gov.au

The authors and publisher gratefully acknowledge the permission granted to reproduce the copyright material in this book. Every effort has been made to trace copyright holders and to obtain their permission for the use of copyright material.

The publisher apologises for any errors or omissions in the above list and would be grateful if notified of any corrections that should be incorporated in future reprints or editions of this book.

'There is another world,' Yeats claims, 'but it is within this one.' This personal and luminously honest account of the over fifty-year-long journey of a Dominican priest looks beyond the curtain of our stories searching for the evidence of that hidden world.

Peter Murnan's search takes us to the writings of Joseph Campbell and Carl Jung, the social activism of Dorothy Day among Manhattan's homeless and of his colleagues' antiwar protests in New Zealand – even to his love of hitchhiking and as he cycles 2000 kms to the centre of Australia.

—Monsignor Tony Doherty

This delightful, wise book is not just another memoir but a pilgrimage searching for the sacred. It traces both a personal and universal journey from birth to death. This journey demands courage to be and freedom to let go.

On the way it presents both the pain of violence and the healing power of love. The trail moves through myth and metaphor, synchronicity and intuition in its search for truth. It identifies the totally interconnected nature of matter and spirit. Love is the motive force and unifying principle of life.

'The wonder is that we do not have to find Infinity. With ultimate care for all that it has made, it will find us.'

—Dr Anna Holmes, author and medical practitioner

Much like Augustine's Confessions, Murnane's fascinating memoir is a blend of gripping autobiography and theology. His life is recounted in searing honesty and fascinating epithets, never ceasing to hold interest. But it is also the raw material for his reflections on the depths of human existence, and never remote. A scintillating and engaging read from cover to cover.

—Dr Mike Riddell, New Zealand writer and film-maker

CONTENTS

Acknowledgements ix

Introduction xi

1. Rondo Alla Turca
First glimpse through the archway 1

2. The Fourth Wall
The Proscenium Arch, origins and analogies 6

3. Strange Connections
The mystery of synchronicity 20

4. 'Deep down things'
Seeing within the everyday 32

5. Doorway into the Daylight
Birth and rebirth 48

6. Dabchicks and Lunatics
Childers Cove and Bundoora 58

7. Golden Square and Gravel Hill
Bendigo, Mepunga East, and Naringal 67

8. 'Just Like the Animals'
Discovering sex 83

9. The Many Halves of My Divided World
Beyond dualism 98

10. The Gates of Hell
The promise of apokatastasis 118

11. 'Now is the Time'
The treasure of the present moment 135

12. 'I Am Not What I Am'
Deceivers and hypocrites 150

13. You Are Not Like Us
Opening towards others 164

14. The Narrow Gate
Journey into darkness 176

15. The Emptiness of the Roadside Beggar
A hitchhiker's guide 185

16. Fruitful Exile
Hunger for justice 197

17. Pilgrimage of Reconciliation
Bike ride to Uluru 209

18. Resisting Empire
When we need to break the law 226

19. Beyond the Last Archway
The doorway of death 239

20. Doorway to The Infinite
The ultimate mystery 256

Bibliography 283

Endnotes 289

ACKNOWLEDGEMENTS

I gratefully thank Anthony Fenelon, who in 1954 unwittingly laid the foundation for this book by playing the piano in the Malvern Town Hall.

Along the way, countless people have helped me to gain insights on our common journey towards the unknown goal. First come my parents, my brothers GERALD AND DENIS (DECEASED) and sister KAYE and a few of my teachers… To the rest with whom I have travelled, impossible even to remember, I offer my thanks en masse, while singling out the many Dominican friars who have accepted me into communities, with all their gifts and challenges, over nearly 60 years.

I can name and thank those particular optimists who for long have urged me to keep writing: notably my Dominican sisters Mary Anna Baird and Liz Mackie, and my friend Jim Nolan, generous hermit of Tenaru in the Solomon Islands.

Thanks also to those who allowed me to use material previously published: to Yvonne Ashkar Matta, for her story from No Stone Unturned: a Lebanese-Australian Family Memoir; to the magazine Tui Motu, Dunedin, for letting me use parts of my article Reality Wedding, Issue no. 102 February 2007 pp. 17-18.

Not least, at Garratt Publishing, I thank Garry Eastman for his encouragement; Publishing Director Karen Tayleur; Structural Editor Catherine Oliver, Editor Greg Hill, and proof-reader Juliette Hughes-Norwood for patiently suggesting improvements and escorting me through the sometimes arduous process of preparing the manuscript for publication.

INTRODUCTION

This book explores an ancient question: is there a world that transcends our senses? If there is such a realm, other questions follow: how separate is it from the material world? Is it neutral, detached, uninterested? Or is it aware of us: can we communicate with it?

These questions emerge from the wonders we find when we look closely at anything from starfish to stars; from vast galaxies to tiny viruses. Our thinkers are proud to have explained – but only partly – phenomena that were once total mysteries: eclipses, lightning, earthquakes, electro-magnetism and even some of the workings of our own body and brain. Other phenomena are still beyond our understanding: gravity; life itself; consciousness; the forces inside the atom, and how sub-atomic particles, hundreds of kilometres apart, can instantaneously affect each other.

Is it even valid to speak of the 'material' world? Contemporary physics reveals that what looks like solid matter is not what it seems. At the deepest levels its most elementary particles – photons, quarks and electrons – sometimes act as if they are waves of energy. When this seeming-solid matter is torn apart in nuclear fission, or squeezed together in fusion as happens continuously in the stars, enormous power is released: matter and light-energy are somehow interchangeable. Beneath all the details, the whole astonishing universe cries out for an explanation as to *why* it is here at all.

This is a personal journey, not a philosophical treatise. I don't try to argue with the likes of Jacques Monod, Richard Dawkins, Christopher Hitchens or Stephen Hawking, but simply follow my own journey through more than seventy-five years, exploring hints of the Transcendent, recalling moments when doorways opened into deeper levels of reality. The first doorway was a theatrical proscenium arch. At age fourteen, when I sat through a dull speech-night in an uninteresting town hall it was through such a structure that I first glimpsed and entered dimensions promising transcendence.

There are many occasions in everyone's life when we gaze through a proscenium arch or pass through a doorway into deeper reality: every story told or drama enacted; the metaphors we use each day; our poetic or mystical experiences. Further depths open up when we are surprised by incidents of synchronicity, or extra-sensory perception (ESP); pass through a *Near-Death Experience*; or, much more commonly, fall in love. Less obvious are the doorways to be found in things that we find most threatening: our mistakes and momentous failures; other people's deceit; trauma and emptiness; but all these too can be archways that bring deeper understanding beyond the world of our senses.

Among all these experiences, the lesser archways simply bring new insights which often lead to further openings, but the greater ones are like the revolutionary discoveries of Copernicus or Einstein, turning our world inside-out as they take us through to entirely new realms. Exploring these many entrances, we discover that the world is not what it seems: that our senses are not limits, but only a horizon.

Because we seem to be separate and independent from each other, we are inclined to assume that the Transcendent dimension – whatever it may be – is also apart and beyond our reach. But when we look closer at the material world we see that our bodies themselves are profoundly inter-penetrated by the breaths we share and the minerals, plants and animals we eat, digest and then recycle. Merely to exist we depend not only on countless humans who sustain our lives, but on billions of bacteria living inside us and around us. The mind or spirit that our body houses is not confined within our skin but reaches through space and time. If we are so closely interlinked with each other, could we also be connected within a reality that transcends our senses?

INTRODUCTION

When we are learning about our world we tend to classify things with their opposites: darkness/light, big/small, healthy/sick, good/bad, friends/enemies; but by taking a step back we can see that each of these opposite pairs is contained within a broader category that includes them both. Could this also be true of matter and spirit, and even the worlds of the living and the dead? The archways recalled here from one ordinary lifetime seem to open towards a singular reality beyond all categories and boundaries. They leave us wondering, or hoping: is there an unfathomable, infinite reality which, incredibly, we are invited to enter?

Peter Murnane

1
Rondo Alla Turca
First glimpse through the archway

On an evening in early summer, towards the end of my fourteenth year, my family set out for a suburban town hall about eleven kilometres from our home. It was rare that we went out together as a family but tonight the town hall was the venue for the end-of-year *Speech Night* of the college that my brothers and I attended.

Our journey was by bus to the train on which we would travel for six stations, and then by tram to the Malvern town hall. As we waited awkwardly at the bus stop at the corner of our street, I imagined that I could see from high above the south-eastern suburbs of Melbourne, the families of the hundreds of boys in our school setting out from their homes and gradually converging on the same building. If they could each carry some kind of special light, I could watch those lights converge on the town hall, slowly forming a solid mass of brightness. My imagining was oddly prophetic. Fifty years later, as I recall that night, almost every person carries a cell phone by which they *can* be tracked to within centimetres of their position on Earth by the watching eyes of spy satellites that feed into giant 'security' networks.

I did not see our school as a place of radiance, or a shining example of community. My life there was generally lonely, often boring and sometimes painful. But on that night, the first Speech Night we had attended, I was to find a door that gave me access to an unexpected and entirely new dimension.

Among the hundreds of families following their converging paths, we passed through the doors of the town hall. With all the other pupils I was directed to the upper gallery. We talked excitedly, less concerned than usual about the stern gaze of the brothers who were our teachers, stationed at strategic positions to supervise us. Some boys called out or waved to friends; others tried to locate their parents and siblings in the main auditorium below.

I was excited by the buzz of hundreds of voices talking at once, but I scarcely knew what to expect of the evening. My childish understanding was bemused by the way life flowed in a big institution and I was content to wait for commands and then follow all the others in obeying.

Like any large auditorium the hall was filled with row after row of seats facing the empty stage, over which towered a huge arch painted with faded gold trim. It was not round like a rainbow, but had a flattened top between its curved corners. A short distance behind the arch was a giant picture of a landscape painted on canvas that was just a little cracked and shabby. It tried to make us believe that through the arch there was a stone-paved terrace with a stone railing supported on low pillars like fat bottles, in a style I had heard called 'classical'. Beyond the painted terrace was a painted landscape, sunlit and fading into a bluish haze of distant hills. On the real stage the only object was a shiny black grand piano, which seemed to have been left there by accident.

The night began with uninteresting speeches, then gymnastic displays by young boys in white shorts and singlets vaulting over a padded wooden box called a horse. Then the bigger, more muscular boys rubbed resin on their hands and dared to swing high on horizontal bars fixed to the stage with wire stays. Choirs of boys then sang songs that had been popular long before they were born, and recited poems whose words were difficult to distinguish amid the dozens of voices trying to speak in unison. It was then that I experienced something that had never happened to me before.

A familiar name was announced, and a small boy walked alone onto the empty stage. I knew him as an uninteresting lad from the class below my own. He wore short trousers and the familiar school blazer, which I had always considered garish with its gold pyjama-stripes on royal blue. Walking across the wide stage, he sat down at the grand piano and without delay began to make it pour out beautiful sounds.

My mind was still wrestling to make sense of the title that had just been announced for the piece: *Rondo alla turca*,[1] but I was forced to put that aside for later consideration, for from the piano's open lid such sounds were coming that I had never imagined possible. While his small hands flew back and forth on the keyboard and the piano was filling the hall with beautiful patterns of sound that astonished me more and more, my eyes wandered to the canvas back-drop that towered above him. As I gazed into it, the sunlight seemed to have taken on a stronger brightness and the dull terrace had become interesting and inviting. I next felt myself *within* the sunny green landscape, travelling by canoe up the blue river that curved into the misty distance. In the next instant, as happens in dreams, I was walking towards the buildings at the foot of the hills, knowing that there were people there whom it would be wonderful to meet.

The waves of delightful sound continued to roll over me, and I became an adult, alone and free in a distant, sunny land. At fourteen I had no idea of what an adult might do, but I was now allowed to do whatever it was. In school I was often rebuked for my childish behaviour or punished for breaking some rule I had never been told about. In my first weeks at the school, when I was not yet twelve years old, the Brother-Principal had caught me and a companion running in an area we did not know was out-of-bounds. The next day, before the whole school assembly, he punished us with six cuts of a stiff leather strap on our stinging hands. Four cuts was the routine punishment for talking in class or failing to complete our homework.

Here, I forgot all that. In this land within the music it did not matter that my family struggled for lack of money; that my parents, having both left school when they were fourteen, did not understand the new subjects I was learning: Latin, French, Algebra, Geometry; or that our home was so far from the school that my few friends hardly ever came to visit.

Everyone was clapping. The music had stopped, and I was suddenly back in my seat looking down on the distant stage where beneath that huge arch the small boy was bowing in front of the piano. I glanced carefully around me, wondering whether anyone else among all these people had also just come back from travelling deep into the green landscape through the arch.

For a long time I wondered how that music could have moved me so deeply when nothing had touched me physically. Its invisible force did far more to me than anything else that night or during the whole previous year. The Speech Night came to an end after a man in a suit had made a dull speech and the Brother who was School Principal had given out prizes. One by one a long line of boys crossed the stage to receive a book for being best in their class or subject, or a silver cup for winning in some sport. I went up to receive my book, but the prize was not nearly as important to me as what I had already discovered that evening and would never forget. After that, the crowds of schoolboys and their families flooded from the hall, and as we climbed into the tram to begin our long journey homewards I was just as uncomfortable as ever that my classmates might see me with the rest of my family. But now I carried a new secret: I had passed through that strange archway into a new land, deeper and richer than the ordinary world around me.

Little Anthony Fenelon playing Mozart, and a tatty painted backdrop, had let me pass through the veil that conceals more of Reality than we can normally cope with. Without understanding what was happening, I entered into a world transcending my familiar senses; a doorway to the infinite. The experience startled me and left me puzzling what to do about it. As family life went on around me I began to wonder whether life through the archway or on this side was more real.

On our way to the speech night I had imagined the families gathering to a focus at the town hall and then afterwards dispersing. My childhood up to that time, like a hidden root-system nourishing a plant-stem, had brought me to a readiness for some new experience. From that night's point of convergence, my mind began to stretch wider and higher, spreading towards the light.

My experience was not unique or even unusual. It is a common way for romantic adolescents to find and enter more deeply into reality. We seem to have a readiness, some innate power or curiosity to find and pass through such archways on a wide range of occasions. While some persons seem more ready than others to do this, perhaps we are all to some degree afraid or unwilling to step through these entrances that lead ... who knows where? We soon learn that they are not always beneficial; that some lead us into difficulty and pain. They scare us ... *humankind cannot bear very much reality.*[2]

Through the millennia of the human journey, many people have tried to describe finding these openings, which seem to hint that we are made for something beyond the present. Some have wondered if there is even some ultimate proscenium arch beyond all our imagining, through which we might pass, if we only had the courage. Perhaps our ancient habit of myth-making and storytelling grew out of memories of the hints of such things. Is death such a doorway, through which we pass to find the meaning of our lives unveiled; or is it simply the fall of the curtain? What *was* the shadowy hint I had received from 'Mozart's rondo' and my trip into the landscape though the arch?

The proscenium arch is far more than an ornamental plaster-stucco frame for the theatre stage. It marks the entrance to the worlds created by every storyteller, playwright and artist; the place of awe, leading to make-believe. The following chapters will explore some aspects of journeys to which the proscenium arch can lead us.

2
The Fourth Wall
The Proscenium Arch, origins and analogies

Somewhere in ancient Greece, in the early days of theatre, the manager of a certain *theatron* decided to improve things by putting up a tent behind the open area where the actors performed. It would provide a convenient place where the actors could prepare, out of sight, before they emerged onto the stage. It would give more dramatic impact to the performances and might even increase ticket sales. It was the kind of idea that other theatres would soon copy. This tent behind the stage – called a *skene* – evolved into a permanent structure, a slender building of three storeys, providing a backdrop on which to hang 'scenery'. It developed windows and balconies as additional places for the actors to perform. The stage in front of it evolved into a narrow, raised platform where most of the performance took place. It came to be called the *proskenion*.

The acting space itself was still in full view of the audience, and remained so into the Roman era, but after medieval times theatre stages became deeper and were framed as if in a great doorway. What we now call the proscenium arch can be seen in a 1560 engraving of a performance in Siena, and the oldest surviving arch is in Parma's *Teatro Farnese*, built in 1615. Both of these are rectangular, but later prosceniuims would be given a more rounded shape, nearer to a true arch.

If our familiar proscenium arch was not present in the most ancient places of drama, or has disappeared from post-modern theatres which might have a projecting 'thrust' stage or no stage at all, this does not remove the unseen 'fourth wall' that separates the actors from the spectators. The story itself is another threshold separating the 'real world' of the audience from the 'imaginary world' of the stage.

Those who have stories to tell have often used theatrical effects to enhance them. Long before the development of the proscenium arch, eons before ancient Greek engineers were building theatres to seat thousands on a semi-circular slope so that everyone had a good view of the stage and could hear the actors' words, the Australian Aborigines were marking out bora rings for their corroborees in which they could tell and dance their stories.

Whether in the open air or in elaborate theatres, the storyteller or script writer takes care to delineate the other time and place to which they are taking us. All they need do is to intone 'Once upon a time …' and we set aside the present moment and willingly enter their world of fable. Homer may have begun the Iliad or Odyssey with a more solemn opening, but no matter how we are invited to pass through the barrier that the proscenium represents, when we do so we enter realms beyond the everyday world. It is not necessary to build an archway, or even to have a stage, for listeners to understand that the storyteller's words are offering a reality different from the present place and time.

The proscenium spans the stage of a theatre, but it also exists in many other times and places as an invisible doorway that frames our entry into the realm of story. We constantly create images 'in our head', using our remarkable power to make internal pictures of things gleaned from our senses or created by recombining fragments from them. We seem to summon up such pictures before every action: before climbing a ladder to put a box on a crowded shelf, we *imagine* the box against the space available among the other objects. When playing tennis or golf, before we hit the ball we *picture* the spot where we want it to land, and try subtly to adjust the force and direction of our muscles' effort. In all of life's processes, we appear to predict, to *imagine* what the next instant may bring.

When going on a journey, before starting out we summon up some image of where we are going and why; a name on a map; an image of a street or house; a person we want to see; and then begin to picture what we need to do to make our journey successful. In speaking, writing or playing music we also seem, however infinitesimally, to 'sound out' the sentence we want to speak or write, or the notes we are about to play. For the beginner learning to read or play music this trial-and-error is painfully obvious, but for the practised speaker or musician the interval between image and action has become so small that it is no longer noticed and may have disappeared altogether. When we learn how to combine these pictures-in-our-head of that which does not yet exist, stories are born. When we attempt to share with others our combinations of pictures, we create proscenium archways into these other, unreal worlds, which let us share with others the realms which we have devised.

This power of ours to create images of what is not there must surely be as innate as sight and speech, for even very young children can distinguish 'make believe' from real, just as kittens do when they carefully hold back their claws in play. It is a source of wonder how a child learns so early to comprehend the pictures that others present to it; to step across the threshold of story and recognise different levels of 'really true'. Even before it is two years old, a child will create little play-stories with its dolls, putting them through situations from its own life: feeding them with a spoon, toilet-training them, pretending to be their parent. This is not mere mimicry. The child-playwright is quite capable of innovating, creating novel interactions, even inventing for their little drama new characters who might be invisible to an onlooker. Children enjoy such make-believe games and know – by what instinct? – the difference between a parent pretending to be a monster and the parent who *is* a monster. To the first they react with squeals of delight, but if threatened by the other they will scream in terror.

Our desire to leave the here-and-now by stepping through a proscenium seems to be intrinsic and insatiable. Not only do we create stories in many kinds of medium; we sometimes take delight in mocking those stories in spoofs or send-ups, thereby constructing a second proscenium beyond the original arch so that the new author and audience can laugh at finding in the original new levels of meaning – or the non-meaning of absurdity.

Merely changing place can take us through a kind of proscenium, into a different story. When in teenage years I first put on a glass facemask and slipped beneath the clear summer waters of Melbourne's Port Philip Bay, it was as if I had travelled to another planet. In those days before colour television or spectacular nature documentaries, I had never seen the underwater world in film or photograph. I was awed that the sea's surface was a rippling mirror overhead and that breaking waves could be viewed from the inside, in confusing three-dimensional negative. Linked to the surface by a snorkel, among fluid-moving kelp I became an unnoticed neighbour to fish, squid, stingrays and even small sharks.

Half a lifetime later, one night after sunset I sat in a crowded mud-brick hut at a village celebration in northern Pakistan. The large room was packed with local people, materially very poor. I was one of a few Europeans whom they had welcomed into their midst. A large part of the evening was taken up by a storyteller, such as could once be found in every culture before mass media began to delete them from society. He played a portable harmonium and kept the people spellbound with stories which he chanted in Urdu, of which I understood not two words. I was told that some were myths from long ago and some were stories about local events as recent as a visit from the Seventh Day Adventist missionaries, which the listeners evidently found quite amusing. I felt privileged to be there, witnessing an ancient and universal ritual, the re-telling of past events so that people could share them again, even for the hundredth time.

The stories we wish to tell others may be re-worked effigies of things we have seen and wish to convey to others, or constructed entirely from our own imagination. Whichever they are, our storytelling is doomed to remain confined in our own mental world unless we have found an adequate medium, a set of symbols to represent effectively the ideas we have conceived.

One hot summer evening, with a storm pending, our living room was full of adults gathered for some serious occasion. Suddenly my little brother rushed into the room, bursting with excitement. At that time he was perhaps four years old, and our parents were already concerned that he was slow in learning speech and other skills because at birth he had suffered some damage to his head. When his noisy entrance had startled the adults into attention, he took a stand and bravely blurted out his news: 'There's stuff in the sky doing this ...!' At which point his childish vocabulary failed him and he had to resort to sign language, but in such a way that the impact he made was recounted in family legend for years afterwards.

He stood before the hushed adults, squeezing his eyes shut as tight as he could, then opening them widely again in succession as rapidly as he could manage. Each time he opened his eyes, he poked out his tongue. He was attempting to mime, with a measure of theatrical genius, the distant flashes of sheet lightning which he had never before seen. His silent narration prodded the solemn adults into laughter, just before they were startled by loud claps of thunder announcing the approaching storm.

We can be thankful that we don't often need now to revert to signs, unless we have reached the limit of our vocabulary in a foreign land, or like my little brother, cannot find adequate words to describe the unfamiliar. Nor do we need to draw pictures to express our meaning, for after millennia of language development we have turned the original sketches into stripped-down pictographs, as in China, or replaced them with a rich variety of alphabets. To tell stories, our various cultures have replaced carved or painted hieroglyphs with thousands of languages with vocabularies of millions of words: interconnected sound-symbols that let us depict with amazing precision whatever is in our mind. Pictures still have their own uses: paintings share the artists' vision; photographs record and remind; comic strips and cartoons entertain and bill-boards try to persuade us. We have even long since learned to bring pictures to life, viewing them through the prosceniums of cinema and television.

⌒

Thinking about language, Aristotle concluded, around 350 BCE, that our senses tell us what is really 'out there'. From what they deliver we form thought-concepts that accurately relate to the real world, and then find words to express these. A thousand years later St Thomas Aquinas built on Aristotle's realism: agreeing that our thoughts and words are *proportional* – analogous – to the things 'out there'. No doubt this accurately describes what happens when we perceive things, but – the philosophers went on – not every reality has a single, simple label.

We have invented rich varieties of words that compete to describe the *same* thing: when we say *clothes* and *raiment*; *whole* and *complete*; *troops* and *soldiers*; *children* and *offspring*, we are expressing almost the same idea with in each pair of labels.

Conversely, it happens in any language that the same word has come to stand for several quite different things: we say *pen* to describe an enclosure for pigs and a thing we write with. This nominal identity is quite accidental: each use of *pen* represents quite a different reality and we use the word equivocally. It is different again when we use the same word to mean things that *are* connected, as when we say that a *person* is peaceful, that certain kinds of *behaviour* are peaceful, and the *atmosphere* in a house is peaceful. The fine difference between these uses might not at first be obvious, but looking closer we easily see that behaviour, person and house are quite diverse, and that when we use the same word to describe them we are linking quite different ideas by this analogy.

One kind of analogy is metaphor. As our languages developed, this invention – another subtle doorway – extended almost to infinity our power to shape narratives and communicate them to others. Metaphor – the Greek word meant the 'carrying-over' of one concept to another – employs the mental picture of one thing to transfuse extra life into our effort to describe another. When a storyteller uses a metaphor he or she transfers an idea to another part of our mental world where it isn't normally found. We say that a person is *lost* for words; a house is *crying out* for a coat of paint; a nation is *born*; a plane *limped* home on one engine; their marriage was a *prison*; he *racked* his brains; health-care has become a political *football*; the land was *blanketed* with snow; my mind was *flooded* with new information; he was *sitting on* 120 kph; education is the *key* to success; when I saw it, my heart *turned to ice*.

People who like to argue about these things sometimes say that metaphor is an inferior kind of analogy because it merely *attributes* qualities to things it describes, and that this is distinct from the three meanings of the word *peaceful* as used above. When we use a metaphor, we might seem merely to *pretend* that an object has the characteristics which the metaphor attributes to it, but this is a little unfair. When, for example, we describe musical notes as being metaphorically ranged on a *scale* – from the Latin *scala*, which means ladder – aren't we using a link between the two ideas that has lain within them since the beginning of the world – or at least since the invention of ladders? Or when we say that we were *lost for words*, surely we are not just 'attributing' this quality to ourselves? Aren't there times when speech fails us, and we feel as if we are in a dense jungle, with no idea in which direction we should walk? If I use the metaphorical expression 'I was taken aback by his rudeness', I am saying that he left me feeling very much like a sailing ship which until now had been driven before a fair wind which suddenly shifted to dead ahead, causing the sails to flap and the masts to shudder, and jarring the vessel so severely that it almost broke apart.[3]

When we transfer the meanings of words we change their original, literal signification, but in doing so we point out instructive and entertaining likenesses that lie hidden in our much-connected world. Is not metaphor a *doorway* which opens up new territories of thought by pointing out similarities previously hidden, and deepens our view of things by revealing their hidden links with other parts of the universe?

Like the ship taken aback, many of the metaphors we use have lost much of their momentum because neither user nor listener knows what they originally meant. They have become just a string of words that we have heard others using, which have worn a track in our brain. We miss now the shocking contrast of the original metaphor: what was once a daring mental leap falls flat because it no longer surprises the listeners with sudden insight.

Metaphors can have great power and beauty because the reality-content of everything is far greater than is expressed in its well-worn name and our blasé image of it. Henry James called this power of analogy to reveal the nature of things a 'tremendous force'.[4] Similarly, in visual art, Van Gogh's profound paintings might seem to distort what you or I would normally see as a sunflower, a starry night or a person's face, but they show us aspects of the world that we might never have found for ourselves. A saying attributed to him describes every metaphor: that there is a truth truer than literal meaning.

༄

When our ability to make and read images turns back to the past, we call it memory. From among the countless sensations that our senses receive and process each day, we recall small fragments or even elaborate structures many years later. There is evidence that we store away every detail our senses deliver to our brain, and if hypnotised could retrieve an image of the face of every person we have ever talked with.

This gift of looking backwards through the archways of time lets us do more than simply preserve and retell our own stories. We can learn from those past experiences by comparing them with our present situation. Even as children we did this, growing in competence and confidence. We can modify the effect the past has had on us by looking back with increased knowledge to understand *why* harmful events happened, and the *motives* of people who did them. We can correct our own mistakes and forgive others the harm they have done. With this increasing control, the choices of our heart give us to some degree the power to travel back through time.

Memory is our treasure-house of experience. By reflecting on its contents we can find more of the meaning we may have missed in what happened around us. It stores all our experiences, but is notoriously fallible, for we can find ourselves combining pictures that did not originally belong together or that others remember differently. We can invent stories of what did not actually happen. Unless carefully checked our memory can lead us hopelessly astray. As we rummage there, trying to be creative, we may accidentally pull out words that are inappropriate or ill-matching, sometimes inventing delightful malapropisms and sometimes sheer nonsense. *Illiterate him from your memory!*; alcoholics *unanimous*; a vast *suppository* of information; having one spouse is called *monotony*.

Such linguistic weakness may fortuitously be a source of wisdom. When we half-understand what we are trying to say, we might actually succeed in wrenching nonsense into sense, revealing hidden meanings that conceal enlightening truth. A mayor of Chicago once solemnly announced that 'The police are not here to create disorder, they're here to *preserve* disorder.'

Children, as they struggle to master language and express themselves are especially prone to recall and mix words inaccurately.

One inspired child has delighted generations by mistaking the line from a hymn: *Kept by Thy tender care/Gladly the cross-eyed bear* ... At age twelve the author Sylvia Wright misheard an old Scottish ballad that lamented:

> *They hae slain the Earl o' Moray, and laid him on the green,*

as

> *They hae slain the Earl o' Moray, and* **Lady Mondegreen**

thereby increasing the romance and pathos of the old song, as well as providing a name – *mondegreens* – for an entire category of misused words. Another child, hearing the 23rd Psalm, found little comfort in being promised the abstract gifts of *goodness and mercy*, even if they come from God. She found it much more consoling to believe that:

> *Surely* **Good Mrs. Murphy** *shall follow me all the days of my life.*

∽

We can picture storytellers at the dawn of human development learning to manipulate their listeners by tales woven from their own imaginations and memories: stories peopled by characters good and evil; monsters, tricksters and gods. But these tales were not wholly 'made up'. They emerged from the forces and conflicts in the storyteller's own heart and found echoes in the hearts of their hearers. Does this suggest that when story-smiths in any culture reach deep into the unconscious and depict realms beyond ordinary experience, they are stirring up our natural longing for – or innate horror of – realms at other levels of reality, beyond what our senses have so far shown us?

The more memorable stories from diverse ancient cultures became congealed into myths. These have surprised modern researchers by the common elements that constantly recur among them. Myths are not false stories, as Post-Enlightenment 'scientific' minds tended to think, but are deeply true. Cinderella; Jack and The Bean Stalk and Little Red Riding-hood are only a few of the hundreds expressing the fears and joys that move hearts in any place and era. Their non-existent characters seem to re-present the divine, the desired and the diabolical within ourselves. Perhaps the nature of myth was best summed up in the perceptive answer given by a little boy to his teacher: 'A myth is something that is true on the inside, but not true on the outside.'[5] From their source in the unconscious, myths may bring forth truths deeply embedded within us, gently couched in metaphorical terms. Scholars like Carl Jung and Joseph Campbell have concluded that myths are ancient attempts to express deep truths about life's origin and purpose, or to explain suffering and fate, which we hardly understand and could never express in literal terms.

David Tacey argues that religious stories, indeed all religious language, *must* be metaphorical, for it tries to tell of things that transcend the senses and so can never be put directly into words.[6] Those who would insist that such stories are literally true are on a road that leads to absurdity and the destruction of belief. Accepting their metaphorical nature might lessen the conflict between those who consider themselves believers, agnostics or atheists ... and the conflict between those elements in the heart of each one of us.

The fundamental stories of Judaism and Christianity – to look no further – were at first composed by oral storytellers at a time when people lived by myth and would not have expected a literal, historical or scientific account such as modern authors might claim to write. Early believers, in every faith, would have received their myths as stories 'true on the inside', revealing the mysterious Transcendent; but not necessarily 'true on the outside', in the miraculous details with which they were adorned. When 19th century biblical scholars began to rediscover this, many religious apologists, already threatened by the advances in the sciences achieved during the Enlightenment, strove vainly to insist that the biblical stories were wholly and literally true.

This inevitably led to a further – unnecessary – parting of the ways, by which faith became separated from reason, and religion split further from science.

~

When we fall asleep, our image-making powers, imagination and memory can range freely. Dreams are partly memories of what we were doing during the previous day, but at deeper levels they are doorways leading into the mysterious depths of our unconscious. Among many other functions, dreams provide a pathway by which significant memories from our earlier life can return to be 'digested'. As our body has a natural urge to heal, so does our psyche, and it brings into our sleeping consciousness situations from the past that have not yet been healed. These can keep returning in bizarre forms which niggle at us repeatedly until we find their key, after which that portion of our life falls into place like a piece of a jigsaw puzzle.

In the late 1970s and early 1980s I had a recurring dream about a strange object: a small, compact black box about seven centimetres by twelve centimetres and about three deep. The upper half of its front side was a screen on which I could see moving patterns of coloured light, vaguely concentric in shape, whose centre receded into the distance as the sides of a tunnel recede when viewed from the back of a moving train. In the dream I knew that the small device was capable of many functions, although I had no idea what these might be.

What was I dreaming about? Some twenty years later I saw similar coloured patterns on the screen of my laptop computer, a display that could run while music was playing. But my dream began about five years before the first personal computers came on the market, and many more years before lap-tops had coloured screens. The thing in my dreams resembled a modern smartphone, though considerably thicker, but I did not see a smartphone until about thirty years after first dreaming about the strange object.

The dream had been recurring occasionally for perhaps ten years when I found myself taking part in a workshop to study dream interpretation. As participants we were invited to recall a recurring dream we had experienced, then lie back comfortably and allow ourselves to fall into a half-sleep. We were asked, if possible, to speak aloud about what came before our minds, while a partner sitting beside us could gently question us to develop the thread of the dream. In a semi-doze I chose to 're-enter' that dream, and realised suddenly that the device resembled the first transistor radio I ever saw. My father had brought it home in the late 1950s, but quite soon I selfishly borrowed it for an evening to show off to my friends. It did not of course have a screen showing coloured patterns, but in my revisited dream I also saw my father wearing his usual hat. In its band was the end of a peacock feather with its beautiful unblinking 'eye', whose shape and rich colours resembled the moving coloured pattern on the device that I had often dreamed of.

Seeing how I had unconsciously combined these images in the dream helped me towards resolving aspects of my relationship with my father. In my teenage years he was often away from home, sometimes working at a second job, with the result that as I approached adulthood I had little time to get to know him. Soon after the transistor radio incident I moved out of home, and less than two years later he was dead.

Evidently dreams can be a doorway leading to deep and entangled memories in our unconscious, offering us opportunities to re-enter and heal them. Does my repeated experience of *that* particular dream also suggest, weirdly, that dreams may to some extent have access to the future? How otherwise could I dream often of that portable device whose functioning puzzled me because the device did not yet exist, and wouldn't until about twenty years later? From what source beyond time did I receive an image of a compact mobile device with a coloured screen? Was it from some 'collective unconscious' that is not confined by our time-flow; or from the influence of minds or spirits of people who are alive but no longer in the dimension that we call 'now'?

Sigmund Freud and Carl Jung began to find that just as people of many cultures share similar myths, so they also share symbols which persistently turn up in their dreams. Jung called these archetypes. But by what mechanism are they shared across cultures? To propose that they are 'in our DNA' does not seem sufficient: thoughts are surely much more than any chemical structure in our neurones. Nor is it enough to say that we all have a propensity to construct our inner world in a similar way, similar to the innate structure that some suggest we have in our brain as a basis for language. The archetypes we share seem to show that we are more than a material mechanism, and that images, symbols and myths are an essential part of our functioning. The 'scientific mind' is obliged to take account of this evidence that we live within a realm of story whose depth and boundaries are as yet unknown to us.

3
Strange Connections
The mystery of synchronicity

All things by immortal power,
Near or far,
Hiddenly
To each other linkèd are,
That thou canst not stir a flower
Without troubling of a star

Francis Thompson[7]

In the fluid years of adolescence, I liked to question what is considered to be normal and necessary, and was much taken by the art of Salvador Dali, who dared to paint his world from astonishing and original viewpoints. I delighted in his drooping clock-dials and melting human faces; the caravan of elephants on impossible stilt-legs, bearing on their backs palaces and obelisks; a caravel with butterflies for sails. Dali could bypass the rules that we trust and expect to govern the physical world. In later years I was to find that the phenomenon known as synchronicity was doing things in my own life as strange as Dali's painted creations. In startling and inexplicable ways, it would open doorways to show that there are links between parts of our world that we never dreamed could be connected.

I had known Yvonne Matta when I was pastor of the Brisbane parish of Carina. Some years later I read her family history[8], whose Epilogue relates a remarkable example of synchronicity. In 1942 her future husband Youssef (Joe) Matta, as a boy of ten, had generously given oranges to an Australian soldier to share with his unit camped near Beirut. The soldier, Arthur, gratefully gave the boy his slouch hat in return. Arthur was afterwards wounded at Tobruk and sent home to Queensland, where he later married and had two sons and a daughter, Anne. In his last years he confided some of his wartime experiences to Anne, including the story of the oranges.

Youssef Matta did not learn the name of the soldier he had helped, but later emigrated to Australia and married Yvonne Ashkar, who was later to write the family's history. The couple returned to Lebanon and raised their seven children, until the 1975 civil war prompted the family to move back to Australia to avoid danger and to educate the children. They chose Brisbane, where other members of the family already lived. Joe, although an Australian citizen, stayed mainly in Lebanon for civic and business reasons, visiting his family when possible. In 2008 he died in Lebanon and was buried there, but soon afterwards a memorial Mass was celebrated in the family's local parish church in Carina, Brisbane. At that Mass, among the many stories about Joe, his son Raymond told the story of his childhood gift of oranges.

After the Mass, Yvonne was greatly surprised to discover that her next-door neighbor, Anne, already knew the story, for she had heard if from her now-deceased father, who was Arthur! Anne and Yvonne had been neighbours and friends for six years, but until that day were quite unaware of the link connecting their fathers. Back in July 1976, when the newly-arrived Mattas had been choosing a house, Yvonne had suggested several but it was Joe, visiting his family at that time, who actually chose their home, quite unaware that next door lived the daughter of the soldier he had helped thirty-four years before. What 'magnetism' had steered him, or what intelligence guided him to choose precisely *that* house for his family?

In 1983 I was back in Melbourne for a few months to work in the parish of Parkville, temporarily replacing its pastor while he was on leave. My first Mass there was to be at 5 o'clock on a Sunday evening, and since it would be my first meeting with the congregation, I was anxious to prepare and present it well. That day I had gone to lunch with the Dominican community some distance across Melbourne, but in the afternoon, returning towards the parish by tram, I noticed with horror that I had badly misjudged the time and would arrive at the church at least half an hour late. When I reached the centre of the city I still needed to catch another tram for the second stage of my journey. By this time I was desperate, and prayed, almost without hope. As I hurried across the Flinders Street intersection, one of the busiest in that city of about three million people, I heard my name called. In a car stopped at the traffic lights a friend was waving to me. Amazed, and enormously relieved, I asked him for a lift and reached the church with a few minutes to spare.

For a few years I was working with a Dominican Preaching Team which gave five-day 'missions' in parishes around Aotearoa New Zealand and Eastern Australia. In April 2006 we were working in the small town of Rakaia, not far from Christchurch. During an afternoon break, some of the team drove up to the nearby Mount Hutt ski-field and, at a sale in the ski-lodge, bought 'windcheater' sweaters as gifts for each team member. I was given mine by Sister Joan Hardiman.

I liked my sweater so much that I was still occasionally wearing it ten years later – although for four of those years I had been working in the tropical Solomon Islands, where sweaters are never worn at all. In September 2016 I had just returned to our Melbourne priory. It was a cold day, so I took my kiwi-embroidered sweater out of storage and put it on. Not many minutes later one of the friars came into the kitchen where I was having a cup of tea and asked me whether I knew a Sister

Joan Hardiman, who had just phoned from New Zealand. I said that I did, and called her back immediately. She was quite unaware that I was in Melbourne, but was very relieved to find me there, for a friend of hers was flying here on the following day to view the body of her brother who had taken his own life. Joan knew it would be helpful if a Dominican priest could accompany the sorrowing woman to the morgue. The unfortunate woman was pleased to have someone with her who knew her good friend Joan.

The term 'synchronicity' was coined by Karl Jung to refer to events like these that happen close to each other in time or space, yet are not causally connected in any way that we can know. He struggled to give them a name and speculated about 'An Acausal Connecting Principle' that might lie behind them. Most of us have experienced synchronicity when we have made a phone call to someone who just at that moment was thinking or speaking about us, or have been rung by someone whom *we* have been thinking about. We are also sometimes surprised when two people run into each other 'accidentally', at a time when the meeting benefits one or both of them. Synchronicity usually seems to be helpful to the persons involved, at least minimally.

We need to approach synchronicity, this archway into the unknown, with a healthy scepticism. Some try to reduce it to mere coincidence; some, by playing with the statistics of large numbers, claim that such occurrences are actually statistically probable. Others dismiss it as merely subjective, calling it apophany[9], meaning *the tendency to perceive meaningful patterns in random data.*

Others have coined the singularly ugly word *patternicity*, describing the human tendency to find – or imagine – meaningful patterns in meaningless 'noise'. At times I have indeed imagined I could hear human speech in a babbling stream or in the agitated water of the older type of washing machine; and I delight in finding human or animal faces in wood-grain, or speckled carpets. But these small feats of *apophany* are ordinary achievements of my senses and imagination, and can hardly be compared to true examples of synchronicity, which are far more spectacular.

It might be possible statistically to 'explain away' accidental meetings: people do run into each other all the time without noting it, until an encounter is so surprising or outstandingly helpful that they take special note. In my experience the most extraordinary cases of synchronicity happen when a person is to some degree desperate, perhaps praying for help or escape.

⁓

Those 'coincidences' that we notice when we telephone someone who is thinking or talking about us may be explained by telepathy, a possible ability of the mind to communicate at a distance without using any known physical means. In Parkville, not long after that remarkable synchronicity had saved me from arriving late for my first Mass, I sat writing a letter to a friend. I mentioned that I had met Sebastian Moore, the English Benedictine monk and well-known author, at his public lecture several days before. Because I was soon to visit England I had asked him about possible help with a theological topic I was researching. He had promised to phone me and give contact details for his nephew, a professor of theology. As I worked on the letter, a few seconds after I had written Sebastian Moore's name, the telephone rang. He was phoning from Sydney, 700 kilometres away, to apologise for taking so long to give me the information he had promised.

While we may call on telepathy to explain such an event – which is quite a different thing from explaining how it works – we may need another term to explain those cases of inner prompting, in which a person feels an unshakeable conviction that he or she should urgently make a choice, such as not to board an aircraft which soon afterwards crashes. The Australian television presenter Mike Willesee relates how he had frankly and sceptically abandoned all belief in a dimension beyond the material, having put aside the Catholic tradition in which he had been raised. He was however surprised to feel a powerful conviction from no apparent source shortly after boarding an aircraft in Africa. The small plane he had hired for his film crew was about to take off, when he felt unshakably convinced that it was going to crash. Knowing that it would appear foolish to cancel the take-off for no visible reason and at great inconvenience and expense, he decided that his only option was to pray, earnestly, for the first time in perhaps thirty years. The plane had scarcely taken off when it did indeed crash, but all on board were spared serious injury.

A similar incident happened to film maker Bill Bennett, who when driving in New Orleans around 3am heard a clear voice telling him to slow down as he approached a green light. He did so, and only by seconds avoided the large truck that sped across his path after running the red light. It would have crushed him if he had not slowed down. He subsequently spent years trying to understand the source of that warning voice, and made a film about it.[10]

Cases like this might also suggest some kind of telepathy, but coming from what unseen consciousness? A faculty called intuition? A 'field' around the person receiving the message? The spirit of an ancestor? An angel? The Infinite Mystery? This is a perfectly scientific question, for the observable effect – Bennett's and Willessee's conviction that they were being warned – must have a cause. With an unbiased mind we need to be open to *any* possible explanation until that explanation can be excluded by convincing evidence. We need to note that whatever 'mind' conveyed the warning messages, it seems to have intended to protect the persons from injury, to save lives by sharing knowledge that those persons did not have. This 'mind' appears either to have been able to know that there was some defect in the aircraft that would cause it to crash, or to 'foresee' the moment when it did crash, perhaps because that 'mind' exists outside our dimension of time. We are shaken by these suggestions. Each of the unanswered questions places us before an archway into the unknown and challenges us to admit that 'something' or 'someone' has knowledge extending beyond the range of human powers as we currently understand them.

In 2007 the Dominican friar Peter Lucas was for some months resident priest in Cobram, northern Victoria. On many Sundays it was his custom to leave after the second Mass and drive for about four hours down to Melbourne, to take the following day off in his Dominican community. On Sunday 11th November he had travelled about half way on his journey when at a rest-stop he found he had left his bag back at the house. Since it contained his essential medication he could not continue, but returned to Cobram. Late that night he had a phone call from the local hospital and went to anoint and pray with a woman who was dying, surrounded by her family. She died as he finished the prayers. What unseen force had prevented him on that day from putting his bag in the car, as he had habitually done many times before? If he had not been forced to come back the woman would have died without the much-appreciated presence and prayers of her local priest.[11]

In 2005 I was cycling with a small group of people on a *Pilgrimage of Reconciliation* from Canberra to Uluru.[12] One afternoon we reached the small town of Morgan. As we approached the town, Ray Wilson (a rider in our party) went ahead. He usually did this to find a suitable campsite and also to meet any Aboriginal people he might find;

our ride was attempting in small ways to promote reconciliation. Ray found a community centre, which was open even though it was Sunday afternoon. Inside, a man was talking on the phone. When he had finished his call, John Ellerton – as he introduced himself – apologised for keeping Ray waiting. He explained that he was studying for the mature-age Matriculation course, for which he was writing an essay on Meister Eckhart, the medieval Dominican mystic. He had just now been trying, without success, to phone a Dominican friar in Melbourne whom he had been told might help him. He was amazed when Ray told him that a Dominican friar would arrive by bike in about five minutes. No more amazed than I was. What – or who – could possibly have arranged that Ray would arrive at the exact minute when John was phoning the Melbourne priory? For long afterwards we reflected on this unusual synchronicity. We could only conclude that, besides the small help that John received with his essay, it was somehow a sign – from where? – that we were both 'on the right course'.

On another day, early in that pilgrimage, Ray and I were riding side by side yarning, for which we had ample opportunity during the 2,700 kilometres. We hardly knew each other as yet, and were surprised to find that although I now lived in New Zealand and Ray in Bendigo, we had once attended the same Melbourne secondary school, although a few years apart. Moreover, on weekends we had both worked for pocket money at the same Metropolitan Golf Club. I mentioned to Ray that my brother had been elevated from caddying there to working behind the club-house bar. Surprised, Ray said that it would have been his own father, as manager, who employed him. 'I was able to finish the story by saying that in my bike's saddlebag I was carrying my brother's latest book[13], in one chapter of which he told the story of his youthful employment and mentioned Mr Wilson by name.' That night Ray stayed awake to read it, burning a light in his tent well beyond a reasonable hour.

～

Sometimes synchronicity might be interpreted as reassuring us that what is happening is part of a meaningful wholeness. This is how I interpreted a bright rainbow that spanned the sky as I emerged from the building where my mother had just died. In this way Indigenous peoples often interpret the timely occurrence of natural phenomena such as rainbows, or the unusual appearing of a specific bird or animal. From 1991 I worked as Parish Priest in St Benedict's church, Auckland. My previous appointment was in sub-tropical Brisbane, where thunderstorms were a common occurrence, so I often remarked how rare it was to hear thunder in Auckland.

When my time in the parish came to an end, I was leading the 10am Sunday Mass for the last time. The climax of every Mass is the final phrase of the Eucharistic prayer, when the celebrant raises the consecrated bread and wine and concludes with words of praise that refer everything to Christ: 'Through Him, with Him, in Him, in the unity of the Holy Spirit… glory and honour is given to God.' To this prayer the congregation solemnly replies 'Amen.' As I declaimed these words I was keenly aware that this was the last time I would be doing it as leader of this congregation, and was more conscious than usual that in the Mass we are in touch with the Divine Mystery in a deeper way than in everyday life. I became even more aware of this when at that precise moment, although there was no storm, a loud but solitary peal of thunder echoed around the sky. I wondered at the strange, hidden unity between our human action and the time, place and atmospheric conditions which might have caused such a startling event.

～

For children, any solemn words or actions, particularly in church, can be made into a source of fun. When we first heard the Holy Spirit called the *Paraclete* we thought it hilarious that the name was so similar to *parakeet*, the colourful bird we often saw raiding the fruit trees or kept as a pet in a cage. During my years in the Western Solomon Islands I would regularly celebrate Sunday Mass on Kolombangara Island, an hour by outboard-motor dinghy from our home near Gizo. On Pentecost Sunday, 2013, when I was preaching the homily, I was alarmed to feel a large object touching the top of my head. I cautiously reached upwards and felt that it was the claws of a large bird, which, to my relief, at once flew out through the open wall of the chapel. As it left I saw that it was a brilliantly coloured parrot, which I learned later was a pet that had escaped from the students' residence. The congregation was laughing uproariously, and was even more amused when I found the presence of mind to complain aloud that in St John's gospel Jesus had promised to send his disciples a new *Paraclete*, but on this Pentecost had sent us only a *parakeet*. I was more astonished, however, by the synchronicity involved: never before or since had a bird landed on my head in a church, but this one came down on the day of Pentecost, at the precise moment that I was attempting to explain that difficult subject.

How does synchronicity happen? Trying to understand what might be responsible raises interesting questions about causality itself. Carl Jung thought that synchronicity was not 'caused', but in saying this he meant that these mysterious coincidental events are not the result of any physical, mechanical energy, which ultimately originates from bodies in motion. He was speaking merely of *efficient* cause, to use the terminology of earlier philosophers – Plato, Aristotle and Aquinas – who also counted *material*, *formal* and *final* causes as responsible for bringing a thing into existence.

Looking at things from all possible angles, they saw that each object, whether made by nature or by craft, exhibits purpose. This *purpose* is its *final* cause, whether we are speaking about the plan in the mind of the craftsman, the life-force that drives creatures to evolve until they find the niche where they can thrive, or as the earlier philosophers would put it, the plan in the Mind that formed the cosmos.

Jung was surprised to observe that synchronistic events often impressed his patients so much that they gained deeper insight into themselves and improved in mental health. Asking *why* the events happened, he concluded that *purpose* was involved. He concluded that *mind* must be responsible: that there must be a knowledge prior to and greater than human consciousness. He suspected that this might be the unconscious area of the individual's own mind and perhaps also the collective unconscious, somehow shared by all people.

When Jung speculated about purpose or *final cause* of synchronicity he was moving beyond the territory of the empirical, observational sciences into that of philosophy. It was quite legitimate for him to do so, for the deeper 'why' is a valid question, beyond the scope of empirical observational sciences, which observe and measure with increasing sophistication what the senses tell us about any part of the cosmos. Philosophy uses distinctly different methods, asking questions that arise from this evidence: questions about causality, purpose, form, and about being or existence itself.

Since the Enlightenment, the empirical sciences have made such spectacular progress that it is not uncommon to drift into thinking that their perspective is the only possible or valid way of looking at the universe. This attitude leads us to forget to ask questions about purpose: *why* things are as they are. It is a theme of this book that many phenomena cannot be explained by our senses, the basic doorways leading us towards deeper areas of knowledge. If we are to be truly 'scientific' and use all aspects of our knowledge, we must include in our observations the fact that phenomena like synchronicity may not be explainable by material causes alone. We need not be afraid to ask the further questions that this raises. Although the empirical sciences cannot provide answers it would be folly to ignore the questions. Why not let them draw us to seek more eagerly for further possible answers, whatever new archways that this might invite us to enter?

4
'Deep down things'
Seeing within the everyday

... There lives the dearest freshness deep down things ...

Gerard Manley Hopkins[14]

Our small house echoed with angry words between my mother and father, with long, painful silences in between. They didn't often fight, but when they did I felt confused and hurt. At the age of six I didn't know what they were fighting about, but I knew my father liked to bet on horse races. That night he seemed to have lost money again, as my mother was talking about how much it cost to buy food and our shoes for school.

She was at the sink, washing the dishes from our meal. My father was sitting at the kitchen table finishing his dinner. On many nights he was not home by the time we had our meal so my mother would put his plate on a saucepan of water boiling on the stove, covering the meat and vegetables with the saucepan lid.

As their bitter comments flew back and forth, I went quietly to the bedroom that I shared with my brothers, opened the wardrobe, pulled out the box where I kept my toys and looked over the small collection. I took my few marbles from their jar, rolled them in my hand then put them back. I pushed aside a worn tennis ball and saw the little maroon Dinky Toy sports car that I always liked to play with. It had a celluloid windscreen; a steering wheel that turned; little doors that opened; and its wheels had rubber tyres that I could take off and put back on again. I pushed the car aside, for I was looking for something else. Soon I found it under some books: a neat black hippopotamus, with a few bare patches of lead showing where the paint had flaked off.

It was heavy, and I could hardly close my hand around its fat roundness. It was my favourite. Feeling around again in the dark wardrobe I found a small pie-dish of white enamel. I took my time to wrap the hippo in a piece of cloth, leaving just its head showing, and lay it gently in the dish like in a bed. I was feeling calm again as I stood up and carried the pie-dish to the dressing-table beside my own bed and placed it ready for when I would soon get under the blankets myself.

I would have been embarrassed if anyone had pointed out that I was doing the same as my baby brother, who would never sleep without that piece of cloth in his clenched fist, tucked firmly against the side of his face while he sucked his thumb. Even during the day he carried it everywhere. It would have embarrassed my parents too if someone had criticised them for letting us play with toys made from toxic lead, but at that time no-one thought of the danger and most children had some lead toys. It is acceptable these days for a boy to play with dolls, but even if it had been back then, my preference for a hippopotamus might have raised some eyebrows. Perhaps counselling would have been advised. It was one of the few toys I had, and I loved it even though it would no longer stand up, for its back legs were bent from often being dropped. The animal was able to lead me through a doorway into a larger world of peace and calm: there were no words, or even imagined pictures, but whenever I felt lonely or hurting, as tonight when my parents quarrelled, it gave me more comfort than my own snug bed.

Other children suffer much worse scenes, far more often. Some are beaten, sexually abused and otherwise traumatised. I relate my small troubles only to recall how this simple object became an archway into a different dimension. Truth be known, don't we all use a variety of things to achieve this, at every stage of our lives?

When my brothers and I were older, the best gift our parents bought for us was a Hornby clockwork 0-gauge railway layout – we called it that because only little kids played with 'train sets'. Older boys might take a long time to afford the extras needed to build up a substantial layout: extra track and points to expand the basic circle; an extra locomotive with a few goods trucks and passenger carriages.

Our joy in trains must have been obvious whenever we returned from playing at the home of our friend John Hanigan. He had a room full of tracks, points and crossings. Like us, his parents could never afford the more expensive electric Hornby Dublo, with narrow 00-gauge that let you fit more tracks into a smaller space, but this did not stop us from gazing often into model-shop windows and imagining that we owned some of the tiny, detailed models. We knew we were stuck with clockwork, and were happy enough.

Does it matter what kind of toy a child has, or even that they can make them only from wooden blocks and bottle-tops? I have watched children in Indian slums who could never afford even a kite, but joyously flew a plastic shopping bag on the end of an unreeled cassette tape. Similarly, in the Solomon Islands, children make model cars from cut-away plastic water bottles, with wheels carved from the soles of discarded sandals. No matter how crude the toys, the child's imagination turns it into a machine from the adult world and lets them escape into a modified copy of that world in which they cannot yet take part.

At twelve or thirteen, I would watch one of our clockwork locomotives whirring around its small network of tin-plate rails, pulling a few trucks loaded with miniature logs, and wheat-bags that I had sewn myself. I *became* the driver of a powerful J-Class steam loco hauling a mixed goods train from Mildura to Melbourne. As it passed again and again through the station, among buildings and papier-mache hillsides we had laboriously made, I could *hear* the pistons huffing and the unforgettable steam whistle echoing across imagined landscapes. When I switched the moveable points – bought with our hard-earned pocket money – I *was* the signal-man pulling the lever that could divert to left or right a hundred-ton steam loco and forty goods trucks, sending them to Kaniva or Yarram, hundreds of kilometres apart.

⁓

Leaden hippopotamus, model railway. Almost any object can become a threshold that opens other dimensions for us. Looking back at some of the things that delighted me for a season, and with which I even fell in love, I am warned that they can also cause dubious outcomes. All around us we see adults escaping, often unhealthily, into another space by squandering time and energy on their favourite pastime: their motorbike, car, computer, camera or bizarre collection. Even an item of clothing can become a symbol of imaginary power and prestige: a child dressed as Batman, or a teen wearing clothes bearing the label of an admired sports star. I can only guess at what women imagine when they bring home the newly purchased dress or hat, but which of us has not sought temporary escape through 'retail therapy' – comforting ourselves by buying something to wear or play with when we don't really need it?

 A uniform or religious habit, proudly worn, can transform a person's self-image and significantly affect their behaviour. Symbolic clothing can empower us for actions as diverse as the sisters of Mother Teresa lovingly caring for the destitute, or soldiers mechanically following orders to torture or destroy the 'others' they have been trained to hate. When political leaders weave the delusion of nationalism, their propaganda can draw vast numbers to follow a square of coloured cloth into an imaginary world, deceived into believing that war is heroic, when in fact it is monstrously evil, mangling bodies and destroying lives.

⁓

When I was about eight years old, during a holiday in Western Victoria we were taken to see an abandoned brick mansion near Camperdown. Westminster Park had forty-two rooms, a tower and extensive stables and had been built at the beginning of the 20th century by a man who had inherited the land of his hard-working forebears and increased it by further purchases. He was imitating many others across Australia, the sons and grandsons of squatters who had become rich from grazing sheep on land leased cheaply from the government. He was aping their custom of building a mansion to anchor his family to the place where they had made their fortunes. Around the time of World War I, when servants were no longer cheap, such houses became too expensive to maintain. The mansion we visited was later found to be a complete 'white elephant'. It was abandoned and later torn down before it was hardly fifty years old.

Property can seduce us. It has deluded many into flaunting their ownership of impressive houses with pretentious gateways through which they hope to find entry into regions of happiness and security. But struggling to grasp and possess it can hinder us from seeing deeper. There is a much richer world to be found, not by pretending to own things, but by glimpsing the truth *within* them. Like Shelley's Ozymandias, the builders of grand houses did not foresee that the domains they thought so secure would soon be broken up by descendants who could no longer maintain them. The wealthy family's dynastic hearth would become a school, hospital or conference centre in an era undreamed-of by the people who built it.

Everything under the sun has its own mysterious being, which can lead us as if through a proscenium arch into a place of contemplation. In earlier cultures, people saw the sun itself appearing to circle tirelessly overhead, and took it to be the ruling principle of the cosmos. As youngsters we were delighted to find a fragment of broken mirror which could project a miniature sun – always miraculously round even when the mirror was a jagged splinter – across the school-yard and into far-off rooms. We enjoyed the power it gave us, from a safe distance, to dazzle and mystify other children and even, if we dared, our teachers.

A more precious find was a discarded lens that we could use as a burning-glass to concentrate the sun's power until smoke arose from a black spot on the paper; or we could use it as a window through which to peer into the magnified worlds of tiny plants and insects. Later I would delight to use more complex lenses, in a dynasty of cameras, to extend the power of my own eye's lens to give access to new vistas of the world. The camera's telephoto could find surprising details in a distant view; and the macro lens became a portal through which I could delve into miniature worlds underfoot. I fancied that these images were art, like visual poems that might lead others to see beyond the boundaries that we wrongly think are limits to our world.

At any point in life we can be surprised to find ourselves looking as it were through the surface of things, seeing them not merely as the furniture around our ego but as they are in themselves. *In se,* the Romans would say; the Germans *an sich*. In these blessed moments of insight – which if welcomed and cultivated can in time become almost continuous – we discover that we can stand back, as it were, and catch at least a glimpse of the essence of things.

James Joyce used the word *epiphany* to describe capturing a sense of the numinous in a moment, or in an object that suddenly reveals itself as extraordinary. St Thérèse of Lisieux is said to have found herself present at an epiphany every waking moment of her day. Perhaps it is not only the thing we see or the music we hear which enchants us, but a subtle partnership between them and ourselves. The doors of our perception are not like mechanical valves that control a flow of fluid. They set up a subtle dialogue between other creatures and ourselves. William James, in his collection of people's glimpses of the transcendent, includes mention of a young boy who was lifted out of depression by hearing and following a drummer in the street. To him the drummer's tattoo showed him a glimpse of flawless perfection:

> It was impossible to conceive more nerve or spirit, better time or measure, more clearness or richness, than were in this drumming ... I was enchanted and consoled ... good is at least possible ... since the ideal can thus sometimes get embodied.[15]

In my late teens, in the freshness of an early summer morning, I found myself astonished by the beauty of an ordinary marguerite bush, almost covered with white, daisy-like flowers. Seeing within them a little more deeply than before, I picked one and took it inside, intending to try to capture what I had seen. Sketching its outline in faint pencil, I took out water-colours and against a jet-black background carefully painted the petals with their subtle variety of creamy whites. I then attempted the glorious sun-like centre. Although I had been taught nothing about painting, my handiwork impressed me; but at a deeper level I felt dissatisfied. The full *reality* of the flower had eluded me, as it inevitably must.

Although all beauty is fleeting, artists spend their lives seeking something timeless in transitory objects: the classical sculptor froze into marble the beauty of the boy pulling a thorn from his foot; portrait-painters struggle to capture the mystery in countless faces; others are enthralled by the dancer; the curve of a nude body; a landscape. They strive to hold and capture a moment of ecstasy in the images they produce. We each have our own visionary power, if we might not have the complex skills to capture in paint, wood, marble or film, or to suggest in clusters of musical notes, the inner reality of the objects that enchant us.

Artists know that they are doomed at least in part to fail, never completely to seize the inner beauty they are seeking. Philosophers too admit their ignorance. The thirteenth-century philosopher-theologian St Thomas Aquinas often admitted, '... the substantial forms which in themselves are unknown to us, have to be known by their secondary qualities'.[16] By *form* he meant the essence or *what-ness*, the nature that makes a mouse to be a mouse, or a tree or a human to be what they are, for a living creature is far more than the sum of all its physical qualities and chemical formulae.

The unique *form* of each species can be seen to be responsible for the intricate processes that cause it to develop as one of *that* species and restore it when that wholeness is lost. The embryos of a kangaroo and of a human may look similar, but each develop into quite different mature creatures through the process of *morphogenesis*. If an animal's body is damaged a similar process allows it to restore itself towards wholeness. We are able to heal bone, muscle and blood vessels after injury or surgery, but creatures like lizards and newts can re-grow functioning limbs, tail, retina or jaws again and again. What *is* the life-force that allows creatures to regain their wholeness so purposefully? What drives this process?

We can most clearly grasp the *form* which makes a living thing greater than the sum of its parts when we see it before and after its death: when – as this philosophical school would say – its *form* as animal or plant has ceased to be and is replaced by other forms of inert organic chemicals. By analogy, we can understand how the subtle *form* of a beautiful melody makes it different from the sum of notes that constitute it; or causes an enthralling story to be far more than its thousands of component words. It is only when we encounter *in situ* this elusive *form* of each thing or person; when we contemplate it and love it, that it will open up the depths that amaze us and lead us into further awareness and joy. Every such encounter takes us in its own unique way a step nearer towards the unfathomable realm of beauty's origins, which must also be our own.

When working as chaplain at Auckland university I rediscovered my fascination with the invisible power of magnets. Finding a piece of strongly magnetised steel the size of a small book, I concealed it in a box that had once held instant coffee and placed it at one side of my office window-sill. I then tied a teaspoon to a length of cotton thread and anchored it to the opposite side of the window frame. The magnet attracted the teaspoon so strongly that it was suspended in mid-air about two centimetres from the coffee-box and a hand's breadth above the sill. It stayed floating there day and night, for years.

Students coming into the office for the first time would cast a casual glance at the floating spoon, then, astonished, do what comedians call a 'double take'. Engineering students might then cynically ask: 'where's the magnet?', but the more romantically-minded Arts students would often become afraid or experience a mild panic attack until the mystery was explained to them. I enjoyed these reactions, which provided a humorous conversation-starter, but never ceased to be in awe, myself, at the apparently inexhaustible energy in a piece of ordinary steel. The memory of it still opens up for me the awesome, unseen world of sub-atomic forces.

What is magnetism? What is a magnetic 'field'? What is the Earth's gravity-field that the magnet had to overcome so that spoon did not fall towards the Earth's centre but remained suspended in the air? What, for that matter, is light, those few frequencies on the electro-magnetic spectrum that our eyes can detect? The argument has raged since Newton's time: is it particles or waves? Or particles that sometimes behave like waves, as Einstein said. There are many such mysteries in everyday things that should shock us out of any temptation to be complacent, or assume that we know all about the 'ordinary' things around us. When we open our mind to mystery every common object becomes an entry into regions of wonder that can end only at infinity.

'DEEP DOWN THINGS'

In secondary-school chemistry class I was surprised to learn that everything on Earth is composed of the atoms from only ninety-odd elements, combined in molecules of enormous variety. It was a greater shock to read that those who study our world at the atomic level constantly discover new vistas, finding that everything in the universe is a whirring arrangement of just a few elementary particles – or are they electrical forces? Although physicists seem to enjoy finding new 'particles' and have so far named about two hundred, only three seem truly basic: *quarks*, which combine to make up the larger protons and neutrons; *leptons*, best known of which is the electron; and *photons*, that comprise all light and electro-magnetic radiation.

I can only gape in awe at how tiny these things are: an atom is no wider than a millionth of a millimetre. Its core or nucleus, which may contain many protons and neutrons, is ten thousand times smaller. The quarks making up those protons and neutrons are at least ten thousand times smaller again, as are the electrons that orbit the atom's proton-neutron nucleus at such a distance that 99.99 per cent of each atom's volume is just empty space.

If we drew the atom to scale, and pretended that protons and neutrons were the size of small marbles, the electrons and quarks of which they are made would be less than the diameter of a hair, and the diameter of just one atom would be nearly 3.5 kilometres. Its outer 'shell' is composed of whirling electrons, which can interact and join with neighbouring atoms, but wondrously, there seems to be nothing between that outer shell and the distant central handful of marbles representing the atom's nucleus. No one has ever seen these things: we only surmise their nature by the effects produced in experiments. Those who deal with them warn us that the things that we have just been calling 'particles' are not at all like marbles, but 'merely' electrical charges, spread-out and constantly changing. It is truly awe-inspiring to 'see' like this into the most intimate structures of our world, and astonishing to find that every different kind of stuff – granite, grass, air; the colour and softness of petals, the texture of flesh and fur; the taste of fruits, all depend on combinations of three basic electrical charges.

People who analyse these things mathematically tell us that every electron and photon, whether in a distant star, in a bacteria on our skin, in the ocean or in a human face, emits its own tiny field of energy which spreads through the whole of space, although the force it exerts diminishes with distance. In some substances, such as iron, these fields can be linked together more or less permanently to produce the force of a strong magnetic field that can suspend a floating teaspoon for years on end. But more wonderful still, the force or field emanating from *every* particle within every piece of matter is in contact with and intermingles with the field from every other particle: we could hardly be more thoroughly inter-connected.

༄

Every object in the cosmos, if we pause to contemplate it at depth, can lead us through to new discoveries, but it is the *person* with whom we fall in love who opens the most profound archways to other realms. Literature overflows with stories of infatuated lovers who overcome astonishing difficulties to find and unite with their beloved. The sound of the beloved's voice or a simple gift sent as token lets the lover glimpse into the heart of this other person who offers to share life with them, and journey into new vistas of mystery.

Perhaps the secret of this revelation and the magnetism that it produces can be glimpsed in the mythical story of *Genesis*, whose narrator states that the human person is made 'in the image of God'. Does the seemingly crazy behaviour of the lover indicate that she or he has seen the Transcendent in the face and heart of the beloved, where others have not noticed it? The union to which this magnetism leads has been endlessly dramatised in story and song but has rarely captured the ultimate truth to which the lovers' quest leads.

'DEEP DOWN THINGS'

Once I had awakened in teenage years to the beauty of the female, I was attracted by many girls but never became adept at relating to them easily. I envied those boys among my peers who had the social skills to move with ease where I trod clumsily. I reduced even further my opportunities to acquire those skills when I joined a religious community at a relatively young age. Our seven years of study – in those days conducted entirely within our own community – reduced almost to nil our chances to meet women, since visits were rare, even from our own families. After I was ordained at twenty-five, I worked in a parish and attended university. In both places I enjoyed mixing with young women – workers, students and lecturers – but I kept my cautious distance, conscious of my commitment as a Dominican friar.

Before making my life-time vows at twenty-two I had reflected long and carefully on that permanent commitment, traditional in Catholic religious orders. I was to solemnly promise to live in poverty without personal possessions; to be obedient to the community's preaching work as directed by its elected leaders; and to live in consecrated celibacy. I still believe that a young person can be mature enough to make this commitment to a spouse or to a community 'until death'; but as the years passed I was to learn much more about the difference between choosing to make such a commitment, and living out in detail what one has promised. Maturity has a price.

I had been professed as a friar for eighteen years when I first met T, through whom I was to discover horizons wider than I had dreamed of. When preaching in another state I had – by chance? – met a relative of hers who told me that T's husband had recently died, that she was struggling to raise young children without her partner and finding it difficult to reconcile her traumatic loss with her belief as a Catholic.

Sometime after returning home, I paid a visit to this unknown woman. Close to my own age, she had that ripe beauty that early middle years can bring. She was obviously struggling with her situation, and in our conversation then and later we found a growing friendship. I was already finding fulfilment in the life I had chosen, but meeting T deepened this, profoundly. Some time after we had got to know each other, I felt compelled to declare that I felt a love for her deeper than ordinary friendship. She confessed the same. Amazed and delighted that she seemed to find me as interesting and lovable as I saw her, I rapidly found myself passing into a new world where two minds and hearts could share almost every experience, where up till then I – and I suspect she – had felt like a lone centre of consciousness. Our backgrounds were similar: we came from families of the same size and at age twenty had both witnessed the death of a parent – she of her mother, I of my father. We shared similar interests, and quite soon found ourselves becoming more deeply in love. I came to see her smile as a sunrise and hear her voice as more beautiful than any music. She was present almost continually in my thoughts. We quickly saw that my commitment as a friar and our new, deep attraction were on a collision course, and talked long and deeply about this. T was as determined as I that our love should not diminish or destroy my existing commitments, my chosen work. Likewise, we were concerned to avoid any compromise to her own reputation.

Reading and questioning, I found that there was ample precedent for celibate friendships like ours. Most famously, St Francis of Assisi with St Clare, but also Blessed Jordan of Saxony – second Master of the Dominican friars – with Sister Diana D'Andalo; and there was St Francis de Sales and St Louise de Marillac among many others, not least of them Jesus, since he was fully human and had many women friends. The gospels do not conceal his unique relationship with Mary of Magdala, but describe it at some length.[17] These precedents were important, but we also knew of many whom the intoxication of love had led to break their former commitments to marriage or to religious community. Could we make it work?

We soon found that intimacy cannot be superficial. Not long after we met, T accompanied me through the process of dealing with a life-threatening cancer[18] which seemed about to put an early end to our love, as it had killed her husband when the children were mere babies. We soon learned that deeply loving someone without living together was more painful for her than for me. She already knew how physical presence and intimacy nourish a relationship. Each parting, after a few hours together, became for her an agony. It meant separation of never less than a week, and sometimes of many months. A wise counsellor expanded my understanding with the shocking warning, whose truth we painfully learned, that all love involves crucifixion. Many have discovered this truth within and beyond marriage, as did the poet Francis Thompson, who wrote that 'no one ever attained supreme knowledge unless his heart had been torn up by the roots'.[19]

Whatever psychologists might conclude about the differences between the way males and females approach life, we found that T saw relationships from a different angle than I. For me our love was strengthening us in lives that remained relatively separate, with me roaming far and wide in various works, while she remained centred around her home, children and a local circle of friends. She naturally felt drawn towards greater domestic stability, which we could never have. We saw this difference of attitude neatly summarised in a painting we admired of an English cottage and garden. Whereas T delighted in its homeliness as a self-contained shelter where a couple or family could live contented and secure, I instinctively focused on an opposite aspect: that at the end of the garden path the small gate was ajar, opening out from this home-base to the unlimited world beyond.

Our growing friendship was soon noticed by T's friends and by some in my own community, for I spoke about it with those closest to me. I had to ask seriously whether it might be scandalous to them or a wider circle, or becoming an unacceptable danger to either of us. Was it prudent, for instance, to take holidays with T and her children? As years passed and the children left home, could we still presume the same freedom?

In the end I convinced myself that anyone who thought it a scandal that we sometimes travelled or holidayed together would have to live with their own judgements. Somewhat illogically we told ourselves that there were scandals more likely to harm people than this positive love between a widow and a man committed to consecrated celibacy. We added to our argument the many church people – even bishops – who were unfaithful to the gospel when they failed to bring paedophiles to justice, or to treat their victims with compassion. We told ourselves of other ways in which the Church in general had failed to follow Jesus' central teaching about love: 'Love your enemies, forgive ...' (Matt 5:44)[20] when it had often supported wars or even waged wars of its own.

As years passed we grew in our love and, we hoped, in wisdom. We felt freed by Jesus' central command: 'Love one another, as I have loved you' (John 15:12) and: 'those who abide in love abide in God, and God abides in them' (1 John 4:16). Our love was as strong as ever when T died of cancer almost thirty-three years after we had first met. During that time my work had taken me to live in other capital cities in Australia then outside the country for twenty years, although I was able to return regularly for holidays. When I look back on our love, I am more than ever moved to wonder at the privilege we enjoyed, and at the sequence of events that led us through this archway in time and space to find such joy. Not knowing a rational answer, I simply praise the unseen Source from whence love must have originated.

If we class ourselves as having a fortunate life, we may reflect with some satisfaction on the many people and structures which have supported us: with whose help we have not only survived, but enjoyed a degree of fulfilment and achieved some creative work. But can this legitimate satisfaction ever be enough? Part of us may want to believe that the place we have reached will permanently content us; but another part, perhaps more perceptive, may still wonder.

This doubt was hesitantly put to me by two women, on separate occasions, during weekend retreats on which married couples sought to deepen their committed partnerships. The women, who did not know each other, had each enjoyed many years of happy marriage, sharing the love of husbands and children. Both were satisfied, at one level, with their lives thus far. The question they confided, from deep in their hearts, moved me but did not entirely surprise me: 'Is this all there is?' They had 'seen through' the good enjoyment of life's delights and survived its sorrows, and were struggling to grasp what more these might point or lead to. As I try to explore in these pages, there are many ways in which the 'ordinary' things in our life seem to be doorways opening to deeper, further reality. In their rich experience of life, those two women had seen hints of realities beyond their present view; openings leading to who-knew-what other vistas and dimensions, like the worm-holes that astronomers postulate might lead from one universe to another. Those questioning women had each glimpsed through the proscenium arch spanning their present days and seen something that moved them to formulate their query and explore beyond the materialist's confident denial, that nothing exists beyond what our senses can detect and measure.

5
Doorway Into the Daylight
Birth and rebirth

Around 10.00pm on mid-winter's night, 1940, the longest night of the year, a baby was born in a cottage hospital in western Victoria. For the baby's mother, not quite twenty years old, it was her third child. As he passed through his first doorway and emerged from the darkness of her body into a lighted room, on the other side of the world it was mid-summer's day. Some people consider that day auspicious. Adolf Hitler believed it was, for just a few hours later he would fulfil his dream of forcing France to surrender to his mad will by signing papers in the same railway carriage at Compiègne in which Germany had surrendered after the First World War. While a baby boy was coming out into the light in the village of Cobden in Victoria, France was entering a long tunnel of suffering and darkness.

Three weeks later the baby was baptised in the little Catholic church in the nearby bush village of Timboon. His parents were living there while his father worked at the new Cooriemungle Prison Farm. On that day I received my name, but at what point had I received the right to use the word 'I'? And what identity could I claim? Was 'I' the fertilised egg that nine months before had travelled towards my mother's womb? Already its DNA formula was unique: protoplasm with *this* particular formula had never occurred before. Was 'I' the thing that lodged in the womb and began to divide rapidly, striving towards its predestined wholeness? Could there be an 'I' before a brain, limbs, eyes and other organs had budded forth? The more these grew, the more uniquely *mine* they were. I still have them, nearly eight decades later: the unique iris, finger-prints, and whorls of my ears; the larynx that was being shaped to produce unique sound-patterns that one day would become my adult voice. And was this 'I' that was coming to be, merely the sum of my chemical protoplasm, organs and brain … or was I something more than the sum of my parts? I am not the first to have asked these questions, but that does not deprive them of their mystery.

Born on the shortest day, I have always enjoyed seeing the days grow longer as spring and summer return, and felt a mild sadness as they shorten into the cold of autumn. I have always rejoiced in the play of light on the surfaces of things: water, leaves, crystals, rainbows, the shining wet skin of children and of seals and a million other phenomena captured by the lens of my eye or camera. But these joys were still to come: a baby's eyes cannot focus, or so they say.

Even before I began to struggle to understand the patches of light shifting around me, enticing me to make sense of them as a first step on my journey towards enlightenment, I would have heard and felt the world around me: the babble of voices in the birthing room; the flurry and anxious activity of the speakers. One of the first sensations I discerned would have been the comfort of my mother's arms, breast and voice. But there would also have been pain, for by the same senses that our body uses to perceive the world it must inevitably learn it can be hurt. The same powers that equip us for ecstasy prepare us to take our part in the human tragedy.

Newly born, I was taken from Cobden, thirty kilometres over forested hills to our cottage in Timboon, by winding roads like tunnels through the bush. Already I would have begun to feel fear and pain from the world around me. It might seem that a baby has nothing to fear, but pain and fear are no less because they cannot yet be named. With good reason, those attending a birth quickly place the baby in its mother's embrace, and with equal justification it complains when it is deprived of that comfort. Did I protest loudly whenever my mother seemed to abandon me to care for her other baby or manage the household? Were these the first steps in the long, slow path that I would have to tread towards letting go of everything, even of what we deem most essential?

What pain can a baby feel? Grof's research shows that our body and unconscious mind form their own memories: that in later life our body at some deep level has not forgotten the stresses it endured during birth. Whatever stresses of mine paralleled my mother's agony in striving to release my 4.5 kilos into the outside world, could my miniature body ever forget the pain it felt when, in the first days of my breathing life, someone cut the entire foreskin from my penis? For no valid reason, more than half of the surface of one of my body's most sensitive zones – was removed. Was I given an anaesthetic? This was not universal practice, for it was believed that newborn babies do not feel pain. Even if I was given the cocaine injection that was sometimes administered, my tiny body would have struggled vainly to pull away from the aggressors, and suffered more acutely during the days and nights that passed as the wound slowly healed.

How could adults be so unfeeling as to mutilate a child as a way of welcoming it into the human family? Could there be a more effective primal lesson in how *not* to trust? Did this experience form a primitive part of my learning to judge right from wrong, or my attitudes towards my sexuality? In cleverly designed experiments it has been found that even the youngest children know the difference between being treated kindly or unkindly; preferring love to rejection. At eighteen months the little person will prefer and favour cartoon figures that it sees acting kindly towards others, and avoid those figures that refuse to help.

Circumcision was practised in ancient cultures, but – at least in the Jewish version – removed only the tip of the foreskin. It seems to have originated in fear and suspicion of the mysterious power of sex, and was perhaps intended to sacrifice to the gods a part of our most ecstatic experience. The modern version, for reasons even less rational, drastically removes every trace of the prepuce. Profit comes into it: from around 1870, in the USA, the influential physicians Sayre and Remondino found that circumcision freed a few boys from pain arising from previously untreated problems of the foreskin. Rejoicing in their 'discovery', they illogically projected its benefits as a 'cure' for a wide range of diseases, blaming the innocent foreskin for poor digestion, constipation, bowel incontinence and much else. They made considerable profit from their determined campaign to remove it.[21]

Since the operation reduced genital sensitivity it was later promoted as a way of deterring boys from masturbating, yet in irrational contradiction was also promoted as a cure for impotence. The two surgeon profiteers crossed to England to preach their doctrine and increase their incomes. Circumcision became fashionable there too among white middle-class gentiles, while poorer folk were left mainly uncut. So it came to pass that the foreskin joined those other unfortunate bits of the body: tonsils, teeth, and even gall bladders that were routinely removed even when completely healthy. The mindless mutilation performed on my days-old body was a ritual dictated by medical fashion. My parents could hardly have been expected to challenge this abuse of medical authority, or withstand any pressure from other family members who had been similarly deceived.

My discomfort as a baby did not end with circumcision. In my first months of life I contracted pneumonia, which before the popular use of antibiotics must have threatened my survival. Did I often fill my small world with wailing, like so many children in countless households an Earth's diameter away in France and other parts of Europe, where entire families lamented as bombs rained down and millions suffered in the insanity of war?

It is mysterious and fascinating to think that our development as an individual, our ontogenesis, runs parallel to the development and evolution of the family-tree of all creatures, or phylogenesis. The foetus that was to become *this* human person, during its early development resembled in turn the foetuses of many other species. When at last it became recognisably human, though still very different from what it would be in years to come, it was ready to make its entrance into daylight. This not-so-grand entrance was to be echoed by many future arrivals into different states of being; new births into new worlds and deeper layers of reality.

Sigmund Freud is credited with first describing the unconscious portion of our mind. His disciple Carl Jung saw that at this mysterious level of our being we are strangely linked to each other, as if we draw from and add to an 'underground river', a shared unconscious that seems to be governed by 'archetypal ideas': the principles of light and dark; of birth, death and re-birth; the hero; the great mother; the child; the trickster; the shadow; good and evil; eros and logos; feminine and masculine. Some archetypes have been given personal forms in mythology: Aphrodite; Oedipus; Dionysus; Prometheus; Saturn; Shakti; Shiva; Kali; Wotan; Isis; Sophia. Jung noticed that the same archetypes occur in the dreams and myths of cultures around the world, and seem to be part of the structure of our psyche.

The research of psychiatrist Stanislav Grof has shed more light on these archetypes. He has found that they seem to be grounded in our body itself and intimately connected with memories of the birth process.[22] During thousands of psychoanalytic sessions with troubled people, in which he used LSD as well as non-drug therapies, Grof observed that patients were often cured after moving back through a series of powerful 'archetypal' experiences, even to the extent of re-experiencing elements of their physical birth. Some of the experiences they reported were more intense and 'universal' than they had thought it possible for a human being to undergo. Grof found a general pattern among the stages of these archetypal experiences, although the sequence varies. At first the person might feel a sense of undifferentiated unity with the mother's womb, which may then be broken by a sudden separation and fall. Next, he or she might feel caught up in a life-and-death struggle with the contracting womb and birth canal; then suffer almost unbearable constriction and pressure, extreme narrowing of the mental horizons and a sense of hopeless alienation and meaninglessness. In this shattering experience everything appears to be lost and the person feels destroyed.

But this apparent death is soon followed by a sudden awakening. The person feels unexpectedly liberated; their horizons dramatically expand and they feel 'connected to the universe' in new ways, which they might describe as being united with nature or the Divine, often in the form of the 'Great Mother'. They have a sense that a shallower individual self has partly dissolved and that they have been healed. Their new awareness far outweighs the agony they have passed through, and not surprisingly they often describe this crisis as a rebirth.

Grof's evidence shows that even though we are not yet breathing when we emerge from our mother, our psyche is already active at a deep level and may later recall parts of the process. By accepting these bodily memories, a person can obtain healing. Reliving some aspects of the birth process seems able to complete what was lacking when we entered the world through that first archway and began to take our part with billions of others in the complex process of human life.

In the lifespan of every person the process of passing through a narrow passage or doorway is repeated in the various *liminal experiences* to which anthropologist Victor Turner has drawn attention. All cultures have created rituals to mark these principal stages of birth, childhood, adolescence, adulthood, marriage, ageing and dying. By analogy, these steps can be seen as re-births and the rituals celebrating them seem designed to ease our entry into the next phase of our life. But besides these experiences common to all, we each meet our own unique, less predictable challenges, which while they severely constrict us, can enable us to grow in new ways.[23]

Teachers of the inner life draw attention to the paradoxical fact that as physical organisms grow strong by struggling against resistance, so does our mind or spirit. The Buddha's *Eightfold Way* calls for us to renounce things that we are naturally drawn towards but which in excess or defect can do us harm: sensuality, ill-will and cruelty, and even one's own home. In order to follow a simpler life, we are called to avoid lying, licentious speech and gossip, and taking what is not given; to abstain from anger and covetousness – which can lead us to injure or kill – o killing, injuring, taking what is not given, and from sexual immorality.

Five centuries after Buddha all four gospels recorded that Jesus of Nazareth stated as one of his chief teachings that if we want to save our life we must lose it. Mark's gospel has: '...those who want to save their life will lose it, and those who lose their life ... will save it' (Mark 8:35)[24] In John's gospel it is: 'Those who love their life lose it, and those who hate their life in this world will keep it for eternal life' (John 2:25). Jesus was not advising us to die or to destroy ourselves, or even 'hate' ourselves in the literal sense, but the strong Semitic exaggerations shock us into seeing that we self-centred persons need to allow our shallow 'self' to be radically changed if we are to learn to consider what others need from us, and to respond in love. Another way to describe this process of our maturing is that we need gradually to *lose* our superficial ego to find and re-shape the deeper elements – our 'true self' within.

~

Around the third century a monastic tradition evolved within the Christian tradition. No doubt there were many social reasons for its emerging, but one element in the motivation of those who joined this dedicated life was to search for the mysterious Transcendent through a penitential life that offered a kind of continuous 'liminal experience'. The men and women who joined monasteries and convents left behind much of their former lives, and spent a period of probation as a novice. They wore a habit, the uniform of that religious order, and in many cases shaved their hair, the men into the monastic tonsure and the women so as to hide their beauty beneath a veil. Often candidates were given a new name and vowed to spend their lives in conditions that were by modern standards starkly penitential.

The Dominican friars had their roots in European monasticism, but radically changed the custom of living in the same monastery for life. They centred their lives around itinerant preaching based on study of Scripture, philosophy and theology and gravitated to the new universities that were springing up in the 13th century. They established their communities in cities rather than the countryside and at first tried to support themselves by begging, which soon proved impractical as their communities grew rapidly.

By the time I became a novice in 1959 the tonsure was no longer required in our part of the world, and after the reforms of the Vatican Council, in the late 1960s, most friars resumed using their baptismal name. At the same time our routine was simplified: the long hours in choir were shortened and the prayers chanted in English rather than Latin. Instead of eating in silence or having a brother read to us while we ate, we began conversing at all meals. Even so, our life itself was still quite penitential, and the restrictions sometimes felt arbitrary.

The relentless daily routine was genuinely penitential, as was the frustration of not being free to go out whenever we chose. Some superiors still censored the few monthly letters of novices and students. Learning to manage my physical appetites was no different than for every young adult, and was probably made easier by living in a community where alcohol was not available to us juniors, and we rarely saw women or girls except in the church or among our few visitors. I began to realise that a greater challenge was to control my desire to be right; to refrain from showing that I knew – or thought I knew – the 'correct' answer in the small disputes that arose among us. This was decades before the invention of the internet, but in me the hunger for facts, the 'lust for certitude'[25], was particularly strong.

Reading had long been a favourite activity and I had many times opened and entered other worlds through the small doors of book covers, gathering and hoarding a store of information which led me to imagine, irrationally, that I knew more than others on most topics. It took many years before I could see that it does not matter who wins an argument, at least outside the courtroom and when life and fortune are not at stake. My own experience, and later Edward De Bono's *I'm Right, You're Wrong*[26], slowly guided me towards a broader understanding of sharing space with other minds. I found that it is not shameful to make a mistake, nor dishonourable not to know everything. This less confrontational approach brought me greater freedom to appreciate and learn from the wisdom of those who thought differently from myself.

It took longer for me to stop clinging, unquestioning, to the several 'orthodoxies' that had formed my mental world up to that time. Precious as it had been to learn a worldview in catechism answers as a child, in adulthood I slowly found the courage to question the meaning of these truths. It was liberating to be freed from a literal interpretation of the Scriptures, to find that they have been shaped by the literary forms and editing styles used by their ancient authors. It was also enlightening to realise that the Church councils were just as limited by the constraints of language as they had tried to transmit treasured glimpses of the transcendent mysteries of the Incarnation and Trinity. Like people of every age, they formulated these in terms of the worldview current in their time.

Our courses in philosophy and theology were largely from the works of Aristotle and Aquinas, taught by lecturers within our own faculty. Astonishing as it now seems, no university in Australia offered a theology degree, and until the 1970s seminaries were not yet combined into clusters like the Yarra Theological Union or the Melbourne College of Divinity. The texts of the ancient and medieval thinkers gave us a solid framework for our thought, but we were not encouraged to be critical of the classical theories, or to read the works of contemporary scholars. When in senior years I began to discover that some of Aquinas' insights could be questioned, especially those based on his limited knowledge of biology, it was both painfully unsettling and at the same time liberating. As I gradually encountered the great minds from other faith traditions and the insights of contemporary sciences I slowly began to see that clinging onto 'certainties' can be a sign of how uncertain we are.

6
Dabchicks and Lunatics
Childers Cove and Bundoora

Robert Frost's image of two roads that 'diverged in a yellow wood'[27] is often used to illustrate the dramatic difference that a single choice can make to our life's journey; but in our younger years it is mainly other people who make choices for us. Our conception occurs at some point in the measureless flow of human and cosmic activity, the result of innumerable physical and genetic factors. We have absolutely no choice in this matter, but from that instant we begin to have power, ever-so-slightly, to re-direct the flow, as the poet did when he chose the path that seemed 'the one less travelled by …'. When I look back at childhood scenes that are etched deeply into memory, I see how others took me through life's archways into places that to a child were unique and exciting, where my body and mind developed as it explored them, with future results that are still not known.

                ~

The wheel of the jinker rose taller than my head. My face was level with the iron hub where the slender yellow spokes all came neatly together, but the hard rubber tyre was higher than I could reach. The horse between the shafts had its long neck down and was noisily tearing off mouthfuls of grass. When he curled his lip I could see his greenish teeth and the silver bit that the reins were fixed to. When he shook his head and snorted at me the harness clinked and jingled.

    The horse waited at the back gate of my grandparents' big stone house near the sea where my parents had brought us for a holiday. Not far behind the house were the high cliffs at Childers Cove, a bay about twenty kilometres south-east of Warrnambool and about two hundred and sixty west of Melbourne. On still nights you could hear the waves thumping on the sand. My father told me that he was born in that house, as were most of his eight brothers and sisters, but one of them, Auntie Kath, had already died. I was told that Grandpa's own father and even his grandfather had lived here a long time ago.

I had watched Auntie Jeanne pack all the letters and parcels into the canvas bag. She tied its neck with a strap and poured on a blob of brown wax that she had melted over a candle, then stamped the soft wax with the seal. If the wax was broken when it reached the next post office they would know that someone had been stealing letters. I thought of the letters travelling in the dark all the way to Warrnambool, like when the train went through a tunnel. When the bag was opened, they would not know where they were.

I was looking forward to going in the jinker to the windmill corner – it was my first time – but I was a bit frightened of Grandpa. He wore braces and big boots and had a bushy white beard. It was hard to talk to him, for he might snort at anything I said about the animals or the farm; about birds, or the dab-chicks that I liked to watch in the swamps. I knew he didn't like boys who were sissies, for when one of my aunts had once let me wear a pretty brooch that I saw on her dressing-table, she warned me not to let Grandpa see me wearing it.

I could not get up into the jinker by myself. I was afraid that Grandpa would growl at me for not being able to climb up; or that he would he pick me up roughly and his big hands hurt my ribs, then dump me where he had already thrown the mail bag. Suddenly he lifted me up – it didn't hurt much – and put me on the leather seat. I wasn't sure if I was allowed to put my feet on the mail bag, but I tried it out when he wasn't looking, careful not to kick the wax seal in case I broke it.

We trotted down the driveway to the front gate. I liked the two deep ruts of hard grey sand, curving like a train line, that the wheels of cars and carts and the jinker had worn across the paddock, leaving a high strip of grass between them. When we came to the white gate I wished I could climb down to help Grandpa by opening and closing it again but I knew my legs could not even reach the metal step, like a round leaf on the end of its stem. I watched Grandpa climb down stiffly, open the gate and lead the horse through, then close it again so that the horses in the home paddock could not wander onto the road.

The road was red gravel, corrugated like an iron roof, but as our horse trotted along the jinker on its big wheels it did not bounce as much as the car did. We passed the school with only one classroom, where my father had been a schoolboy many years ago. After that we went past the swamp where the little waves were playing in the sunlight and dabchicks swam among the bull-rushes. As we trotted past I saw one of them dive, and I knew it would come up a long way from where it had gone under. After a while we came to the Windmill Corner and the tarred main road. Grandpa said that further to the east this Great Ocean Road ran beside the sea and went all the way to Melbourne. We stopped at the milk depot, a reddish-brown shed set back from the road. It was built on poles as high as the jinker; open at the front and full of silver milk-cans. A big semi-trailer from the butter factory was stopped there and the man was tilting and rolling empty cans from his truck onto the depot. They were marked with painted letters so that each farmer could find their own. Soon he would roll the full cans onto his truck. Grandpa took the new mail bag from a hook and put ours in its place, then picked up a few rolled newspapers. In the bag there would be letters and parcels for people in the farms around our district. Grandfather was not allowed to open it: he had to bring it back to Auntie Jeanne.

Auntie Jeanne was lighting the kerosene pressure-lamp, forcing air into it with a small brass pump. When it was hissing and burning properly she left the pump lying on the table, so I took it out to play with. It was about as thick as a broom handle and a bit longer than a pencil, with a snout like the end of a little trumpet, but the wide end of the trumpet was fixed to the pump and air came out the narrow end. I pumped the piston back and forth and liked the solid, metallic 'cluck' sound at each end, and the jet of cool air that it squirted into my face.

I took it out into the garden. The path was lined with petunias, and I saw that they were almost the same shape as the end of the pump, fitting them almost exactly. I began to pump air into one petunia but the vigorous movement of my little hands soon reduced the fragile flower to bruised mush. This did not deter me, nor did my aunt's gentle rebuke that I was hurting the petunias. I kept trying to 'improve' more of the delicate blooms, but was disappointed each time, and soon lost interest.

I can look at any time through the tunnel of memory and see moments from those holidays in the house at The Cove that became for me an ideal of security and peace. Such moments may have served to anchor me, despite numberless upsets and turmoil later in life, within a stable psychological context. One morning I was lying in bed beside my father and two brothers. We were snug and warm as we talked and laughed, even though the wind rattled the big sash windows in their frames. Outside, magpies were carolling in the sunlit green paddocks. This scene, although it may have lasted only half an hour and never been repeated, has remained with me all my life. I have loved the song of magpies ever since.

When visitors came to my grandparents' house they were not received in a parlour, but went straight to Annie's room. Auntie Annie, older than my father, had caught polio when she was a girl and had been in bed ever since, but her room became the family parlour, where news was exchanged and morning or afternoon tea served. Annie was friendly to us children and always listened when we told her where we had been and what we had discovered, and she answered all our questions, for she had read many books. Her cramped hands had difficulty writing with a pen, so someone had bought her a black portable Stott & Underwood typewriter, the first typewriter I had seen.

⁓

One of the best things about those holidays was that my brothers and I could explore around the farm. There were high box-thorn hedges that served as wind-breaks. The roaming hens feasted on their bright orange berries and made their nests deep among the thorns. Rabbits too made their burrows there. We were warned not to put our hands down a burrow, because often snakes lived there after the rabbits had left. We knew how far the clever rabbits could dig their branching tunnels, because when we went rabbiting our uncles' shovels had opened them up to find the ferret when it caught a rabbit and stayed down to eat it.

Away from the house there were sheds full of farm machinery, and joined to it at the back was the Old Kitchen and laundry, two rooms of silver-grey weather-boards that were the only part left of the original home. The laundry was still used, but the old kitchen had become the family storeroom, filled with the junk of generations. We wondered at the bits of old harness and machinery; the hand-operated washing machine, the discarded sporting gear and books; but the best treasure of all was the wind-up gramophone with its stack of 78 rpm records.

The only music I had previously heard was from the radio at home: the current 'hits', mostly from the United States, and songs that today would be called Country and Western. Here, as we cranked the wood and silver handle and placed the needle with its crackling speaker onto the spinning black disc, a window opened onto a world of amazing new sounds. We heard the wavering tones of a few operatic arias – the *Anvil Chorus* from *Il Trovatore*; bits of Mozart; some of Wagner's *Lohengrin*; *La Paloma*; and many traditional songs like 'O Dem Golden Slippers'; 'Red River Valley'; 'The Big Rock Candy Mountain'; 'The Streets of Laredo' and 'Birmingham Jail'. This entrance into the world of music was for me the best of all tunnels to explore. The scraps we heard from those scratchy 78s enchanted me. I had no idea from what part of the world the melodies came, or from what era, but I let these sounds from some other world carry me through many strange doorways. They lodged in my mind – or heart, or spirit – and remained there until nearly forty years later I taught myself to play a flute and found great enjoyment in once more bringing them to life.

For a few years in the mid 1940s we returned from our earliest holidays at Childers Cove to our home in Plenty Rd, Bundoora, where my father worked as Assistant Farm Manager at the Mont Park Lunatic Asylum. Our brick cottage there and the Childers Cove house are the place of my earliest memories.[28]

What sort of archway do I pass through, to look back more than seven decades at myself, a little blond boy playing in the hedge at our front fence along Plenty Rd? This is more than looking at slides or a video, none of which existed then anyway. Looking back now from far in the future the edges may be dim and cloudy, but I enter a still-living world. My brother and I are breaking dry twigs into lengths, because we are operating a match factory. In that distant scene, we are passing together through a further archway of imagination, leaving behind the garden and the hedge to enter a fictional dream-factory for making imagined matches. How do a four and three-year-old find the power to travel to such a place? We were inspired by the real Bryant and May factory far across Melbourne which we had never seen, but had heard of as the place where several of our aunts and cousins had found jobs during the recent Great Depression. There they made real matches from pine-wood and phosphorus; and one aunt found a real husband.

No memories of pain mar those days of peace and sunlight. I lived low to the earth, rejoicing to ride a half-broken tricycle along the dirt path on the eastern side of the house and up over a low mound where someone had left a pile of dirt that had turned hard. Beside the path, in the foundations of the brick cottage, were interesting terra-cotta ventilators where spiders lived. We played at being road menders, using our baby brother's pram as our truck, and spoons as shovels.

Inside the house were the 'mynah spare-room' and the 'block spare-room'. In the former a trapped Indian mynah-bird had made a noisy fuss and a very visible mess; in the latter, wooden blocks were stored, builders' off-cuts, which made wonderful play-things before being burned in the kitchen stove or the living room fire-place.

My younger brother Denis was born while we lived in this house. I recall him in his canvas bassinet, which hung on a collapsible wooden frame that socketed together in a way that fascinated me. Sometimes my father would take us to where he worked in the large brick-paved dairy that supplied milk to the asylum. Within its whitewashed walls many cows were being milked by inmates from the asylum, amid a great din of clanging buckets, shouted orders and floors being hosed down with water rushing at frightening pressure. We visited the piggery, where pink snouts poked through the railings of pastel green angle-iron, from which the powdery paint coloured my hands when I touched it.

Across the fence from our backyard sprinklers sprayed the large vegetable garden. Here and there more inmates worked, digging new beds or gathering vegetables that sometimes arrived in our kitchen with the damp soil still on them. At the backyard tap, above the 'gully trap', my father sometimes filled square, bright silver kerosene tins. The rushing water and the echoing tins made this a noisy, exciting process. Believing I was helping, when the water was about to reach the top I would loudly call: 'flowing over!' I could never comprehend how he carried a full tin in one hand.

Some of the more 'trusty' inmates were allowed to work in our garden. We knew and addressed them by their surnames. For many years afterwards we recalled the quaint stories they would tell: that a noisy car passing along the road had the motor of a fire-engine, or that the ear-wigs among the flowers would strive to get into our ears. We could tell that they had passed through some strange archway to live in a world of their own, from which they seemed unable to return.

Lying in bed, my father often read farming magazines, with black-and-white photos of pigs, cows and farm machinery. There were diagrams of carcasses showing how to cut them into joints for the kitchen. One night I saw that the pictures were of the various types of bombs which might fall on Melbourne if the Japanese came any further. The Second World War began to colour everything. Where once the only heavy traffic past our gate had been the bus and occasional timber jinker hauling just one big log from the Kinglake forests, now we saw occasional convoys of military vehicles: trucks loaded with soldiers; even tanks and guns.

One night we were taken out to see searchlights far away to the south. Like long fingers they moved back and forth across the sky over Melbourne, feeling for aeroplanes. A family we visited in the suburbs showed us the air-raid shelter they had dug in the backyard. Like most of the Australian population, none of us knew that Darwin had already been destroyed by multiple air-raids or that Broome and Townsville had also been attacked; that a boat in Sydney harbour had been torpedoed and the US and Japanese fleets had been locked in combat not far away in the Coral Sea, and further off near Midway Island. My Uncle Louis, then in his early twenties, visited us in khaki military uniform. He sat in the kitchen while I was stood, naked in the 'tin dish' on the table, to be bathed. Later I heard my mother saying that Louis was embarrassed by this, and wondered what 'embarrassed' could mean.

My first memory of a church service is of being taken to Mass in the Sacred Heart church in Bell St Preston. We drove there in our Nash sedan, which had tasselled roller blinds and an oval rear window. It would have been a new car, twenty years before. On the altar in the church there was a brass stand holding a red book from which the priest was reading. Sometimes when my father was reading and I wanted to talk or play with him, he would make me wait until he finished a chapter and I would try to calculate the thickness of pages still remaining. Looking at the altar I saw with alarm that in the book from which the priest was reading, a thick wad of pages remained on the side that he still had to read, and I grew depressed, thinking we would have to endure this boring process for a long time before we could return home.

In nearby Coburg I recall entering new zones of experience on an outing with my Mother and brothers. Denis, the younger, was in his 'pusher'. We followed an interesting footpath beside a railway line, separated from the tracks by a white fence. I enjoyed the neat arrangement of silver tracks and the stones of the road-bed stained brown by rusted brake-dust. A high red train rattled past us, making a great din, but behind the fence I was not afraid. Was it on that same outing that, in a park, I ate strawberry ice cream for the first time? The delicious flavour is still with me, more than seven decades later.

7
Golden Square and Gravel Hill
Bendigo, Mepunga East, and Naringal

As a young man in the 1920s my father left his family home at Childers Cove and travelled north to Queensland, working at a variety of jobs. He had not long recovered from severe peritonitis, which in those days before antibiotics was usually fatal. During the Great Depression he joined the prison service and worked in Melbourne's Pentridge Jail and at the prison farm on French Island in Westernport Bay. Soon after his marriage in 1938 he was one of the officers who pioneered the new Cooriemungle Prison Farm near Timboon in Western Victoria. Sometimes, because of his restless searching for adventure, sometimes because of his horse-racing debts, he was prompted to move his young family in search of better opportunities. He left the prison service for other government jobs: as Assistant Farm Manager at Mont Park asylum, then as an Attendance Officer in the Education Department. At his father's death in 1949 he returned to the family farm but later again went back to the government job in the Education Department. Even here he sought to improve his lot by moving from one district to another, and later 'moonlighting' at a second job.

After a few years at Mont Park, my father must have seen in the Government Gazette a vacancy which seemed to offer better conditions. He had no secondary education, but abundant optimism and skills in dealing with people, so he successfully applied for the position of Schools Attendance Officer. In 1944 he moved his family to Bendigo, a provincial city a hundred and sixty kilometres north of Melbourne.

We packed all our family's goods into plywood tea-chests and sent them off in a furniture van, then at Spencer Street Station caught the train to the north. To me as a small child it was a supreme adventure to climb once again into one of the red carriages behind a huge, panting steam locomotive. We walked down the narrow corridor to find our seats of green fake leather, deeply embedded with buttons that begged children's fingers to explore them. On panels beneath the woven-wire luggage racks were sepia photos of Victorian scenic spots that could be visited by train.

As we pulled out through the railway yards I stood near a window, my face pressed against the glass. I could not take my eyes from the silver rails below, which were moving sideways! They slid back and forth amazingly as we picked up speed, hitting against and seeming to pass through one another. I had never seen anything like it, for I knew you could not *do* that with pieces of steel. I tried to ask my father, who was busy talking to my mother, how the rails could move like that. He said that men at the signal box moved them. Taking him at his word, I tried to imagine strong men sitting on the end of the platform, each holding a large wooden handle attached to the end of a free-moving rail which they somehow moved back and forth; but even at the age of four I knew that no men were strong enough to move heavy rails from hundreds of metres away, especially with trains running on them. Anyway, what would be the use? I could only conclude that my father had not understood what I was trying to ask. It was not the first time an adult had done this. I asked him again later, but he still did not understand, so I left it at that; one day I would find out. Later I understood that he thought I was talking about the points which the signal box operator moves just a few centimetres to direct a train from one track to another. He had not seen what I was seeing, the wonder of silver rails seeming to slide rapidly sideways as the speeding train crossed over several tracks to find the one that would take us to Bendigo.

With its many stops, the journey seemed to last the whole day, but probably took only about four hours. I was shocked by the sudden darkness as we entered each of the two tunnels, then shot out again into sunlight. They were apt thresholds into the new worlds of awareness that were soon to open up before me. Almost at the end of our journey, the train passed through Golden Square station, whose beautiful name caught my attention; I would have liked to leave the train there and find our new home in that place.

In Bendigo we stayed at first with friends of my father, the Ward family. I recall their white house as palatial, with French windows leading onto a tiled terrace; pergolas with vines; a lawn with berry bushes; but it was probably a modest suburban home. There was a daughter some years older than us – she might have been eight – who played with a few girls of her own age. They played a game with orange berries from the cotoneaster bush. I had difficulty playing, either because I could not follow its rules or because I could not do the counting it required. I was hurt that the girls teased me for being incompetent and babyish.

We lived out of suitcases and had our meals in a single room cluttered with our clothing and other belongings. At one time my brother Gerald was sick with pleurisy. Our parents made poultices of unpleasant grey clay, heated over a pot of boiling water, which they applied to a cloth on his chest using a knife as trowel. This fascinating sight became unpleasantly connected with watching Mr Ward some time later clearing a drain that ran into the gutter outside the house. When nauseating grey gunk emerged, someone remarked that it could cause diphtheria.

We soon moved into a cold bluestone house in Mundy Street. I felt confined there, for the concrete backyard was small, ending against a high factory wall. But every stage of our journey has its compensations: at that house I delightedly crunched my teeth for the first time into a toffee- apple, bought at the shop across the street. Not long after, we rented a small wooden cottage in Neal Street for £2 a fortnight, which in today's values would be around $200. This one had a broad yard and was more lightsome. My brother had begun going to school and my days felt empty, so I looked forward to starting school myself. To encourage me, my father asserted that I would be more intelligent than any other child in the class. His well-meant attempt to affirm me had the unfortunate effect of confirming in me a false sense of superiority that he had already inspired. I suspect that my father felt awkward dealing with children. At thirty-four he had married an eighteen-year-old wife to save her from a disgrace that was none of her own doing. I remember him as often absent. Perhaps he was unconsciously using work and horse-racing as excuses to avoid the domestic scene. When at home he would alternate between preoccupied silence and occasional loving displays of affection. He was generous, and after a win at the races would bring home lavish treats for us, but his generosity led him to make promises to us children that he could not always keep. Wanting to give us joy, he would cause disappointment, so that while feeling sad for myself, I would also feel sorry for him.

At last I began school at St Kilian's, and each day would walk the few blocks, just over a kilometre, with my brother. We would gaze up at the railway bridge high above us, occasionally admiring a steam train thundering and smoking on its way north towards the Murray River at Echuca or perhaps Kerang. Near that bridge we could look far down into a creek that except in flash floods was merely a trickle in a concrete channel. When I re-visited the place as an adult I was astonished that I could almost touch the iron girders of the rail bridge, and that the concrete drain passed barely two metres below the roadway.

Bendigo's climate ranges from winter frosts to blazing summer heat. It seems now inexplicable, but at no season did we wear more than short trousers, shirt and pullover. We never had jackets, and like all other children wore no head covering in winter or in days of century heat. Paradoxically, adults wore hats at all times. On frosty mornings we would play with the panes of ice that formed on puddles and horse-troughs, perhaps contributing to the frequent painful chilblains from which we suffered despite the woollen socks and gloves that our mother knitted for us.

The school-yard was bordered by peppercorn trees and paved with yellow gravel in which flashed occasional bits of pure white quartz. Like most of the children I would often graze my knees and hands on that sharp gravel when I fell at play. The quartz was a feature of golden Bendigo, which had been a main centre of the nineteenth-century Gold Rush. After making many people rich on alluvial gold, its deep mines continued to produce tonnes of the precious metal for almost a century. Mullock heaps surrounded the town, and while Golden Square was evocatively named, so was the suburb and the State School that bore the name Gravel Hill.

At St Kilian's the Sisters of Mercy were frightening towers of black with rosaries clicking at their leather belts. All we could see of their flesh were their hands and pinched faces framed in stiff white oval coifs. They were the source of all rules about what must be done in the classroom and playground. Sitting in our long 'forms', we chanted prayers to learn by heart:

> O Angel of God, my guardian dear,
> to whom God's love commits me here;
> ever this day be at my side
> to light and guard, to rule and guide. Amen.
> Hail Mary, full of grace, the Lord is with you …
> Glory be to the Father, and to the Son, and to the Holy Spirit, as it was in the beginning, is now and ever shall be, worldwithoutendamen.

My small, puzzled mind struggled to make sense of the last word, as indeed, for centuries, far greater intellects seem to have done.

The 'Bubs' class was taught by pretty Sister Tarcisius, perhaps still in her teens. To teach us letters and words she used a thick pad of hanging charts, from time to time flipping over a page to reveal another set of pictures and words for us to chant and learn. To emphasise each word she tapped it with her wooden pointer, making a soft 'thup' sound, which I loved and waited eagerly for her to repeat.

Like most educators of that time, the sisters had a limited understanding of children's psychology. When we were at the tender age of five they told us about the sufferings of Jesus. In every classroom and hanging from every sister's rosary there was a crucifix, surely the most horrible method of execution ever devised. Only as an adult did I realise how inappropriate this was for children, and began to ask what had become of the central Christian belief that Christ is risen? Being constantly taught that one of life's keynotes was the death of God must surely have led to much pessimism, even depression.

It is easy to criticise the Catholic school system, but it was built almost entirely on the unpaid labour of many religious communities of Sisters and Brothers, few of whom could afford proper training. They were supported mainly by the coins given as 'school money' by poor families who for a hundred years had received nothing towards their children's education from the taxes they paid to the government for that purpose.

In Grade 1 we moved into the care of Sister Collette, and were now considered old enough for the higher technology of slate pencils and chalk. Each child brought a wet rag in a jar to clean their slate and a dry rag with which to wipe it. I particularly loved the rare times when we were allowed to play with plasticine. Once I created a tree bearing a public notice, for which I pressed a penny into its plasticine trunk, and was sent to show the Grade Twos, to inspire them with my creativity.

I had looked forward eagerly to starting school, and found, as I had hoped, little friends who were attractive and pleasant to be with. A few of us would walk happily around the playground, arms across each other's shoulders, delighting to share each day our miniature discoveries. In this happy atmosphere, I had no idea that it was possible to walk through an ordinary doorway to find a region of incomprehensible hostility.

Early in Grade 1 I endured one of the most traumatic experiences of my school days. My younger brother Denis had suffered a head injury during his birth, and had difficulty learning. When he started in his first year at school, I became a kind of guardian for him, although scarcely a year older. It was my duty, for instance, to meet him at play time to make sure that his glasses were clean.

In the days before the zip fastener, men and boys had to cope with awkward concealed buttons to fasten the front of their trousers. To make life easier for him, our mother had made him trousers with a simpler way of fastening, a flap of cloth that tucked into a small opening.

On his first day at school, I accompanied him on his initial visit to the boys' toilets to make sure that he could manage this. I did not know that some boys had been misbehaving around the toilets and that teachers were trying to catch the culprits. While I was helping my brother, several older boys poked their heads around the door and watched us. When they saw me checking to see that he had properly fastened his trousers before returning to the school-yard, they began to shout accusations. I had no idea what or why they were shouting but they were obviously hostile and I soon realised that they were accusing me of doing something improper. They quickly surrounded me, demanding that I go to the head teacher. Even as a First Grader I knew that this was not good news, so I strongly resisted. Three of them easily overpowered me and dragged or carried me, literally kicking and screaming, through the crowded playground to Sister Gonzaga's office. Every child in the yard stopped their playing to watch this spectacle and I was deeply ashamed. I don't recall what happened when we got to the head teacher's office, or how I explained myself. I received no punishment, but the experience had already been so traumatic that for a long time I could barely allow myself to look back at it, much less tell anyone else.

※

Later that year, at the end of the war in the Pacific, every child was given a commemorative medal and – more importantly – a free ice-cream to celebrate our victory over Japan. I have a clear memory of a newspaper's front page with huge headlines over a picture of a mushroom cloud. It seemed to cause awe in my parents, for they kept it for a long time afterwards.

Mrs Johnstone took charge of us in Grade 2. The dull hours dragged, and classes became a kind of torment. I could find only limited amusement in imagining pictures among the cloud-like swirls left on the blackboard after it had been cleaned with the duster. My most enjoyed classroom achievement that year was learning to sew together pieces of blue felt to make an animal of uncertain species, stuffed with bits of rag.

When the time came to prepare for our First Holy Communion I knew that something important was about to happen. Whatever thoughts I already had about a world beyond this life were further awakened by the ancient teaching that this bread somehow contained Jesus, who was God. This ancient truth came to us in a setting somewhat distorted from the original context of Jesus' last meal with his friends. After much instruction to prepare us, we received, in the middle of a Mass in Latin, a small circle of bread refined beyond recognition and tasting like ice-cream wafer. It was given to us from a gold vessel by a man wearing coloured garments seen nowhere else but in church. Much later I came to understand that the ceremony did not look at all like the Jewish Passover meal where Jesus told his friends that he loved them enough to die for them; nor did we receive the wine that featured in that meal.

Despite these large differences, something of a profound reality reached to my depths. Beyond the boring vista of the classroom a precious doorway was beginning to open, through which I could reach towards and even speak to the ageless God who had made the world, who from now on I could receive into myself. On Sundays our family would walk the few blocks to St Kilian's Church, 'the largest wooden church in the southern hemisphere', dating from 1888. On some special evenings I would go there with my mother to Benediction. From the nave of the long church I would watch the altar boys lighting many candles on the altar. They appeared to carry a globe of light on a stick, with which they silently touched one candle after another, wonderfully transforming each into another globe of light. The smell of incense enchanted the air and the golden-rayed monstrance with the sacred Host at its centre seemed like a window into God.

Rituals can lead us towards the Transcendent, but I have come to see that the emphasis on worship of the Sacrament apart from the Mass distorted our understanding of what Jesus was doing. Deeper understanding shows that the Eucharist (first known as the Breaking of Bread) is a shared *activity*, a meal in which just before he was murdered, Jesus symbolically gave himself to his friends and to future generations. The purpose of this central celebration is not just to produce sacred food to sustain the individual Christian but to *unite* the community celebrating it. As the members of this community struggle to serve each other and try to bring about God's reign, they draw on the presence of the Risen Christ to transform them even to the point of being ready to die. However imperfectly I or my mentors understood it then, the ceremony of the Eucharist offered me, at seven years of age, entry through an archway into a deep mystery of never-ending life, challenging me in ways that I would only slowly come to understand.

Other doors were opening, to reveal mysteries in my wider surroundings. On some clear summer nights my father and his friends would stand for hours in the backyard, talking of horse racing and other things unintelligible to a little boy. Backyards were not then flooded with glare from nearby street-lights, and even kitchen windows were not brightly lit. As the men talked on, the stars shone splendidly overhead, and sometimes even became the subject of their conversation. The sky seemed to me a domed roof over the obviously flat Earth. Although I was eager to learn about the world, it would be fifteen years before I heard that the stars were moving away from each other at unimaginable speeds, but at distances so vast that even after centuries their positions seem unchanged. It would be many more years again before anyone knew that there were at least a hundred billion galaxies like the majestic Milky Way that we admired, each of them containing some hundred billion stars.

Miss Bourke taught Grade 3. When I visited the St Kilian's parish more than thirty years later, in the early 1980s, she was still teaching it. Third Grade students were considered mature enough to use pens with steel nibs which we dipped into white ceramic inkwells. I recall the exciting tension of doing competitive mental arithmetic, and the comfort of sitting next to a friendly boy called Peter Gill. Companionship was becoming important. One morning I asked to leave class, trying to conceal the fact that I could not stop crying. It was probably the first day of term, for I was desolate over the departure that morning of the large and lively family of cousins, the Matthews, who had been staying with us. In their ancient car they had made an epic journey from their farm near Warrnambool, returning our visit of the previous summer.

Bendigo summers were hot. On the most blazing days during the long holidays, when the thermometer climbed well above 100 Fahrenheit, we would lie shirtless on the lino beneath the kitchen table, the second coolest place in the house. Before household refrigerators, our butter, milk and occasional lemonade was kept cool in the ice-chest, where a large block of ice slowly melted. It was delivered twice a week by the ice-man's horse-drawn cart, but in midsummer the ice-block would not last until his next visit so the butter had then to be wrapped in a damp cloth and stored in the brick fire-place, which was cooler than the kitchen floor, but too small to lie in.

In the long summer evenings, on a few rare occasions, we walked as a family to the swimming baths. I did not care that the unfiltered water, crowded with unwashed people, was silty brown; or that my woollen bathers itched; or that I could not swim; I loved being immersed in its coolness.

Scattered through the suburbs of a Bendigo much smaller than it has become today were small corner shops and not a few hotels. We were often sent on a 'message' to the local butcher, or to Randall's corner grocery shop where goods like biscuits, sugar, flour and rice were measured and weighed into brown paper bags as each customer required. An ice cream cone cost sixpence and the luxury of a milkshake one shilling. Besides money we had to hand over rationing coupons, for during the war and for several years after, a fixed number of coupons were allocated to each family for items like meat, butter, clothing and petrol.

We were frightened to walk past the Limerick hotel just before six o'clock closing time when the roaring din of many voices poured from its open windows and doors. Its bar was crowded with men gathered for the 'six o'clock swill', for the irrational closing time was meant to force family men to be home for the evening meal. Instead it forced them to cram their drinking into less than an hour after work and sent many home rolling drunk.

To go into the town centre of Bendigo we would wait for the small black-and-white bus that turned into our street. It would arrive uttering its frequent but unusual cry of *tooka tooka tooka*, which the driver sounded by pulling on a string. Nowhere else have I heard a bus with that ability. In the big department stores it was exciting to watch the shop assistants send cash from each counter to the central cashier, who returned the customer's change and receipt. Some stores used capsules propelled through tubes by air pressure, but others more excitingly used overhead wires on which small containers were propelled across the shop when a cord was pulled to release a strong rubber spring.

My mother, new in town and hampered by three young children, had few friends. There were no play groups or auxiliaries that she could join. Mrs Burtonclay would occasionally call, a neighbour who also had three young sons. To 'call' did not mean using a telephone, for we had none. It meant to drop in, or send a child with a message to arrange a shopping expedition or a rare visit to 'the pictures'. Before I was seven I had seen *Bambi, The Sullivans, How Green Was My Valley, Stand by for Action*, and some Westerns and cartoons. I barely understood them, but many decades later was surprised, when watching again *How Green Was My Valley*, that the one scene I remembered in full detail was that on his first day at a new school the young hero was bloodied in a fight with a bully.

Once, as a treat, we were promised a boat ride. I had never seen a real boat, and certainly never ridden in one. After what seemed a long trip to Lake Weeroona – it was only a few blocks past my school – I was deeply disappointed that the boat was not something approaching the size of an ocean liner, as I had been expecting. It was merely a dinghy, and not even a proper wooden one, only canvas stretched on a frame. But I did enjoy the ride, and watched with interest the rippling water-level half-way up the canvas, as seen from inside the boat.

I was adept at building up expectations that were doomed to be dashed. On another weekend we walked a long way from our house to see an aeroplane. I was again disappointed that it was not an airliner that you could climb into, such as I had seen in magazines, but just a small yellow biplane which could carry one passenger in an open cockpit behind the pilot. I was aware that my sorrow at being let down by such events would also disappoint my mother, so I tried, probably without success, to conceal my dashed hopes, thereby adding secrecy and depression to my confused emotions.

Another memorable outing was to the Wax Works. I was fascinated by the various tableaux, but that night I woke from a horrible nightmare. I could not clearly remember its contents, except that it involved blood and mutilation. My mother could not have known beforehand all the details of the displays that we were going to see, but my reaction showed clearly that six or seven is not an appropriate age to introduce children to the gruesome alternative world of crime and mangled bodies.

⥲

All children are sensitive. Fear or brutal treatment may make them hide their feelings, but every little person is capable of profound depths. My mother was then a young woman of 24 or 25, and had already given birth to four male children. The first of these, conceived in violence when she was not yet seventeen, she had been compelled to give away for adoption. To us she was remarkably loving and kind, our daily emotional support. This beautiful, reliable woman was always there, providing three meals each day; bathing us; dressing us with clean warm clothing; mending what was torn; knitting us socks, gloves and pullovers against the winter cold.

On occasion she would delight to share some of the ghost stories she remembered, and we would enjoy the thrill of the terror they aroused. But on a few rare occasions she would look at us with a particular expression that seemed to show, or pretend to show, maliciousness. Did she put on that look to tease us? I could not decide whether she was merely playing, trying to give us the same thrill as we got from the ghost stories, but for the brief intervals that she maintained the look I was terrified, fearful lest she withdraw her irreplaceable, loving support. Were we seeing traces of some black mood, recalling the emotional pain of her youth? These episodes would not last long, but while they did I would suffer agonies more terrible than any other. Here was the source of all the tenderness and care that I knew, apparently turning against me. It was inexplicable, beyond the horizons of my world. I could not deal with it.

I knew our mother could be very afraid. When occasionally our father was absent for a night or two she would make a bed for herself in the room where we children slept, and at bed-time attempt to jam the keyless old lock with pieces of our Meccano set. I trembled to imagine some faceless man trying to open it from the outside – as no doubt she did herself – for it was less than ten years since in her teens she had suffered rape. Fortunately, we never had occasion to know whether the lock, or the door, would hold under the imagined onslaught.

At times I felt a deep pity for my mother. I recall her attempts to make us a kite. While she had brilliant skills as a cook and at knitting or crocheting, she had not been trained with a hammer or other tools, although would no doubt have taught herself if her husband had possessed any tools of even moderate quality. She chose the lightest pieces of wood she could find and tacked them crudely together in the form of a cross, then put string around their ends and glued newspaper to the frame she had made. She attached a tail of grocer's string with pieces of cloth knotted to it at frequent intervals.

Just by looking at it, child that I was, I felt that it would not fly. All its components were too heavy. How did I know? Had I seen other kites? I cannot be sure, but when the kite fell miserably from her hand each time she launched it I felt a deep disappointment, indeed shame, for my mother. I felt a similar pity for my father when he attempted to repair or build something. Although he was a consummate gardener, when by sheer determination he succeeded in building a primitive fence or even a chicken coop, it looked as if it had been put together by some stone-age human who had for the first time picked up the battered hammer and the borrowed saw. This pit of bleak, seemingly unfathomable sorrow was the strongest feeling of my childhood, probably more painful to me than any embarrassment felt by those whose limited skills I was pitying.

In each of the many houses we lived in, my father always kept poultry – chooks – and was proud of his pure Sussex strain. He considered these the best for laying and eating, although he also experimented with the colourful Wellsummer breed. In Bendigo he bought a part-share in a grey racehorse called Zimmy. To house it in the backyard, he had someone build a 'loose box' which – unlike a stable – leaves the horse free to move about its shed and roll in its small yard. When Dad was away, we were trusted with mixing Zimmy's food. I recall the strong aroma of the thick black molasses that we mixed into his crushed grain. Before my father's groupbought him, Zimmy had won the only race he was ever to win, before my father's group bought him, and eventually had to be admitted an expensive failure, by no means unique among my father's adventures on the racecourse.

Besides the chook pen and the loose box, our backyard also contained the outdoor lavatory, which was linked with the town sewage system, a luxury we would not enjoy in the rural places where we were soon to live. Behind the lavatory was a lilac bush and along the side fence a row of tamarisk trees. I would sometimes join my brother in his games of building farms with wooden fences made by hammering wood-chips into the dirt, and was awed by his elaborate dreams about the life and management of such farms which comprise part of his first book.[29]

Our neighbours on one side were a large, seemingly dysfunctional family. While the mother was a helpful friend to our mother, the father was often drunk. In that condition he would engage in noisy verbal fights with his wife which would sometimes last through the night. Sometimes he was violent.

On the other side was a Protestant church, divided from our house by a tall wooden fence which we could peek through in places. We were fascinated and a little scornful of the fact that other people went to church but did not have the real Mass. One Sunday I was in the backyard playing with the hose, perhaps filling the chooks' water dishes. A little girl climbed the fence in her Sunday best and looked over into our yard. Without hesitating, acting on some instinct that told me I would not have such a chance again, I pointed the hose at her head and drenched her. While I found this not-very-ecumenical experience quite satisfying, it was not prompted by the fact that the child was from the Protestant congregation, but that she was looking into *our* yard, and besides, she was a *girl*. Many years afterwards I was troubled by the crime, but only a little, and wondered what effect it might have had on her church attendance, or even her faith.

8
'Just Like the Animals'
Discovering sex

We meet our first sexual desires as one who rounds a bend in a path and finds a new and unexpected doorway that is at once attractive, exciting and dangerous to enter. We feel compelled to find out what lies beyond this tantalizing entrance, for we instinctively know that unless we do, we might not find our own self.

With desire, comes exploration. A very early memory records me sitting naked in an armchair, probably after a bath. It must have been a cold day for I was half wrapped in a towel, while across the room a fire was glowing. Draping the towel over the chair-arms to make a roof, so that I sat like a sheik in my private tent, I began to observe the interesting sight of my penis, the study of which led me to link two ideas in poetic conjunction, perhaps for the first time in my life.

Its smooth little head had nowhere to hide, having been ruthlessly circumcised soon after I was born. The coldness of the day made it bluer than usual, which caused me to notice with some surprise that it was quite like a policeman's helmet, of the kind then worn by constables in Melbourne streets. Its acorn shape, taller than a half-sphere, had that slightly flared slope at the back, which on the officer's helmet protected the neck from the sun or against assault by any blunt instrument. Like the constable's headgear, my cock also had a little thing on the crown of its dome – for them, a silver button; in my case, just a pee-hole. It astonished me to discover that I had a little policeman between my legs. Had I – then a mere toddler – been able to express my poetic insight in the conservative Victorian press of the early 1940s, how might the constables who kept law and order have reacted to the embarrassment of being told by a little child that each of them was in fact a dick-head?

༄

About the subject of sexuality, perhaps silence has more often been demanded and speech more often suppressed than in any other area of life. Such was the general prudery in society at that time, especially among the less educated, that sexual matters were treated with almost total silence. My mother, for her own valid reasons, found any mention of sex quite impossible. For my father, these matters were not totally beyond discussion. He was proud that his children had experienced life both in a farming milieu – 'on the land', the truer way to live – and also in the city. When we were about six or seven, recalling that on our grandparents' farm we had often seen animals copulating, and perhaps prompted by the randy behaviour of the rooster among his hens in our back-yard, we asked our father: 'How do people mate?' He replied, frankly and generously enough, 'Just like the animals', but he then evaded our further curious questions, promising to give further details 'when you are older'. He might have done better to continue at that point, for his embarrassed failure to elaborate left us busy during the following months observing how dogs, chooks and cattle did it, speculating between ourselves about detailed possibilities that quite destroyed his attempt to keep us in modest ignorance.

In our Bendigo Catholic school, taught by the Sisters of Mercy, we sat in class with little girls, but in the playground segregation was enforced: there was a boys' yard and a girls' yard. At lunch time, after the children had eaten their sandwiches and fruit, one boy, prompted by a teacher, would run around calling aloud: 'All around the boys' yard'. At this, every boy would move in a stampede around to the other side of the school building for the remainder of the lunchtime. Much later in life the memory of this custom struck me as resembling the Victorian era's after-dinner custom by which the ladies would withdraw to the drawing room, leaving the gentlemen to their port and cigars — although in the school-yard it was the males who relocated themselves, galloping with rather less decorum.

For the first nine years of my life I had no sister and we would meet our female cousins only on rare holiday visits. I was almost completely ignorant of what the naked body of a girl, even a baby or toddler, looked like. If when out visiting one of us might sneak a rare glimpse of a baby girl having her nappy changed, we would later attempt to report back what we had seen. This seems incredible in today's mass-media-soaked world following the sexual revolution of the 1960s, where nudity is common on public television and movies, and older children do not satisfy their curiosity as we did, with pictures from men's magazines where genitals were air-brushed out of existence. They have access to centrefolds of bodies totally exposed; and primary school children can find on their mobile phones videos of the most degraded sexual acts. We were profoundly ignorant, but could not ask our parents for more knowledge, for it was their own embarrassed silence and protectiveness that kept us uneducated, and — naturally — increased our curiosity.

One memorable summer's evening, when I was seven years old, two little girls who lived nearby happened to stop at our front gate during the long hours of twilight. We soon found ourselves playing a game in which we chased and caught each other in the fading dusk. Being older and stronger, my brother and I did most of the catching. After one capture, I began to hold and tickle the little girl I had seized. Since she did not complain, but only giggled, I soon began to explore her body further, reaching her more intimate place. The activity excited me in a new way. It stirred my own small sexual thing, giving a surprising new pleasure, which I wanted to continue as long as possible. Did I catch the girl several more times, or did it happen only once? Memory is fallible, even about the first opening of a door to such an exciting and important new world.

Was it a subtle intervention of Providence that soon after that evening we moved to a distant part of the state? I was seven years old and wondered for a time whether the move was prompted by my parents finding out about my precocious sexual activity, but since I had received no embarrassed rebuke I finally concluded that we must have moved house for other reasons. In fact, we were moving because of my father's gambling debts, and our new home was a dilapidated, lonely cottage standing by itself in a bleak flat landscape with the nearest neighbour almost a kilometre away. For the remaining weeks before year's end we were enrolled at the Mepunga East State School, which we reached by walking, morning and evening, more than three and a half kilometres along a straight, flat road. The prevailing westerly winds would often sing eerily among the dozens of telephone wires strung from pole to pole down the long road. On the way home each evening we took reluctant turns to carry a heavy billycan of milk which our father – at that time working on a nearby share-farm – had left for us to collect at the milk depot near the school.

In this State School playground there was no thought of segregating by gender the earthy farmers' kids. During one lunch-time I felt an urge to recapture something of my experience with the little girl in the summer twilight. Naively imagining that I could choose such an experience at will, I chased and made a grab at a girl whom I knew from my own class, failing to note that she was bigger and stronger than I. Annoyed that I dared even to think of invading her privacy, she threw me face-down onto the ground and sat on me, her legs astride the small of my back as one would ride a horse, while other children looked on and my ears burned in dire humiliation.

This defeat by no means quenched my childish lust, nor my curiosity. I would listen eagerly when any group of older boys began to talk about sexual matters. My brother and I made plans with a boy who lived on the farm nearest to our house. He had a number of sisters, and we plotted to visit their house when their parents were at the milking shed and try to get his sisters to show us their bodies. Some days later during the milking hour we trekked across the paddocks to their house. The three girls came into the wash-house as had been arranged. Standing side-by-side and quite unembarrassed, like an unconscious parody of the chorus line at the *Folies Begère*, they obligingly raised their skirts and lowered their panties. The totally new spectacle caused in me such awed delight that my abdomen began to turn to jelly. But even while I revelled in the forbidden sight and enjoyed passing through this archway to new knowledge, there seemed to be something dishonourable about it. It did not seem a noble thing for us to be staring at the girls displaying the pale, secret area between their legs, as people inspect cattle or sheep in pens at the annual show.

I had made my First Confession in the preceding year. Although the twilight incident with the neighbourhood girls had occurred after that time it had not occurred to me to seek absolution for chasing and tickling them. Now, however, when my parents suggested one Sunday that I join the queue of people going to confess their sins to the priest before the start of Mass, I was deeply confused. I may have connected our new adventure with some recent warning from the pulpit about 'impurity', for I began to feel pangs of guilt at that terrible wrong, which was how I had begun to interpret that simple attempt to settle my curiosity.

One Sunday I walked hesitantly to the front of the crowded church, and when my turn came stepped into the sacristy. The gruff, irascible Irish priest was sitting with his back to the door. There was a kneeling-stool beside him. I knelt on the hard wood and after the opening prayer summoned up the courage to confess that I had 'done something rude', for I had no name to describe what we had looked at. He may have asked for further details, but I became tongue-tied, and could say nothing more. I cannot recall how the encounter ended, but I formed the idea that for lack of accurate reporting, my sin had not been forgiven. Moreover, for several years afterwards, because I could not clear up this matter, I thought that every confession I made was a 'bad confession', making my reception of Holy Communion 'unworthy' and adding terribly to my guilt.

There seemed no way out. Guilt has a way of diffusing and spreading. I could not have known, nor could the adults who controlled our lives, that to prohibit children from looking at things sexual only burdens with guilt the simple need to compare one's body with others; to learn what humans are. My sin seemed to grow beyond the one incident and had become a nameless dread that I could not put words to. During those years of confusion and vague belief that God would severely punish me, I was isolated and unable to seek help from parents or teachers who themselves had unwittingly contributed to my fearful darkness. Should anyone have to go through such a distortion of truth? Childhood is struggle enough without the small person having to cope with a distorted image of the world as less than beautiful and of the Transcendent as less than completely loving. I don't blame my various teachers, but the question remains: how had our Church through the centuries lost sight of the welcoming, all-forgiving child-friendly God that Jesus of Nazareth had shown to people of his time?

His best description of God was the well-known comic-serious story about a father and his two sons (Luke 15:11-32). The father, a caricature of the stern Semitic patriarch, allows the younger son to abuse family tradition by demanding his share of the inheritance. Not only did this gravely insult the father, being a wish that he was dead, but involved the unthinkable folly of selling half the family's precious land. But this unusual father indulged his wastrel son and, long after he has gone, watches longingly for his return. When the profligate eventually does come back, penniless and intending to ask for a job, the father interrupts his confession of guilt, restores him to full dignity and freedom, and throws a huge party to welcome him home.

Jesus was showing that God loves us without limit, but his Good News reached my teachers via the tainted thought-stream that came from Saint Augustine, an ex-Manichean, which was further filtered through puritanical French Janesism and the Irish Catholic Church. The prudish attitudes about sex may have been reinforced by conditions in the crowded cottages of generations of Irish poor, where there was an urgent need to avoid incest, but the fear and ignorance that those attitudes generated did not help children in my time who inherited the distorted teaching. It may be that guilt serves a vital purpose, as do death and decay. Jung's pioneering work with archetypes suggested to him that guilt may help us become aware of our 'shadow', which is the obverse, darker side of our healthy instincts. We are inclined to suppress and deny this real part of ourselves, but until we recognise it are less than a whole person.

Guilt may help us to face our lust and our ruthlessness, our ugly impulses to dominate and take power over others. Only by recognising and integrating these dimensions can we pass through to healing and emerge into psychic maturity. Even if Jung was only partly right, perhaps my imagined or artificial guilt and the painful process of working through it was a dark but necessary tunnel, an extended archway which I had to negotiate if I was to grow. Perhaps it helped me to avoid who-knows-what greater disasters in teenage years, in which I might have harmed not only my tender conscience, but also the lives and innocence of others.

Learning to manage our sexual urge is vital and central to our personality, but other moral rites of passage are just as important. It was because I had absorbed a strong sense that truth is fundamental that I had felt so keenly the unjust accusation at St Kilian's school. A similar testing awaited me at Naringal State School, which we three brothers attended for some time in 1948, for we had moved house yet again when my father found better working conditions on a different dairy farm.

The school was located among wealthier farms in a mainly Presbyterian part of the district and we were among the few Catholics attending it. The principal, Mr Wilkinson, took a strong dislike to me, and showed this in a memorable incident during an arithmetic class. The details are now blurred, but I recall being questioned about my homework, which possibly I had not done. I do not remember what explanation I gave, but it enraged Mr Wilkinson. He strode down to my seat and pushed or dragged me to the rear wall of the classroom, several rows back from where I had been standing. He was holding me by the hair, haranguing me about the evils of lying, which I was sure I had not been doing. During his harangue he was bumping my head backwards against the wall. I was eight years old. I have sometimes wryly wondered whether this might explain my subsequent dislike of arithmetical tasks and my poor ability at bookkeeping.

Soon after this event I was faced with a choice that was more important than briefly viewing the naked girls a few months before. It brought me to the threshold of the world of serious moral decisions. Mr Wilkinson's son Lindsay, who was in my class, owned the first fountain pen I had ever seen. It was dark blue, and he had boastfully shown a group of us how it was filled by pressing a black button, normally concealed by a small screw-cap on the end opposite the nib. One day at playtime I was alone in a row of young cypress trees that served as a windbreak along the edge of the school ground. Just as the bell rang for class, I saw Lindsay's fountain pen lying in the grass at my feet where it had evidently fallen from his pocket during play. I had often felt angry that he was favoured as the son of the principal, and envied him this wonderful writing implement. I could scarcely have begun to name my feelings about the abuse his father had inflicted on me. Now I had only moments to decide: should I keep the pen? Or throw it away? Or smash it? I imagined myself stabbing its sensitive nib into a nearby tree-stump, but somehow I understood that this was a decision that would influence my future. I picked up the pen, unscrewed the cap covering the refill button and emptied the ink onto the ground. Replacing the cap, I put the pen on the tree stump and returned to class.

At Naringal school we were at the bottom of the pecking order. Perhaps that is why one evening, when most of the children had gone home, Charles Burleigh, a large boy in my class, felt he could attack me in broad daylight in the driveway beside the school. He easily overpowered me and wrestled me to the ground. While I lay on my back, helpless beneath his weight, he lay on top of me, grabbed at the crotch of my trousers and began to knead my testicles. My feeling of helplessness and indignity as his victim was worse than the pain he was inflicting to give himself perverse pleasure. The ugly memory of the incident stayed with me long after I had left the school. Much later I understood that I had experienced a small fragment of what children, women or men feel when they are victims of far worse sexual assaults.

After we had moved back to Melbourne, as my years at Secondary School began I was excited by the opening of new doors to knowledge: the worlds of Latin and French, Geometry and Algebra; English literature and science. But just when I naively began to think that studying new subjects would soon let me fully understand the world, I was surprised by knowledge of quite a different sort. Hair began to grow on my body in places I had never expected, and a part of my body I had not paid much attention to began to grow in size and perform in odd ways. At awkward moments and for long times my penis would stand to attention. Sometimes I would gaze at it in awesome wonder, knowing that it was so designed that it would one day join me with a woman who was right now, somewhere, a girl of my own age; but how to find her and form such a partnership seemed a state of delight quite impossible to attain.

Yes, I had heard some explanatory talks about adolescent development, but my body's mysterious growing and my awakening imagination were well ahead of any explanations. The talks and booklets seemed to leave unsaid most of the things I wanted to know, and I could never read enough or find enough explanations of the mystery. Where I only wanted to do what was right, the dominant tone seemed to be caution, danger, fear and guilt.

Every time I read an article about some aspect of sexuality in a science book or *Readers' Digest*; every time I saw a nude statue or painting in a museum or gallery – and I went out of my way to see as many as humanly possible – my physical reactions, with the fascinated enjoyment they gave me, would quickly rebound as feelings of guilt that I had 'taken pleasure' in those sexual feelings. Taking pleasure in such things, we were often warned, was the measure of sin.

When I heard that it had been fashionable in some ancient civilisations for women to go in public with one or both breasts exposed, I regretted, possibly more than Hamlet, the 'cursèd spite' that I was *not* born in those times. Living in the mid-20th century, in Victoria, that most 'Victorian' of states, was for me a tragic accident of history. At that time no one could have dreamed that within ten years the 'Age of Aquarius' would bring a revolution in *mores* that would accept women baring much more than their breasts on beaches, and that full nudity would be common in movies and even on television in our homes.

As is true for any of life's natural archways, adolescence is impossible to understand before you have passed through it. How could you explain mature physical desire and romantic love to a pre-adolescent? Back in 1950, as a ten-year-old child, I had greatly enjoyed a hit-song called 'The Can-Can Polka', played by the Billy Cotton Band. I did not know that it was reviving a popular dance of the 19th century – in turn based on Offenbach's splendid operatic music from Orpheus and Eurydice – which had become increasingly bawdy and suggestive in French music halls until it reached the Folies Bergère.

I can-can and you can-can so why should not we two can-can,
Who can-can like you can-can; who can do can-can like you can ...

Its fast, exciting music and rapid-fire words enthralled me, although I was quite unaware of sexual implications. I knew however that it was exciting to adults in some way that I did not comprehend but liked to think that I did. Like the baby in the womb, pre-adolescents cannot understand what lies on the other side of the archway through which they are about to pass, nor could anyone describe it to them. They cannot possibly comprehend the utterly changed situation that they will soon enter. Such doors cannot be entered until we are given the key.

The key came like a grace in my fifteenth year, when after dreaming of a beautiful girl on a swing, I awoke to find a sticky wet patch the size of a saucer on the front of my pyjamas. I was awed by the knowledge that I was now capable of joining with a woman and bringing other human beings into existence. Because of the deeply-ingrained taboo imprinted by religious teachers, I waited for sleep to bring again the occasional ecstasy of an orgasm. I don't at all regret this abstinence, for I could accept as valid teaching that 'sex is sacred' and we ought not seek to enjoy that union until we had made a lifelong commitment to a carefully chosen partner, but in my young adulthood I felt keenly the lack of such a female presence.

It was an accident of genetics that I did not have sisters as playmates, and our family's mobility prevented me from having time to make friends among girls in the neighbourhoods where we lived. No one is to blame for this, but the lack was destructive. Nor did our single-sex secondary school help. Even if it is true that boys and girls do better academically in such an environment it is surely foolish to maintain this type of school on the sole basis of academic results. If the goal of schooling is human development, can segregation and taboos be a good way to teach us how to relate maturely?

In old age, through the powerful telescope of hindsight, I can see serious deficiencies in the way we were taught. We were not given the impression that sex or marriage was bad: on the contrary, as created by God it was of great value and to be strongly protected; but most talk of it in classrooms was piled high with its associated dangers. The worst error was to stress that – outside of marriage – all sexual pleasure was 'a sin'; and sin was the offence of rebelling against, or at least turning away from our Creator. It now seems to me that it would have been much more helpful to emphasise the positive, and more effective to accept the obvious truth that children need to learn by experiment, including with their own bodies. A temperate balance will sooner be learned by accepting the natural pleasures of our body, rather than by fearing and shunning them and trying to force abstinence by total prohibition.

Because it was so strongly forbidden and at the same time elevated as sacred, sexual intercourse became in our minds something belonging almost to a separate world. I was struck by imbalance in our formation when in our final year at school one boy asked during a question time: 'How is it that we are forbidden to enjoy all sexual activity, even thoughts about sex, until the night after a person is married, but then all is permitted?' The question seems naive, and can be answered simply, but it was revealing that the best efforts of his educators had left him and many others with this dualist, all-or-nothing understanding of life. Although it is proper to shield young children from even the news about the horrors of war, violent crime and the harsher facts of sexuality and death, it is folly to try to keep them for too long ignorant of these realities. If we are to emerge from a swamp of ignorance, we must eventually face and deal with all the realities in our world. Only by doing this can we work to heal some of them.

The dramatic personal changes that every young person discovers as adolescence progresses can have devastating emotional repercussions. As a child I had enjoyed writing creative essays or 'compositions' and received praise for them, but when adolescent hormones began to reshape my body, throwing my emotions into turmoil which was not helped by unbalanced guidance, I lost my skill at putting words together. Essay writing became an agony, and if asked to debate or speak before a group I would freeze into incoherence or silence. Too often I found it difficult even to conduct a conversation with an adult.

My adolescence was by no means an emotional desert. There were large oases of joy and delight as I explored new regions of place and of human experience, and even if my time was more often spent in solitude than among companions, I rejoiced at the goodness of it all. Mostly alone, I revelled in art, poetry and music; swam in the beaches of Port Phillip Bay and explored parts of Victoria's western coast. I enjoyed learning to dance and attended school dances. Alone and with a few good friends I travelled roads around and beyond Melbourne's suburbs on a bike that I had assembled with slender earnings from golf caddying. There was a background of music, both light and heavier classical – 'Invitation to the Dance'; *The Thieving Magpie* Overture; Strauss; Tchaikovsky; 'The Swedish Rhapsody'; Beethoven's Emperor and violin concertos and more, from a seemingly boundless supply. There was also the endless flow of popular hits. If many days were tainted by misery, many others were full of rejoicing, often for no known reason.

Through the innate power by which our bodies and minds heal themselves, I somehow learned to rejoice in female beauty and the feelings it stirred in me. One day I noticed as if for the first time a large hoarding which was common on railway stations. To advertise Vincents headache powders it showed a shapely young woman in a one-piece swimsuit diving from a springboard. Even though I could see no connection between her beautiful body and aspirins, I felt suddenly grateful to the sponsors for choosing her as their way of boasting about them. Likewise, hearing a song called 'Sweater Girl', whose lyrics some radio stations banned as too shocking, I felt a thrill that the female form was part of reality, of *my* world, and I had moments of genuine, calm delight in the reality of which sex was an integral part.

Sex is surely one of the most spectacular archways into another dimension: not just the pleasure of copulation, but the intimate, sustained love of a cherished partner that transports a person into another world from that of the pre-adolescent or the lone adult. My Catholic culture had taught me that choosing to be celibate, to live *without* a sexual partner for the sake of one's search for God, can lead a person into a deeper kind of relationship with the Transcendent Mystery. Christians were not the first to have discovered that choosing a disciplined life of prayer, meditation and sexual abstinence can make 'space' for an adventure no less deep than the love of the happily married, and among the followers of the Risen Christ, some have always chosen to remain celibate 'for the sake of the Kingdom of Heaven' (Matt 19:12).

Having taken this risk, as the years passed I would learn more about the depth of this search: that 'God', as the source of the created universe must be the *source* of our sexual attraction, and seeking to relate to this Being can be at least as fulfilling as a lifelong human partnership. Just as parents' love can grow stronger when for a time they willingly deprive themselves of sexual enjoyment in order to attend a sick child or to work in a distant location to support their family, a committed celibate tries to base his or her *whole* life on total abstinence for a similarly noble purpose.

Married persons can and ought to grow in the depth of their prayer, but putting aside marriage can create something unique in the heart. Even as a teenager I had been convinced by the example of this generosity in the lives of nuns, priests and brothers, although whenever it occurred to me that I might choose such a life myself I felt quite reluctant. I did not want to miss out on the pleasures and joys of a sexual partnership and family life. As the years of my secondary education came to an end I faced the inevitable question of what to do with my life. I took the choice seriously, and against the good advice of my father to take up a scholarship at university, at least for a year, chose instead to try living in a community of men vowed to celibacy.

What I thought was a noble conviction was no doubt a complex blend of needing a community of friends; simplifying – by side-stepping – the complex decisions of courtship and career building; wanting to 'work for God' as the best career choice; and perhaps an unhealthy trace of self-immolation. Whatever the complicated reasons may have been, I decided to see whether I could survive life in a religious community. Amid my mother's tears, I went off to join the novitiate of the Dominican Friars.

9
The Many Halves of My Divided World
Beyond dualism

The happiest times of my childhood were holidays on our grandparents' farm on the ocean coast at the bottom edge of Australia. During a few weeks that seemed never to end, I moved through wide paddocks, played with dogs, watched horses and rode in drays and jinkers. I hung around the milking shed where cows jostled and mooed and the numerous cats were never short of milk. I delighted in visits to the beach and drives along red gravel bush roads where the trees joined overhead. Then one morning the dream would burst and we would be on the early train back to Melbourne.

Approaching the city through its depressing western suburbs, the train rolled through Spotswood and Seddon where treeless streets of workers' cottages lined the railway tracks and I struggled to recall paddocks where the next tussock might be hiding a treasure of skylark's eggs. Near Footscray, the stench of stockyards and abattoirs penetrated the carriage; we could see and hear cattle that were no longer free. The despoiled banks of the Maribyrnong River muddied my memories of a gold and emerald bay. I saw the city as entirely miserable and felt I was being dragged backward out of a story, my idealised country fading to mist. But the nature of the proscenium is to create illusion and sometimes it can deceive us. The story I had composed for myself was not entirely true. Not that it was false to rejoice in my romantic view of our grandparents' farm; the untruth was to see it as *separate* from the other parts of the world. When I succumbed to my childish romantic prejudices I was nurturing in myself a deeply dualist pattern of life.

As city-dwelling consumers we have largely succeeded in separating ourselves from nature. We are shocked if we see a cockroach in the kitchen or a slug in the bath. We fear, hate, spray, kill, and fail to understand. This schism between human being and nature would seem to be but one of the many artificial splits that we have created between the self and the world: mind and body; intellect and soul; spirit and matter; secular and sacred; science and the humanities; science and religion. But more of this later.

As a five- or six-year-old I was drawn towards the side of nature, believing that the rustic world of cow-yards, kerosene lamps, bush and ocean was sublimely good and lovely, while factories and treeless streets were obnoxious beyond bearing. Many years would elapse before I could accept and reconcile these opposites, and see the world as in fact profoundly and essentially one.

Except to attend the annual speech nights held in the town hall close by, my parents never came near our secondary school. When I was eleven our father had taken us to be enrolled, but did not return there during the following seven years. Or only rarely, in the course of his work as Attendance Officer, for it happened to fall within the huge district where he was responsible for seeking out truants.

Our mother and father had little idea of most of what we were learning. Although they were eager readers, both had quit school at fourteen to help their families survive. They did not know much about our school subjects and my father's occasional comments mocked their apparent lack of relevance to 'real life'. This separation between the two worlds was as much our fault as theirs, for teenagers are notoriously non-communicative. The situation was compounded by the fact that we lived far from the school and it would have been difficult for my mother and father to attend the infrequent parents' meetings even if they had wanted to. I suspect they felt a sense of inferiority, for although they both mixed easily with strangers they must have wondered what they could have in common with parents who – they wrongly imagined – had all spent years in secondary school or university.

Our mother and father were companionable and shared an excellent sense of humour, but my father was often away, and on the rare occasions when I had a relaxed conversation with him or my mother, I did not share my feelings, nor did they enquire much about my inner life. When adolescence began to develop my body, I withdrew more deeply into my own thoughts and emotions, trying to make sense of a territory in which no one else seemed interested. In fact, if anyone tried to enter my private emotional world I would become alarmed and evasive.

This division between my inner and outer worlds intensified as adolescence progressed. Not fully understanding myself, I hated to think others were discussing me. When I realised that the brothers who taught us must discuss the senior boys in order to choose Prefects and House Captains I inwardly quailed. Although I was doing passably well in studies I knew I would be seen as hopeless in competitive team sports, which in our school seemed equally important, but I had no more interest in them than in the struggles between political factions in remote Communist China.

∽

The contrast between life on the farm and in the city; the disjunction between home and school: and my strong defensiveness about my inner life, were only some of the ways my divided self was split. Despite the daily presence of my mother and younger sister, I lived in a world that was almost entirely male. This could not last forever. I was becoming aware that there existed girls of my own age, and began to admire them from a safe distance: pretty, some of them, in their school uniforms, as they rode the same trains on their way to and from their convent schools. Rarely could I manoeuvre to find or create an occasion when I could speak with one, and I regularly cursed my misfortune that Catholic secondary schools at that time were strictly single-sex.

When the old priest who was school chaplain announced that he would start Saturday *Learn to Dance* classes in the church hall near our school I was enthusiastic. With the energy of youth, I thought nothing of repeating on Saturday night the ninety-minute round trip from Huntingdale to Malvern that we made each school-day. At first it was daunting to enter a hall full of girls adorned much more attractively than in their school uniforms. For the first few occasions I struggled, awed and tongue-tied in the close presence of such creatures, like beings from another world, with whom I could scarcely believe we were allowed to join our left hands, while placing the other discreetly on the small of their back as we moved more or less gracefully around the hall. I noted with amazement how small – and beautiful – were the hands of one of my first dancing partners as I trembled to put my clumsy hand around her waist.

My world was further and decisively divided when I entered the novitiate of the Dominican friars. My father did not accept the common Catholic view that clergy and religious were somehow the holier section of a dual world, and tried vainly to persuade me to spend at least one year at university after leaving school, but in 1959 I took the decisive step of leaving home. For a callow youth of almost nineteen such an idealistic step was relatively easy.

In the months beforehand, my mother and I spent a lot of time buying clothing, including a black hat, to fill an unrealistic list that must have been drawn up by some unworldly cleric several generations earlier. Suddenly the day came when on the morrow I would leave my family home forever. Only then did the finality of my choice hit me. My thinking did not include the possibility that I might weaken and return home. Although the first four years of novitiate and temporary vows were a period when the Order and candidates would mutually discern whether they were suited to be a friar and priest, in the Catholic community there was a strong sense that candidates who pulled out had failed. I did not even consider this possibility, feeling convinced that I would not leave – that this was 'for life'.

As we were preparing for bed that night in the room that we three brothers still shared, I surprised myself by having the maturity to ask my older brother what he thought of my decision. A student at Teachers' College, he was at that time putting aside his belief in the Catholic worldview which we had been taught was the only true way to find God. He told me that he thought I was making a foolish choice; that he had no respect for the clerical profession. His answer neither surprised nor deterred me.

On the following day, a Sunday, my father accompanied me to the priory. We had no car so we set out to make the fifteen-kilometre journey by two buses and a tram. But first I had to say goodbye to my brothers, my ten-year-old sister, and mother. For the one setting out, departure is usually an exciting adventure, but not so for those left behind. My mother's grief at parting was profound. While I found it relatively easy, physically, to move out of her embrace then turn and walk from the room, she continued to weep bitterly and I knew that there were deeper dimensions to this simple human scene than I was able to deal with at that time. Nothing that I could do would make it easier for her, so as usual I kept my feelings hidden until at some later time I could find an opportunity to examine and release them.

After our two bus journeys we found that no trams were running that day because of a strike, and our only option was to walk the last kilometre and a half carrying my two heavy cases. We were both strong, and had recently carried hiking packs together, but it was a hot February day and there were several steep hills to negotiate, so we were grateful to reach the priory. This short journey was one of the last times I was alone with my father. Sometimes he was able to come with the family on the monthly visiting days, and he was present a year later when I made my temporary vows, then in August 1960 our last brief conversations were in the hospital room where he lay dying.

The Camberwell priory was as it is today, except that the high cypress hedges have been replaced with less gloomy shrubs, and tall trees now grace the lawn. Beside the high bluestone church was the two-storey house of red and black brick, built in 1891 and occupied by the friars since 1925. At the rear had been added an ugly three-storey block of red brick, for novices and students.

I passed beneath the Romanesque arch over the front door into a new stage of my life. The Master of Novices who greeted me – I later found – was linked to my family by a curious synchronicity. He was a young priest of thirty years with the uncommon surname of Northeast. I had already met him when enquiring about joining the friars and my parents had at that time asked whether he came from the village of Cobden where I was born. In the week before my birth my Mother had stayed with a family of that name, to avoid a rushed journey to the cottage hospital along bush roads from our home in Timboon. This Fr. Northeast was indeed one of the sons of that family, and I later found that he had been born on the same date as myself, but twelve years earlier. Both of us became Dominicans and eventually I too would become Master of Novices.

My room in the novitiate was stark, containing only a bed, desk, prie-dieu and sink. Only in the coldest winter spells was it heated, for the community's budget did not stretch to running the furnace continuously. Silence pervaded the house. Stillness at various levels was wisely seen as a valuable and necessary context for prayer and study. For long periods it was punctuated only occasionally by the sound of a brother's shoes in the corridor as he passed my door, or the distant trundling of the trams along Riversdale Road.

The novitiate year was not intellectually demanding, but nonetheless arduous. It focused directly on the reality of the Transcendent God, to whom we prayed every day in the choir stalls around the church's main altar. Our community of about thirty-five friars spent long hours there, chanting in Latin the hymns and psalms of the *Divine Office* or the *Prayer of the Church*. On feast days, and each night at Compline, we sang these to a Gregorian chant, but at other times used a curious monotone.

Besides the hours in choir, we novices gathered in the novitiate chapel several more times each day to recite the *Little Office of Our Lady*. A large bell clanged to wake the community at 5am, and through the day to summon us to community events. In our corridor a little hand-bell called us to other novitiate events – *Little Office*, classes, recreation and outdoor work periods. Some found it annoying to have life governed by frequent bells, but I did not mind. For me it was a honeymoon period and I was enthusiastic about it all, especially the prayer. On the cusp of adulthood, I was leaving behind the pleasant options that I presumed my former school-mates were enjoying: university life with its parties and the adventure of pursuing girlfriends. I would miss going to movies – only about once a year the community would hire one for a film night – but I thought I was entering through a portal into a place of peace and quiet where I had no great responsibilities, cushioned in an ancient institution where I would be guided more-or-less automatically towards a role then seen as the highest in Catholic society.

From the earliest times the various forms of monastic life have proved effective in strengthening self-discipline and enabling people to become efficient and productive, but they have always contained the risk of being psychologically unhealthy. It was assumed that the institutional regime was capable of forming us into mature adults. While we had some supervision from the directors of novices and students, and were critiqued by our peers in regular chapter meetings, this was not adequate for everyone's human development, and isolation from normal family life could have a negative effect on our maturing.

I took it all seriously: I knew that soon I would make vows to give up ownership of goods and the free direction of my life by promising obedience to our elected leaders. I would surrender the delights of sexual relationship: of ever having a wife and family. All this I recognised as a way of dedicating my life to the unseen, transcendent God. During our novitiate year we only rarely had conversation or contact with the priests of the senior community. Even with the professed students we shared only a daily period after lunch for gardening or sport, and we novices had another short period of recreation after tea. Our days began at 5.30am with a half-hour meditation and were filled by prayers, classes, meals and more prayers. Meals were almost always eaten in silence, or accompanied by a brother reading to us.

∽

We seldom left the priory grounds, but on Thursday afternoons were permitted to walk as far as we pleased into the endless expanse of Melbourne's south-eastern suburbs, and once a month shared a much-enjoyed picnic with the professed students. We would walk to the local station and go by train to the Dandenong Ranges, then hike further to a suitable picnic spot. We had – for once – more food than we could eat, and in those ignorant days were supplied with cigarettes, which many tried for the first but by no means the last time. On such outings I began some strong friendships among the students, bonds which were strengthened during our long summer holidays at Portsea, where we occupied the empty dormitories of the Dominican Sisters' School for the Deaf.

On rare occasions novices might have reason to travel – with a companion – into the city: a half-hour journey by tram. On my first return into the bustling world which I knew so well but had turned my back on, I was strongly stirred by the familiar sights and sounds of crowds and traffic. No doubt I was inwardly struggling to justify the giant step I had recently taken, for on our way home, as we gazed through the tram window I commented to my companion how unfortunate were all these people who could not enjoy the life of closeness to God in a religious community, to which we were returning.

My fellow novice was already aware of my strong tendency to a kind of legalism, to manage life by laws and rules rather than what people need in order to live in a relaxed, human way. It was a deep flaw that I would not easily shed. On top of this, my scorn and disparaging comments about the majority of ordinary folk who had chosen marriage, suburban homes and nine-to-five commuting must have been too much for my companion's common sense, for I recall the stinging rebuke in his reply. I was building my world on a dangerous schism.

Towards the end of my second year my father became seriously ill. The Student Master kindly drove me the eighty kilometres to Geelong, where my family now lived. I was allowed to stay with them and visit my father in the hospital for the remaining few days of his life. This humane concession within our sometimes-medieval system contrasted with the regulations then governing congregations of women religious. Most of them were not permitted to attend a parent's funeral or the wedding of a brother or sister. Mercifully, the reforms of the Second Vatican Council humanised these rules imposed long ago by male clerics or Vatican committees.

I returned from my father's funeral in Warrnambool after only six days. Although I could have stayed longer, my attitude to our 'regular life' drove me to seek refuge back in the community routine. I scarcely noticed how heartless it was to leave my mother so soon when many practical arrangements remained to be completed. The gap between my two worlds was depriving me of practical realism. Community life has many advantages, but part of its dangerous 'shadow' side is that it encourages the worst characteristics of institutions. For instance, at that time 'lay' brothers cooked all our meals, so clerical students and priests never shared the cooking. I was not developing adult responsibility, but beginning to encase myself in the world that the clerical caste had evolved for itself; expecting things to be provided; living in a state of entitlement.

On returning through the back door of the priory I saw the familiar stacked baskets of laundry that we paid others to wash, something unheard-of in the small family home from which I had just returned. I felt as if I was returning through a portal into a safe zone that I was happy to embrace, but thankfully it had not killed the deeper roots of my humanity. Before I could reach my room, the massive grief I was carrying burst forth in a flood of tears.

∽

From childhood until some years after I became a priest, religion divided my world into two quite separate realms. Each Sunday night during my teenage years, probably at my request, our family radio would be tuned to *The Catholic Hour*. I remember little of its contents, but recall that it was introduced by Jeremiah Clarke's majestic Trumpet Voluntary, followed immediately by a sonorous male voice announcing 'Thou art Peter, and upon this rock I will build my Church, and the gates of hell shall not prevail against it' (Matt 16:18-19).

This 'triumphalism' was partly a reaction to earlier persecution, especially in Ireland, where for centuries British colonial rulers had confiscated land, impoverished the native Catholic population and persecuted their religion. In strong reaction we still saw the rest of the world rather dismissively as *Non-Catholic*. Most Catholics saw it as reasonable that we were forbidden to attend the church services of other Christian denominations unless we had received the bishop's permission. We were discouraged from marrying *Non-Catholics* but if a couple did get the necessary dispensation they were penalised by having to exchange their vows not before the altar, but in the sacristy, the vesting room, while the congregation waited outside and saw nothing of that crucial moment in the couple's lives.

This vast institution to which we belonged had evolved out of Jesus' teaching, but at that time I did not see that in many ways it had drifted seriously away from it. It was the environment in which I grew as child, youth and man and which strongly influenced my life. I remain grateful that I learned within it that the world extends far beyond the material, and that the Transcendent dimension is real. The Catholic belief system provided a solid framework from which I began to try to comprehend and question my life.

Although the Church possessed great wealth in real estate and who-knew-what international assets, at the level of parishes it was poor. It had chosen to build up a vast network of schools, for which – until the 1960s – it received none of the taxes that Catholics paid to support education. An army of volunteers taught in these schools: men and women religious from abroad, and later mostly homegrown, had sprung up for this purpose. They struggled. I had sat in primary classes of more than fifty children, taught by one harassed Sister. Our large secondary school in the late 1950s could still not afford a rudimentary library. The Brothers who taught us lacked training, so after a full day in the classroom many would attend evening lectures at university. They taught us Christian Doctrine in a fairly simplistic way, for the Church still held literalistic interpretations of the Bible, and the overall outlook given to us by clergy and teachers lacked optimism about the goodness of the world and had inherited a Jansenistic puritanism about sex. Not always unconsciously, they used fear to motivate and urge Catholics to lead a moral life.

Now free of overt persecution, clergy in Australia – as in Ireland – generally established themselves at upper-middle-class standards, the bishop's house even being referred to as a 'palace'. Splendid neo-gothic cathedrals and churches were ambitiously planned and erected, paid for largely by the willing donations of the poor. The grand architecture of these holy status symbols did inspire people with some sense of the sublime. The soaring spires and arches of St Patrick's cathedral in Melbourne and the stained-glass in many churches reinforced my youthful search for the Transcendent, as they were no doubt meant to do.

Although my father expressed healthy criticism of Church structures and clerical leaders, I – like most Catholics – looked up to the clergy. They represented the Sacred, for they had received the power given by Christ at the Last Supper to consecrate the bread and wine of the Eucharist, and to absolve us from sin in the Sacrament of Reconciliation. They attended the sick and dying and often quietly gave material help to the poorest. Priests had received a tertiary education when most of their flock had not, and generally worked hard to serve large congregations in parishes that were vital social centres for young and old. We revered the clergy, and accepted their human failings, but tragically this reverence made people reluctant to complain even when some committed serious offences. This, combined with the lack of accountability, has proved to be a huge flaw in the Church's structure, as recent revelations have shown. Lacking my father's worldly wisdom, as I prepared to join the ranks of the clergy I was unquestioningly sure that I could serve worthily in this prestigious position.

The evangelist Mark recorded that when Jesus died, the curtain of the Jewish temple was 'torn in two, from top to bottom' (Mark 15:38). Whether it actually happened, he made it a symbol that the Holy of Holies was no longer needed. Jesus had confronted the hypocrisy and injustice of the leaders of his religion and they had murdered him. I accepted the Catholic belief that he completed his work by passing through death, making real his declaration that 'the Kingdom of God is among you' (Luke 10:9, 17:21) and fulfilling his promise that the temple was no longer needed because the Spirit of God would henceforth be powerfully present in his followers. *We* are God's temple.

It is curious then that in Catholic churches from sometime in the first millennium until the Second Vatican Council, a fence had been re-erected between the altar and the people. Although Jesus clearly rejected the Jewish temple and priesthood, the Church had gradually re-built the 'sanctuary'. Where Jesus had defined leadership as humble service: 'the greatest among you must become like the youngest, and the leader like one who serves' (Luke 22:26); and had washed his disciples' feet, serving them as a slave (John 13:3ff), the Church had worked hard to re-create a privileged clerical caste.

From the fourth century the Church became closely allied to the Roman Empire. Church buildings began to resemble Jewish and pagan temples, suggesting that the area reserved for cultic worship and the men who led it were more holy than others who could not enter their domain. Religion was once again becoming a profession, or worse, a business.

Until the late 1960s, during the whole of Mass, no female was allowed into the fenced-off 'sanctuary' around the altar because of the ancient prejudice that women are somehow inferior, even unclean. This was a major reason why all Western clergy from the end of the first millennium were forbidden to marry, and why women are still not allowed to be ordained. As a young Catholic I was hearing clearly that the 'secular' and the 'sacred' were two separate worlds. It would take me half a lifetime to understand that we had somehow by-passed a central truth of the gospel and betrayed the Incarnation, our most fundamental belief that the Mystery of God has joined itself intimately to us; that in the Risen Christ 'there is no longer Jew or Greek, there is no longer slave or free, there is no longer male and female; for all of you are one in Christ Jesus' (Gal 3:28).

~

During my school years I carried the impression that a secular world and a sacred world were in conflict. This basically theological idea was intermingled and probably magnified by my unquestioning acceptance of the popular propaganda of the Cold War era, which fed us daily on the so-called menace of atheistic Communism and the necessity to fight against it. In Australian politics, I presumed from my uncle's involvement with the strongly Catholic Democratic Labor Party that the battle was real, and a serious one.

Eager as a teenager to learn science, I enjoyed the discoveries we made in chemistry and physics classes. Our teachers, committed religious brothers in black gowns dusty with chalk, were opening for us new corridors of knowledge and we avidly explored these insights into the world. But I felt a gradually increasing disjuncture: on one side there was the world of atoms, elements and the laws of motion discovered by Galileo, Kepler and Newton, and hints of Darwin's evolution of species. On the other hand, in our Christian Doctrine classes we were given the stories from the Bible as if from a different stream of truth. We were learning about the unseen God who had directly created the world and from whose revealed commandments we had acquired our knowledge of right and wrong. To their credit, the brothers made attempts to connect the two worlds: I can recall a lesson on the 1950 papal encyclical *Humani Generis*, which accepted the possibility of evolution, but logically enough rejected the idea that chemicals alone had given rise to life, or that mutations in material bodies had produced the conscious human mind.

We discussed the gospel stories of miracle healings as proofs that Jesus could draw at will upon the infinite power of God. At the same time, it was obvious that science had harnessed other kinds of power: the electric trains that carried us to school; the jet airliners that were almost ready to carry passengers around the world; the first submarine fuelled by a nuclear reactor. The British government was just then arrogantly testing nuclear bombs in Central Australia; and the USSR and USA were competing to shoot bigger satellites into orbit around the Earth, the latest ones carrying human observers. Even after I had completed my schooling and the novitiate year, this apparent split between science and religious faith continued to widen. Studying philosophy and theology as a young friar in my early twenties, I still struggled to fit together the two sides of the education I had received: the ancient doctrines of my faith and the world-view coming out of the Enlightenment and the Industrial Revolution. The worlds of material development and of the spirit seemed quite separate. Did they fit together? If so, how could I show this to others when I could not reconcile them myself?

It was to be many years before I was able to see that my struggles with this dualism were part of a much broader human conflict. Ancient Indigenous peoples, before being changed forever by colonisation, saw the world as complex but united, in which they lived in harmony with its web of species. This was in extreme contrast to our post-Enlightenment mind, which has come to see the external world as unconscious and impersonal. Although I was taught to see and value the world as beautiful, we were inclined to explain it mechanistically, as simply matter in motion, purposeless, ruled by chance and necessity and altogether indifferent to us who study it. Post-Enlightenment scholarship tends to study the world mainly to control it and draw more profit from it. Our crowning mistake is to presuppose that our 'scientific' minds are themselves the exclusive source of meaning and purpose.

It has been interestingly suggested that humanity's ancient way of seeing itself as intricately united with the world's complex ecological web began to change radically in the 6th century BCE, in what has become known as the Axial Age.[30] With newly-awakening analytic thought, our ancestors began to speculate about the empirical world of flux and finitude and about its causes. They began to see it as distinct from the divine, eternal world of eternity, separating the measurable world from the supposed realm of the gods.

In that era of remarkable originality, new belief-systems emerged: Confucianism, Buddhism, Taoism, Zoroastrianism, Jainism and the Hebrew prophets, all of which began in various ways to define the individual person's responsibility to choose to relate more personally to the Divine, rather than conforming as previously to communal norms.[31] At the same time, they began to express in new ways the 'will' or plan of that unseen divine Cause of the world, the determiner of our future after death.[32] In the same era, but with different emphasis, the earliest Greek philosophers began to analyse the visible world seeking to know its causes and the mathematical structures underlying it.

However it may have begun, this division in thinking certainly trickled down to affect me. But my divided view of the world began to evolve soon after I was ordained, when I began further study at Flinders University while working as curate in an Adelaide parish. I studied psychology, geography and more history. I came across the works of the first scientists to warn of the global warming and ecological damage that the Industrial Revolution had precipitated. I was also meeting students and young workers who reconnected me with areas of the world that I had been shielded from in the seminary. It was the era of world-wide student protests against authority, largely in response to the USA's war in Vietnam. When that war had begun I had not questioned Australia's sending of conscripts to die in what was actually Vietnam's struggle for independence, but now I began to see it as a vast moral evil which I should join with others to speak against.

In the youth group to which I was chaplain I heard young shop-girls, mechanics and nurses struggling to see how the Church, and the books of the gospels on which it was founded, were relevant to their daily lives. One of the commonest questions that cropped up, as in most discussions about God, was the ancient question of evil: if God is good, where does evil come from? If God is all-powerful, why allow it? This primal question had already influenced my choice of reading since teen-aged years. I had immersed myself in Charles Dickens' novels depicting the wretchedness of England's nineteenth-century poor. I read Victor Hugo's *Les Misérables* at such a precocious age that there was much in it that I did not understand. I read graphic descriptions of trench life in the First World War, and when in our final school years we studied Alan Paton's *Cry, The Beloved Country*, I empathised with those who suffered under the apartheid regime in South Africa, where even as we read about them, the Black population was bravely boycotting buses and police were massacring women, children and youths like ourselves.

I imagined I had an extensive knowledge of the world's darker side, but when I came across Lord Russell's book on Nazi atrocities[33] I saw a depth of evil that I had never imagined possible. It was the same with a visiting Japanese artist's exhibition of paintings depicting what he had witnessed in Hiroshima after the atom bomb had destroyed it. Shocking scenes from Russell's book and from that exhibition deeply affected me and informed my thinking. When I eventually visited Europe in 1975 I made it a priority to visit Dachau and Auschwitz. In a much later visit to Japan, I visited Hiroshima.

In those earlier years I was becoming absorbed by human suffering – although I saw it largely as existing in a separate world from myself. My interest took a literary turn when a school poetry competition was announced. To complete my poem, I took myself off for an afternoon in Melbourne's State Library, whose great domed reading room replicates that of the British Museum. In a way that was only partly self-mocking, I was aware that I was imitating Karl Marx, T.E.Lawrence and other authors who wrote in the British prototype. Despite distractions from the many interesting books around me I finished my poem, 'Job', about a homeless alcoholic. It won the prize.

As for the origins of suffering, we had no option then but to take the story of Adam and Eve as literally true, but to young people it seemed outrageously wrong and unjust to punish the whole human race because two people had failed a simple test. History studies were telling me about the greed of empires, colonialism, slavery and war as root causes of many of the world's evils. What was it though, that *first* moved people to abuse power, exploiting those weaker than themselves? In the first instance, why were we greedy?

As for the millions of victims of exploitation and war, was it enough recompense that they were promised happiness after death? Would all victims, from prehistoric times until contemporary Vietnam, even reach that goal? What chance did those millions have to prepare themselves for death if they apparently never thought of God, let alone went to church? I had still no choice but to accept the teaching that the human race would end up in two groups: the saved, and the damned who had not repented. It was not daily at the forefront of my mind, but I was aware that somewhere out of sight there was a great archway leading towards immeasurable despair. I could make no progress in trying to think my way logically through this, but deferred the problem for later. God must somehow make sense.

As we chanted the psalms each day in choir, a few texts about evil caught my attention. For instance I regularly puzzled about a line in Psalm 139: 'even the darkness is not dark to You; the night is as bright as the day, for darkness is as light to You'; or as the Jerusalem Bible put it: '... for You, darkness and light are one' (Ps 139:12).

Was the poet saying that God did not distinguish between good and evil? That: 'It's all one to me.' From our study of Aquinas a possible answer emerged to the ancient quandary: God creates all beings, so every *thing* that exists must be good. However, because creatures are material and composite, defects can and must occur in them. On a global scale, the Earth's surface has cooled into continental plates which drift together to push up mountain ranges. These give us rain and climate; glaciers, rivers and soil which make life possible on Earth. But when the plates move, as they must, they cause earthquakes and *tsunamis* that can kill thousands of people.

Similarly, the life-force in living cells is good, and the mutations that sometimes occur, when inherited by following generations, have enabled the evolution of the millions of species that populate the Earth. Among the species that have evolved are viruses and bacteria, most of which help us, although some can destroy us. Mutation in our own cells can cause cancer, or in a foetus, spina bifida, blindness, deafness or mental retardation.

Aquinas perceived that phenomena like earthquakes, sickness, mutations – evils at the physical level – are actually a deficiency, a gap or a no-thing where there is meant to be a whole being. In the case of moral evils though, he saw clearly that we cause these ourselves when we use our freedom – which like all our faculties is good – to choose some good for ourselves which causes serious harm to others. The thief desires something good and may get to enjoy it, but his action hurts the shocked and deprived owner of the goods stolen. At the same time his betrayal weakens the level of trust in wider society. It is the same with adultery, murder and all our ghastly crimes up to genocide and ecocide, when we injure large parts of our planet.

Whenever I had read about the experiences of mystics of any religious tradition – people who through prayer and meditation have gone beyond the margins of ordinary sensation and thought – I found that they reported that in moments of ecstasy they reach an awareness that all creatures are linked in one complex and beautiful web. If we can trust their insights, they seem to have glimpsed how at a higher level the good-evil duality is somehow transcended, and that the gross defects in Earth and humanity will somehow be healed. Considering the fearsome things that we do to each other, theirs is an awesome claim.

William James noticed this. In his 1901 Gifford Lectures[34] he noted that the mystics' vision of cosmic unity occurs among a wide range of cultures and religions. He was disturbed by the possibility that this might be showing that 'evil' is a *species* of 'good', as if the two were parts of the same genus, and therefore somehow equivalent, but

Aquinas' explanation avoids this dilemma, clearly identifying evil as a privation or *lack* of the good.

One of the mystics who most impressed me by her remarkable optimism about cosmic unity was Dame Julian of Norwich, the 14th century English mystic who reported seeing a glimpse of the whole universe, no bigger in God's hand than a hazel nut, and heard God tell her that, fragile as it seemed, it is being kept safe from perishing. Julian is renowned for her memorable conviction that 'All will be well, and all manner of thing will be well.'

In later life I have found my several once-dualist views of the world converging like the twin images in an optical range-finder, revealing a picture of the world that is ultimately one, although it had at first seemed irreconcilably divided into opposing sides. I began to find a deeper optimism hidden at the heart of my Christian heritage, and to escape from the dualist beliefs that had greatly confused me. These were first steps: I still had a long way to go before I would find unity, leading to a treasure of unquenchable joy.

10
The Gates of Hell
The promise of *apokatastasis*

One hot February night in 1979 I stood outside our Dominican priory on the northern edge of Canberra and watched the spectacular sight of a mountain on fire. Mt Majura, a 350-metre hill about three kilometres from our house, was being consumed by a fire that had raged for several days in the lands behind it. Flames flared above the eucalyptus forest and the mountain eventually became a fearful but beautiful heap of burning coals. As we watched the red light shimmering from within its depths, we nervously wondered whether the fire might come down into the suburbs, but put the thought aside as too frightful to be possible as 'There are green areas in between that would stop it.' There weren't: the grass was mostly dry. 'Bushfires never come into the city'. They do: only the lack of wind was keeping us safe. Twenty-four years later, despite improved fire-fighting technology, a massive bushfire *did* rage into the western suburbs of Canberra and in ten hours destroyed more than 500 homes, injured 490 people and killed four. As we watched Mt Majura blazing, the too-horrible possibility compelled us, irrationally, not to think about it.

Four years before that night, on a freezing winter's day in Poland, I had walked through the gateway of what had once been the Auschwitz extermination camp. Its curving wrought-iron archway still carried the motto that had welcomed millions of victims to the camp: 'Arbeit Macht Frei' – Work Makes You Free. I spent most of that day descending deeper into sadness, depression and anger as I saw more and more poignant reminders, preserved to show the evil things done there. I felt only a tiny fraction of the pain suffered by millions of good, ordinary people who were there stripped of all dignity before

THE GATES OF HELL

they died under forced labour or were murdered in their hundreds of thousands in the gas chambers.

We have become accustomed to describing such places as 'a living hell'. The phrase turned in my mind as I moved through the camp, wondering how human beings can design systems to funnel those they call 'enemies' into increasingly narrow spaces until they disappear from our sight.

༄

In my Catholic family I had learned from childhood that death was a doorway to another world. We learned about 'heaven' and firmly hoped to go there, but my Church also gave me the obverse of this beautiful teaching: that people who have led bad lives go to a place of flames and torment where they will suffer forever. Until sometime in my thirties I believed it possible that I might end up in this literal hell of eternal fire, for it was orthodox Catholic teaching that although we had been created to reach heaven, many of us might fail to reach the goal for which we were made.

As a child I had been afraid of going to this hell, of which I was often reminded by the priests who preached on Sundays, and especially in the occasional 'parish missions'; by the Sisters of Mercy who taught me in two primary schools; and by the De La Salle Brothers in my secondary college.

James Joyce was strongly challenged by this doctrine, and in his *Portrait of the Artist as a Young Man* he included a horrific sermon on the subject, given by a Jesuit to schoolboys on retreat:

> 'Hell' – the preacher said – 'was said to be a dark and foul-smelling prison filled with fire and smoke, where the countless damned prisoners are so heaped together that they are not even able to remove from the eye a worm that gnaws it. They lie in a never-ending darkness, flames and smoke of burning

brimstone, and awful stench of all the offal and scum of the world and of the bodies of the damned themselves ... The fire is an even greater physical torment. A finger placed in the flame of a candle feels pain, but ... the fire of Hell is of a different quality and was created by God to torture and punish the unrepentant sinner. It burns forever with unspeakable fury, and preserves that which it burns ... The blood of those wretched beings seethes and boils in their veins, the brains are boiling in the skull, the tender eyes flaming like molten balls. The intensity of this fire proceeds directly from the ire and vengeance of God ... the immortal soul is tortured eternally ... by the offended majesty of the Omnipotent God.

The torment is increased by the company of the damned themselves ... [They] howl and scream at one another ... They blaspheme against God and hate their fellow sufferers and curse those who were their accomplices in sin, but it is too late now for repentance ... the devils ... mock and jeer at the lost souls whom they dragged down to ruin. Why did you sin? ... Why did you not leave that evil companion; give up that impure habit? ... listen to the counsels of your confessor? God spoke to you by so many voices, but you would not hear or obey the precepts of your holy Church. How dreadful to hear ringing in one's ears the awful sentence of rejection: 'Depart from me, ye cursed, into everlasting fire which was prepared for the Devil and his angels!'[35]

There were also said to be spiritual torments in hell: the pain of loss ... the damned fully understand what they have lost forever by their sins. They are perpetually but fruitlessly remorseful at the memory of past pleasures, and they rage that they have lost the bliss of heaven merely for money; for vain honours; bodily comforts; a tingling of the nerves. The crowning torture is the eternity of hell. Here, the preacher excelled himself:

> ... the divine majesty, so outraged and slighted by sinners, demands boundless extension of torment, incredible intensity of suffering, unceasing variety of torture. It would be a dreadful torment to bear even the sting of an insect for all eternity. What must it be, then, to bear the manifold tortures of hell for ever? Imagine the tiny grains of the sand on the seashore: now imagine a mountain of that sand, a million miles high, reaching from the Earth to the farthest heavens, and a million miles broad and a million miles in thickness. Now imagine such an enormous mass of sand multiplied as often as there are leaves in the forest, drops of water in the ocean, feathers on birds, scales on fish, hairs on animals, atoms in the air. And imagine that at the end of every million years a little bird came to that mountain and carried away in its beak one tiny grain of that sand. How many millions upon millions of centuries would pass before that bird had carried away even a square foot of that mountain; how many eons of ages before it had carried away all? Yet at the end of that immense stretch of time not even one instant of eternity could be said to have ended. Eternity would have scarcely begun ...

Joyce's preacher left no doubt about the endlessness of torment by saying that even if his imagined mountain were restored and removed countless times, the eternity of punishment would not have been lessened by a single moment. He then concluded:

> Human beings are astonished that God should mete out an everlasting and infinite punishment in the fires of hell for a single grievous sin. They are unable to comprehend the hideous malice of mortal sin, which transgresses His law and God would not be God if He did not punish the transgressor.

In *Portrait* Joyce describes the struggle of Stephen Dedalus – possibly Joyce himself – to cope with the dilemma which this doctrine presented. He found the courage to confront this ghastly teaching, eventually to reject it and the Church which taught it. When I read his book in my early twenties I piously regretted that a man so brilliant as Joyce had 'left the Church', having apparently 'lost his faith'. Much later I came to understand his reaction and saw that Joyce was one of those independent, indeed heroic figures who in their time had a clearer vision than the Church did, and was able to recognise that this, among other teachings, had been distorted and manipulated by religious authorities to enhance their power over people. They had ended up teaching things diametrically opposed to the Good News that Jesus announced. Joyce saw that when religious leaders misinterpret the myth-stories in this way, they not only traumatise young and old: they abuse Truth itself.

It now seems difficult to understand that I accepted this teaching, along with most Catholics and Protestants and the younger Stephen Dedalus; that every day of our lives we walked around under the real threat of ending up in that ghastly torture chamber from which there was no hope of escape. Like spectators watching a bushfire; or the thousands of good German civil servants and railway workers who every day sent a stream of victims towards the extermination camps, we hardly dared to consider, but trembled at the possibility, that *we* might also become its victims. We pushed the thought to the back of our minds, a reality too terrible even to look at.

In my mid-teen years, I was becoming vividly aware of this horror. A mortal sin, my Church taught me, was any action bad enough to cause me to lose 'sanctifying grace', the life of God within me. Typical mortal sins were murder, adultery, large-scale theft and, most pertinent for me as a teenager, 'sins of impurity'... *any* misuse of sex. Who was I to deny so fundamental a doctrine, supported by minds like Augustine, Aquinas, Calvin, Knox, and by the Catholic Apologetics texts we used in senior classes. I had no option but to accept: surely the Church knew best. At that age I did not dream of questioning it.

At that time the behaviour of my male member often intrigued me as it chose to become rampant of its own accord. When it took the initiative in this way I enjoyed the new sensations that it brought. I well knew what its purpose was, for I had observed pets and farm animals mating; joining their bodies to reproduce the next generation of calves, foals or puppies. I did not know where my arousal might lead me, but there was no shortage of severe warnings from the school chaplain and our Form Master, that 'playing with yourself' would inevitably become a sad, enslaving habit. I was loyal and conforming by nature, so I willingly obeyed the given rules and took care not to let it get out of control.

My educators were teaching me that sexual acts outside of the protective fortress of marriage were among the worst deeds one could commit. We were strenuously warned against pre-marital sex and all close contact with girls that might lead us in that direction. Self-stimulation was totally wrong, and although sins like adultery or 'unnatural sex' – homosexuality – were less-often mentioned there was no doubt that they were all gravely evil. Yet at the same time our school ran training courses – the military cadets – in which its young men were trained in the use of deadly machines that killed indiscriminately. They were taught how to murder.

In the early weeks of each of our senior years at school, army officers would visit to call for volunteers. If you joined the Cadet Corps you would get to wear a soldier's khaki uniform with boots and webbing and learn to use a .303 rifle and bayonet. You had the choice of joining the Vickers machine-gun squad or the trench mortar squad. Another option was the medical corps. In the term holidays you would attend a camp for further training in Mildura, reached by a long rail journey.

All these exciting adventures were offered free of charge, so very few boys stood back. Soon, on one day each week, almost the whole of the senior classes came to school dressed in khaki and stayed back after school to drill at marching and the use of weapons, shooting .22 rifles at a sand-bagged target in the handball courts.

I was eager to be part of all this, and earnestly told my father, expecting that he would share my excitement. To my surprise, he quietly but strongly refused to let me join. I tried asking him on a second occasion, but could see that he was unshakeable. A man of few words, he did not or could not explain his reasons; but on looking back years later I realised that he had learned enough about war to see through its absolute folly and the fraudulent reasons that governments give for persuading citizens to take part. I am deeply grateful now that he wanted his sons to have nothing to do with it.

Later, at the age of twenty, I came across Leon Wolff's *In Flanders Fields: The 1917 Campaign*[36], and Alan Moorehead's *Gallipoli*[37]. They showed me what rifles and machine guns were actually used for, and opened windows onto war's ruined landscapes. The theatre of war, I learned, was not for entertainment. Its scripts contained such vile deceit as I had never imagined possible. I was shocked to find that when war seemed likely, government propaganda strove to portray 'the enemy' as monstrous: those ordinary German or Japanese people who had recently been neighbours, friends and trading partners. Politicians and the media began to speak of military tradition and glory, in order to seduce the young into letting themselves be trained to suppress their humanity so as to kill 'the enemy' as efficiently as possible. The bigger the killing machines, the more they were glamorised: battleships, huge naval guns; aircraft carriers, bombers, fighter planes and eventually the atomic bomb. I discovered that war is legalised murder, whether by bullets, bayonets or high explosives; and that when politicians and mass media speak about it they adopt values that are the complete reverse of what is expected from citizens in ordinary life.

I soon learned the cliché that in war the first casualty is truth, and I was appalled by the unblinking way in which governments and newspapers told the public the opposite of what was happening at the front. When incompetent generals sent tens of thousands of soldiers to be massacred in what – even by their own definition – was a failure, they used censorship and blatant lies to tell the public of 'successful advances' and 'hopeful gains'. The poet Siegfried Sassoon, who saw the First World War in all its front-line horror, said that when a country is at war: 'People who tell the truth are likely to be imprisoned and lies are at a premium.'[38]

Soldiers who have survived war are usually unable or unwilling to describe their experiences, but if they do they often use the metaphor 'Hell on Earth'. It was curious indeed that a Catholic secondary school, indeed a whole network of these schools, was willing to prepare their pupils for such a destination.

My youthful naiveté was further destroyed when I discovered that war was hugely profitable for business and was often sought for that reason. Financiers and manufacturers in the USA and countries that were later its allies in trying to destroy Hitler, had earlier helped him to build up Germany's armies. By selfishly excluding Japan from trade they had given its militarist party the leverage to persuade that nation to invade other countries for essential resources. I was no less shocked to learn that in 1945, after fire-bombing dozens of Japanese cities, the US government falsely claimed that it was necessary to kill several hundred thousand more civilians in Hiroshima and Nagasaki 'because it would shorten the War'. At that time Japan was ready to accept peace, so long as the emperor was spared, but we, their enemy, insisted on unconditional surrender.

As years passed I learned that from within the shelter of bureaucratic institutions, human beings are skilled at constructing versions of hell. Governments seduce their young people by portraying war as exciting; then when they are gruesomely killed or their lives ruined, describe their destruction as a 'glorious sacrifice'. By such lies they divert resources away from people's real needs for food, shelter, health and education to splurge it on armies and weapons that destroy all these necessities.

I began to see that war is a collection of sins on a scale cosmically different from adolescents enjoying the discovery of their bodies' new sexual powers. It seemed obvious that young people's fumbling mistakes as they learn to relate to each other were minute in comparison with the hellish destruction of thousands of persons in Gallipoli, Fromelles and Paschendale, or twenty years later in Dresden or Nagasaki. Why was our Church more concerned about our sexual exploration than about the machinations of financiers and politicians arranging unjust wars or, in peace time, about unjust wages and interest rates that caused poverty, sick children and the deaths of millions?

But it was the real possibility of ending up in hell at the end of my life that most haunted me. What sins had I committed? As already mentioned[39], even before adolescent hormones had begun to stir, I had suffered agonies of guilt about small acts of sexual curiosity. Now that my body was beginning to exert its new powers I was being taught to be obsessed about my sinfulness, but in fact there was not much to it. At this point in my life I had never seen an adult female body naked, even in a photograph, yet the puritanical education I was receiving told me that even my imaginings and feelings about human sexuality were putting me in danger of eternal punishment. What worried me most were sexual thoughts. I found few opportunities to form serious relationships with girls and lacked confidence when they occurred, so I observed life mainly from the background, gathering and hoarding information, avidly reading anything about sex that might enlighten or entertain me.

I developed a skill for sniffing out sexual references from chapter headings or by speed-reading dozens of pages of text. In bookshops I came across such titillating facts that in Eskimo tribes, overt sexual play among children was liberally tolerated, even with adults present in the igloo. I envied Eskimo children enormously. In childhood I had never had girl companions with whom such play might even have been suggested, and if it had been, our adults seemed so vigilant that any such experimentation was unthinkable. Things would have been different, I day-dreamed, if I had been born into an extended Eskimo family and spent long winters in the Arctic Circle. I was also stirred by reading about an African native ritual, involving every young man and woman of the tribe. When all the village had assembled, the ceremony began with a warrior publicly 'fecundating a donkey' by way of inspiration to the rest, and ended with a night of general copulation.

These were among my more notable discoveries, but long hours of searching were rarely so fruitful. Such findings as I made I kept mostly to myself, too embarrassed to share them with any but closest friends. But whether it was some astonishing revelation from my library research decades before the internet, or merely prim articles in the *Readers' Digest* about anatomy or pregnancy, such arousal as I felt would cause me to burn with guilt that yet again I was 'giving way to impure thoughts'.

We were taught that such thoughts were not sinful unless one had 'taken pleasure in them', but this advice was itself destructive, for not only was it almost impossible to discern whether one had taken pleasure in what was innately pleasurable; it also designated as morally evil this natural, good pleasure of a body discovering its sexual powers. While the young do need to be helped towards self-control, countless adolescent Catholics must have been distorted in their emotional lives by being told that they must not rejoice in the feelings that arise naturally in us as we grow to adulthood.

One night in my fifteenth year I sat at the kitchen table cutting from white cardboard a rectangle a little smaller than a matchbox. As knights of old had mottos, and modern corporations design logos, I was trying to compose a suitable phrase to inscribe on this small plaque, to express in a few words the consequences that faced me whenever I was tempted to do wrong. An equivalent practice among contemporary youths might be the plastic bracelets with the cryptic acronym WWJD (What would Jesus do?) I was trying to prevent myself from making wrong choices that would send me to eternal punishment. I intended to wear this warning always, on the medal chain that already hung around my neck.

I cut a rectangle from the card, then rounded its corners to form what I felt was an ideal shape, something like a miniature version of the first television screens, although I had never seen one, for they would not arrive in Australia for several more years. This was also before the era of plastic laminating, so I planned to conserve my epigram by varnishing it with the clear nail polish that my mother sometimes used. Having made the tablet I found it difficult to come up with a suitable lapidary warning that would always remind me to choose to act so as to avoid the eternal flames. Instead of first drafting it on scrap paper, I unwisely wrote my first effort on the tablet, then varnished it, only to discard it as not good enough.

I made another, then still other tablets, but however urgently I wanted to compose a dire, sin-stopping admonition, the warnings I composed seemed either weak and inadequate or too wordy. In the end, driven by weariness and by guilt at the piles of homework that as usual waited to be done, and half-stupefied by the fumes of the nail-varnish, I abandoned the task and went off to bed. I never approached it again.

The fear of hell went underground, into my unconscious, and not until my thirties did I find that I could question the Church's teaching about it. Some theological writers were beginning to soften the harshness of the doctrine by saying that if any person is in hell it was not God who condemned them to the torment of infinite loss: they put themselves there by their own choice. The active divine 'just punishment' that James Joyce had heard preached was being quietly forgotten. But this seemed like a cop-out: God was still responsible for not helping sinners in their own folly. Other theologians accepted that hell exists – as Church documents insisted – but suggested no one is actually there! Still others, among them CS Lewis[40], suggested that persons who chose to turn away from God would eventually wither away to nothing. Against this, Aquinas had taught that the Creator would never annihilate a creature that he had made. Allowing them to disappear seemed to me much the same thing, a serious conflict with God's Love. CS Lewis also speculated that in hell people remain free to visit or to choose to live in heaven, but that their previous choices have made them unable to see this as desirable. Lewis was suggesting that hell is a place that we choose.

Other theologians were reviving the ancient belief, held by a few early Christian writers, that Infinite Love would not allow us to miss out finally on the purpose for which we are made: to be united with the One who made us. This hope, that all will be saved, was based on St Paul's statement that the work of each person who builds on the foundation of Christ will become visible on The Day [of Christ's return]:

> ... the fire will test what sort of work each has done. If what has been built ... survives, the builder will receive a reward. If the work is burned up, the builder will suffer loss; the builder will be saved, but only as through fire (1 Cor 3:13-15).

This optimism is echoed in an ancient Easter homily that speaks of Christ entering the world of the dead to free Adam and Eve[41], who in the understanding of the time were the greatest sinners because their sin led to all subsequent sins. The same optimism is preserved in the Apostles' Creed, which states enigmatically that Christ, no doubt for some effective purpose, 'descended into hell'.

I was helped by reading a small work on this hope of 'universal salvation' by the Jesuit Bill Dalton and by a conversation with him. I wrestled with longer works by John Hick[42], Ladislaus Boros[43], and Hans Urs Von Balthasar[44], contemporary theologians who were again proposing that 'all could be saved'. Up till then I had been loyally accepting the Catholic literalist interpretation of the Bible, but it had prevented me – and so many others – from finding a greater loyalty to what the gospels were actually teaching: that God is infinitely forgiving and merciful. Like Saint Augustine centuries before, and so many others, including James Joyce, I had wrestled with the ambiguity of a God whom the New Testament declares 'wishes all people to be saved' (1 Tim 2:4.), but who – Matthew's gospel tells us – will punish wrongdoers in 'eternal fire'. I was delighted to discover texts in writings attributed to St Paul that showed a much larger vision, that God's plan was '... to gather up all things in [Christ]' (Eph 1:10; cf. Col 1:20), and to read that St Peter, as reported in the Acts of the Apostles, referred to '... the time of universal restoration' (Acts 3:21), or *apokatastasis*. This word came to be used to express the belief that all people will achieve salvation. These optimistic writers could see a wider picture, a Transcendent Love planning to bring it all together, whereas the pessimists accepted eternal punishment for a large part of the divided human race. Who had found the truth?

The optimistic vision does not delete human responsibility or say that we are not accountable for our actions. To damage another person in pursuing our own desires is plainly evil. It is indescribably more horrible to do this on a large scale, as we see in widespread child abuse; in the fire-bombing of whole cities and in genocide. Nevertheless, we cannot deny that those who take part even in the most terrible atrocities are still 'children of God' and are included in God's mercy and healing. As for those who die unrepentant – the optimistic theologians are saying – would not God, who is infinite Patience and Love somehow enlighten them at their death, in the timeless moment of eternity? Although Aquinas' philosophy ruled out any change of heart at death, I dared to suspect that he might be wrong on this point and struggled towards an explanation that fitted with convictions forming in my heart.

I found a key to resolving the apparent contradiction between my instincts and the 'punitive' scriptural texts when I discovered that the Gospels take us through archways of metaphor, exaggeration and myth. Only since the 1950s have Catholic biblical scholars been free to use the full depths of scholarship to interpret the Bible in a scientific and critical way. It took longer for ordinary Catholics to come to understand how the authors of the ancient texts used various literary forms of expression, and that if we cling to a too-literal reading of the Scriptural texts we will misunderstand much of what they are trying to tell us.

For instance, in teaching us how to bring about the Reign of God, Jesus warned what will happen if we harm each other:

> ...it was said to those of ancient times, 'You shall not murder' ... But I say to you that if you are angry with a brother or sister, you will be liable to judgement ... and if you say, 'You fool', you will be liable to the hell [Gehenna] of fire (Matt 5:21-22).

The translators of the Catholic Douai Rheims New Testament (1582) and of the King James Bible (1604-1611) chose to replace *Gehenna* with the word *Hell*, which came into English from the Germanic *haljō*, literally 'the hidden place', the underworld. The translation was quite deceptive, for by *Gehenna* Jesus was referring to the valley of *Ben Hinnom* outside Jerusalem, the smoking local rubbish dump, which was additionally repulsive as the place where children had once been sacrificed.[45] Jesus was tossing off one of his powerful metaphors, telling us that anyone who hurts the community by their hatred or spite will end up on the rubbish tip, among its smoke and stinking garbage. It is disappointing and misleading that translators of most modern versions of the Bible still translate *Gehenna* with the English word *Hell*.

Like all metaphors, especially those used with exaggeration, *Gehenna* invites us to peek through its entrance door to see a highly colourful and frightening, but *figurative*, consequence of our actions which pushes us towards understanding the *actual* result. Jesus was not threatening us with some underworld cave of horrors, but beguiling us to look at the serious consequences that our self-indulgent and anti-social actions bring about. By these we distort our own person and cause wretched chaos in the community. Worse, we lose sight of the transcendent mystery behind life.

In another metaphor Jesus warned us to beware of dangerous temptations:

> If your right eye causes you to sin, tear it out and throw it away; it is better ... to lose one of your members than for your whole body to be thrown into hell [Gehenna]. And if your right hand causes you to sin, cut it off and throw it away; it is better ... to lose one of your members than for your whole body to go into hell [Gehenna]' (Matt 5:29-30).

I have not yet met a Christian with only one eye who had taken Jesus' advice literally, so we have cause to wonder why generations of Christians have ignored his advice there, but persisted in taking literally the Gehenna statements and similar threats of 'eternal' fire.

Myths are not false, as many people tend to think, but are deeply true, and symbolise what happens in everyone's life. It is curious that 'believers' often make a mistake comparable to those that they scorn 'unbelievers' for making: where the latter reject miracles as impossible because their senses cannot perceive a cause, hyper-credulous 'believers', ignorant of the mechanisms of language and culture, accept things that were never meant to be *literally* believed. They want mythical stories to be literally true, even if it means accepting a world-wide flood that destroyed Earth's entire population and animal life except the Noah family; a fish that can swallow a prophet; and a human race ultimately divided, with some perfectly happy in God's presence but forever forgetting that their brothers and sisters, in some other place, are being endlessly tortured.

I knew that Christians believed in a literal hell mainly because of the great judgement scene near the end of Matthew's gospel, where the Son of Man judges all the nations, separating them:

> as a shepherd separates the sheep from the goats ...Then [he] will say to those [the goats] at his left hand: You ... accursed, depart from me into the eternal fire prepared for the Devil and his angels; for I was hungry and you gave me no food, I was thirsty and you gave me nothing to drink ... And these will go away into eternal punishment, but the righteous [the sheep] into eternal life (Matt 25:33-46).

When the puzzled goats ask *when* did they fail to welcome the King or give him food or clothing, he will reply 'just as you did not do it to one of the least of these, you did not do it to me' (Matt 25:45).

This extended metaphor, constructed from several different stories that Matthew blended together, states clearly that the way we treat each other has enormous consequences. Its main point is that every person is linked to everyone else because we are each part of the mysterious whole, the 'Body of Christ'. When we help – or fail to help – *any* person, we are helping or damaging this total network. If we fail to see this close relationship, we hugely miss the point of the parable, and of human life. We are so incurably individualistic that the main thing we notice in Jesus' story is his metaphor about the *individual* punishment we might receive. We fail to see his much more important point.

Once we can lay aside any literal interpretation of the Last Judgement story, we no longer have to believe that the great trial will be conducted by a ruthless tyrant who condemns to eternal torture those who have broken the rules. In these metaphors Matthew seems to be offering three truths: the first is that when we fail to help people in need, we make ourselves fit to be cast away from God; the second explains that all victims are somehow identified with the Risen Christ himself: 'Whatever you did to the least of these, you did to me' (Matt 25:41, 46). A third implied truth is less obvious: even those who are ignorant or malicious enough to hurt or neglect their neighbour are *still included* among those whom Christ identifies with himself. Even though in the metaphor he calls them goats, God cannot fail to love them, infinitely.

At death, what might happen to us if we have led a destructive life? We must certainly face the consequences of the harm we have done, but this will happen in the presence of the God who Jesus elsewhere consistently described as totally merciful. Jesus himself, during his life, did not shun those whom the Law called 'sinners', but chose to mix with them. He told them about a God who forgives and welcomes them. The most moving of all his stories was about a father and his two sons.[46] This God whom Jesus is portraying does not torture or abuse his own children! It is a tragic fact that for generations the opposite doctrine was set before me and most young Christians. I can hardly begin to understand the depth of harm that this abuse has caused.

For the quarter million or so folk who, around the world, die each day, whatever happens after death takes place in a state beyond all our present knowledge. Those who have been through a Near-Death Experience[47] tell about their profound encounters in metaphors of their own. These often include being judged, but with extreme, life-changing compassion, which tallies with Jesus' own teaching that infinite love oversees our lives. At life's end, outside the square of our present experience and logic, the apparent conflict between God's justice and mercy may cease to appear contradictory but come together in the beautiful truth that even in our most flawed condition Love cannot reject us.

11
'Now is the Time'
The treasure of the present moment

Like earthworms or little burrowing animals in their familiar soil, we bore through time day by day, unconscious of any great progress; being busily engaged with our daily tasks. Only occasionally do we break through into clearer vision, whether by choice or after some disaster – like the earthworm flushed to the surface by rain – and are astonished to discover the distance we have come, the difference that time has made.

For nearly forty years I had not lived in my home state of Victoria, although I had sometimes visited it briefly. When recovering from peritonitis I returned to Victoria in mid-2016 and asked for some sabbatical leave in which to convalesce and to write. The diocese of Ballarat offered me the use of the empty presbytery in the village of Timboon, not far from my birthplace, where I provided Sunday Masses and other assistance in four rural churches.

I arrived during a run of bleak, cold weather, so when the sun at last came out I drove, for a break, to the coast at nearby Port Campbell. It was exhilarating to watch the wild ocean, brown with the silt from flooded creeks, foaming like a giant cappuccino and tossing spray high over the sandstone cliffs. I drove further east to the spectacular Loch Ard Gorge and London Bridge, which I had not visited for perhaps fifty years. Things were different now. I had already heard that one of the arches of the remarkable Bridge had collapsed into the sea. Looking at the gap that remained I shivered to recall that I had once walked across that arch, careful but confident as I looked down to the foaming waves below. Just now I felt my confidence crumbling like the shattered rocks.

When I was last at Loch Ard Gorge fifty years earlier there had been one or two cars parked in a bare, sandy patch amid the scrub on the cliff top. We struck up a conversation with the few intrepid pilgrims who had travelled to that remote spot to see the scenery of which we locals were so proud. Now I was amazed to find an extensive paved car-park with scores of cars and seven coaches unloading and reloading tourists from Korea and China. A river of pedestrians flowed down the new stairway into the gorge and the beach itself was like a city square, with groups using mobile phones on sticks to take selfies against the backdrop of towering cliffs and incoming waves.

I drove back to my quiet home, feeling that I had just stepped through an archway of time, from the world of memory into one that my eyes could not deny but my mind struggled to accept. Time usually creeps past slowly, but today it had crashed catastrophically around me, like the arch of London Bridge. I was startled as one is when visiting a family after a long absence and is greeted by handsome young adults who, when last seen, were children at play. I was stunned by the changed landscape of my birth.

When I had lived as a child on our family's farm in that part of south-western Victoria, we thought the district was and always would be ours by right. Hadn't our grandparents cleared the forest with their own strength to establish dairy farms? Weren't the local bays and roads named after our families, the first white landowners? How could it ever change? We had quite forgotten that before us a previous population had fished and hunted, eaten and slept in those places not for two or three generations, but for hundreds of lifetimes. Could *they* have ever dreamed that a new race with paler skin would one day cruelly drive them all away, taking it all for themselves and radically changing the landscape with their axes and saws, their seeds and chemicals; their machines, and tens of thousands of dairy cows?

The events of daily life can be astonishingly beautiful, but we have a curious habit of idealising pleasant times in our past. We recall them as if they lasted for longer than they did. 'We always had picnics down in that bay …', 'In the summer holidays, Dad would always take us fishing …', 'Every Christmas we used to play backyard cricket…' Such reminiscences might mean that our memory has expanded just two or three, – or perhaps half dozen – occasions into a well-entrenched tradition. We expand into an endless, blissful era a few happy occasions in a childhood that is now long passed.

When I was pastor in a large Brisbane parish, one mother lamented that, 'The priests often used to visit us, but they never call these days.' She recounted a happy memory of looking from her kitchen window to see that the parish-priest had just arrived and had joined in the children's backyard cricket game. I recognised her veiled hint that I ought to visit parish homes more often, even as I groaned inwardly at the thought of nearly four thousand Catholic households on our census list and the impossibility of dropping in casually to their homes, many of them apartments three floors above the doorbell and intercom. I reflected – but only to myself – that the cricket-playing pastor had probably arrived just two minutes before she noticed him from the kitchen window, and probably stayed for a visit lasting ten more. Almost certainly he would not have returned more than once.

Creative artists labour to capture and express the timeless. They often confess that they fail to reach the perfection that they have glimpsed, but occasionally they *do* capture something of the real beauty of things. Sometimes, in a still life, they show how non-moving objects can declare their enduring relationships with us and are waiting for us to use them: cups hanging from their hooks; the bridle hanging from its nail; the work-boots tossed aside; foods half-prepared on a table.

Like the artist, we all seem to have an instinct to hold on to experiences that satisfy, bring pleasure, or delight us with their beauty. When the experiences inevitably pass, we try to repeat them. We want to stop *here*, now that we have found the job we wanted; the partner we hoped for; have built our ideal home where we are happy and think we will be happy forever. But if we imagine we can make things last, we deceive ourselves. We cannot stop the flow of time anymore than a cyclist can stop moving and remain upright. Even if we enjoy some experiences on hundreds of occasions, in our heart we know there will inevitably be a last time when we must let go. Time is simply the measure of the moving flow of the physical world, and one of our few certainties is that the universe, including this planet and our whole life on it, is temporary, changing every second. It is our privilege to revel in its beauty, and wise of us to accept its passing, even rejoicing as it leaves. Perhaps this is the only true way to grasp things.

No matter how often we repeat a daily routine on our turning, speeding planet, every moment and every position in space that we occupy is absolutely unique. So radical is this total flow of change that in our unconscious fear of it we sometimes try to save ourselves, as if from drowning, by grasping at floating twigs. Even when we claim to believe in an unchanging God, we are tempted to make symbols of permanence and cling to them as if *these* were unchanging – basilicas, cathedrals, dogmas, creeds and forms of words in liturgy – in a vain attempt to describe or hold on to the One 'with whom there is no variation or shadow due to change' (Jas 1:17). We tend to become afraid when people use new words to talk about the Transcendent or suggest new ways to worship. Trying to cling to some past practice or return to a past era does not – as we mistakenly think – bring us to the ultimate destination. It is merely at attempt to dig in and build a fortress somewhere along the road in a vain attempt to defend ourselves against besieging time.

Our big plastic rubbish bin had not been cleaned for some time and black sediment had formed at the bottom. The bin wouldn't fit under the tap at the back of the house, so I filled a bucket with water and threw it vigorously into the bin. It surprised me by rebounding up above the sides. In mid-blink, my eye caught the splash as it hung for an instant at the top of its leap, splayed out into irregular tongues of water and clouds of droplets. I was reminded of a photo of the Crab Nebula, the remains of a supernova, an exploded star that was first seen bursting in the sky in 1054 AD, although it had actually exploded six and a half thousand years *before* then, so long did its light take to reach the Earth. So huge was the star's bursting that nearly a thousand years after we first saw it explode, the Hubble telescope still sees its leftover fragments spreading out in a colossal cloud of glowing gas 94 trillion kilometres across.

As I went on cleaning the bin, I wondered whether there are minds that see time on a different scale than we do, for whom the exploding of a star and the following millennia are a momentary process like water splashing up the sides of a rubbish bin. If so, they might watch the debris from the Crab Nebula continue to spread, then in what is for us a distant aeon, fall back together again to form another star which could develop orbiting planets where after billions more years living species might evolve. Could those ultra-minds see such cosmic developments in the way we watch a quarter-second water splash, or a rose opening over a few days? Is time the same for all minds?

⌒

When the suburban train stopped at a station, big schoolboys bounced through the door into the carriage. They were talking tough to each other and acting with bravado to impress the few girls present. Some even swung from the overhead bars, heedless of the watching security cameras. A few elderly passengers seemed shocked, even alarmed, as the students noisily exulted in their new freedom, for – I began to realise – these were final-year students on their last day of term and of school life. After a week or two of study they would endure their final exams and then be free of school forever. It was a most special day, a milestone in their lives. Only a few other times in their future would compare with it: the day of their graduation from university or their exchange of wedding vows; or even more certainly, the last hour of their breathing.

I enjoyed watching them as they moved around so energetically, probably not realising that they were paused – as it were - in the archway leading from this unique day into the next stage of their lives. But – I thought – is not *every* day like this? Don't we enter, each moment, a new territory made up of elements that may look the same as yesterday's but which bring us to a different point on the web of our relationships with other people and with our own body and mind? Isn't time like a long corridor lined with doorways? We have no choice but to pass through it, but we can make an almost infinite number of choices about which doors to enter as we pass. If we catch from the side of our eye any individual day or moment, we might notice that its complex pattern is unique among the billions of sunrises and sunsets that have measured out the history of this planet since the time when its molten surface slowly cooled, so that one day millions of species of plants and animals, like us, could each have here the time of their lives.

⁌

Feeling as weak as the proverbial new-born kitten I slumped in an armchair beside the hospital bed. A breakfast tray had just been placed beside me, but I had not the least desire to eat. My stomach was painfully bloated with air and my lower belly completely full of fluid, and neither showed any sign of emptying. At times the distension was agonising. It was three days since the operation on my abdomen, the second of its kind in just over a year. The first, in December 2015, had saved my life after my appendix had burst and filled my gut with infection; this second was to repair that previous wound, which had not closed properly and had become herniated. I was shortly to learn that this wound too had now become infected. A bloated stomach can usually be relieved by simply walking about: eventually some of the wind will escape. But I felt too weak to walk, or even to stand. I knew that if the bloating did not lessen I would again need a tube poked up my nose and into my stomach to relieve the pressure, as had been done on the previous night, until it became so uncomfortable that I asked for it to be removed. 'To reduce the wind, I need to walk; to get stronger, I need to eat.' I try to focus: 'Get up! Walk a few paces ... It's your only choice ... Just five or ten steps.' I don't want to ... I can't.

My thoughts were circling, locked into the same track, looking for a way out: how to get stronger? By eating ... but I could not. How to reduce the painful distension? By walking ... not able. The closing spiral led downwards into darkness. I felt stuck, barely conscious, in this moment of time ... But my mind was not quite completely locked in. I nodded awake and found myself looking outward, beyond my pain. I had remembered a name: the name of a man who had suffered far more than I ever had or would. I knew him by name only, for my friend Harmeet had told me the story of Maher Arar, his friend from student days in Montreal who had become an item of world news. Born in Syria, Maher had come to Canada aged seventeen and obtained dual citizenship. After university he had become a successful telecommunications engineer, married and had two young children.

In September 2002 he was returning home to Canada after a holiday in Tunis. His wife and children were on a previous flight, and when he failed to meet them at John F Kennedy airport they did not know that US authorities had detained him. Acting on false information from Canadian police about 'terrorism', the FBI agents held him without charge, secretly and in solitary confinement for nearly two weeks. They continually questioned him, but denied him any useful access to a lawyer. The US government, in its largely phoney 'war on terror', suspected him of being a member of Al Qaeda, simply because they suspected, also falsely, one of his friends. Their suspicion came from the 'evidence' of a man tortured in Bagram prison in Afghanistan, who had 'identified' Maher's photograph, telling his interrogators whatever they wanted to hear, as tortured people usually do.

Instead of releasing Maher and allowing him to go home to Canada, United States officials illegally sent him to Syria, although he begged them not to, knowing he would be tortured there. Like many others he was being 'renditioned' abroad to be tortured, for US agencies were afraid of being caught acting in breach of their own Constitution. Maher was imprisoned in Syria for about a year, locked in a cell he describes as a three-foot by six-foot 'grave' with no light and many rats. He was beaten regularly with shredded cables, and through the walls of his cell could hear the frequent screams of other prisoners being tortured. His torturers asked him the same questions he had been asked in the United States, and passed his answers back to US officials.

I can scarcely imagine what Maher Arar suffered in the 374 days that passed between his arrest and release. On October 5th, 2003 he was returned to Canada and reunited with his wife and children. The Syrian government later admitted that he was completely innocent and a Canadian enquiry publicly cleared him of any links to 'terrorism'. Arar sued the Canadian government for neglecting to protect him as a citizen and in 2007 it settled out of court, awarding him C$10.5 million with an additional million for legal costs. Prime Minister Harper formally apologised to him for Canada's role in his 'terrible ordeal'. He is still not allowed to enter the USA, whose government keeps him and his family on the 'no fly list' and whose courts steadfastly deny that his constitutional, civil or international human rights were violated or that he has any right to damages. In June 2010 the Supreme Court declined to review the case.

That morning beside the hospital bed my thoughts lingered on Maher Arar. I imagined the coffin-sized cell where he woke morning after morning to the threat of that day's torture, clinging almost without hope to the slender thought that one day he might see his wife and children again.

～

Later that day I thought of my aunt Annie, who had not come to mind in a long time. Born in 1900, she was a child of twelve when my father's family sold their farm near Warrnambool in western Victoria and made a great trek northwards of more than 1600 kilometres to richer farmland newly opened up near the Tweed River in New South Wales. Their stay at Crabbes Creek was to be short, for the buyer of their Victorian farm was unable to pay up, and Annie's situation probably contributed to their decision to return.

She had contracted poliomyelitis, which left her paralysed below the waist and confined her to bed. She spent the following fifty-five years in that condition, without the technical aids that disabled people can use today. Even if a lightweight wheelchair had been available, beyond the veranda of her home there were few paved surfaces where she could be wheeled, and although beautiful coastal scenery was no more than a kilometre away, she was rarely taken to see it. During my many visits to the house, only twice did I see her carried outdoors. She was in her forties when I first saw her, already greying, but strikingly cheerful. This joyfulness seems to have continued during the following twenty years. She knew everyone in the district; her bedroom was the place where visitors were received and cups of tea shared. If perhaps her moods swung downwards at times it would be entirely understandable, but I never saw a hint of it. I used to wonder what heroic choices she – and her hard-working mother – must have made every day, to accept her condition and lead a fruitful life among that small rural community.

I thanked Maher Arar, whom I may never meet, and my aunt Annie, who died fifty years ago, for giving me, through their different stories of seemingly timeless imprisonment, a clear sight of my own doorway to freedom at a difficult time.

~

Only a few times in my life have I been bored, felt imprisoned and been profoundly discontent in the present moment. Routine and repetition are useful tools to help us to learn and to do our work efficiently, but if boredom has snared us in its net, sameness becomes a torment.

In 1947, as the school year was drawing to its end, my family moved from Bendigo back to Western Victoria.[48] I was not yet eight years old and did not understand why we had left and moved half way across the state. Among the several reasons was the fact that my grandfather was nearing the end of his life. My father was the eldest of his four sons, who must have often discussed the future of the family farm. Perhaps it was with a view to claiming his share that my father had brought us back near his birthplace and found temporary work share-farming with strangers.

In later years I wondered what impact the move, and especially our arrival, made on my mother. After a long, hot journey travelling in the furniture van with our goods, we reached our destination: a ramshackle wooden building beside a long straight road with no other houses in sight. One or two neighbouring farmhouses might be guessed at among clumps of trees far across paddocks of dried grass. We had been told that our new home was known as 'The Butcher's Shop', for remote as it was, it had once served that function. In the front wall was a wide window, now closed with a wooden shutter, like a blinded eye, where customers had once been served. In the days of slower transport it must have been more convenient for local farmers to buy meat there rather than in Allansford or distant Warrnambool.

Hearing my mother's sharp comments and sensing the tension between her and my father, the van driver quietly but ineptly offered to take us back to Bendigo, whence he was about to return when we had unloaded the van. For my father this was unthinkable, for another reason for our departure was his gambling debts to bookmakers. So we unpacked and spread our belongings through the rooms which were vacant. Even though it was a small building, several locked rooms were filled with the stored furniture of the previous occupants.

For the few weeks remaining before Christmas we enrolled at the Mepunga East State School, to which we walked three and a half kilometres each morning. Then the school closed and the long weeks of summer holidays stretched ahead. We three brothers had to find our own entertainment, for we had no neighbours or friends, few toys and no transport to go anywhere: prisoners in our own house until school resumed at some time in the distant future.

Our natural urge to learn and create was taxed to the limit: there were no books, so we read and re-read a small stack of tattered, second-hand magazines: *Saturday Evening Post, Outdoors and Fishing, English Women's Weekly.* Although most of their articles and stories were beyond my seven-year-old understanding, I gazed longingly at the cabin cruisers advertised in the sporting magazines and day-dreamed about owning and riding in one. On the short front veranda we devised running games which began and ended with a leap down from or up onto the sloping lid of the chook-food bin. Among the infrequent traffic that passed our front gate, we counted and classified the different kinds of milk trucks: semi-trailers loaded with hundreds of rattling cans from the several small butter factories then operating in the district. On the hottest days we played in the water-drum under the hand-pump at the back door. To add interest to the game we vandalised our school pastels, crushing them to make bottles of brightly-coloured water, with which we stocked an imaginary chemist's shop.

As the weeks dragged on we could not keep back the grey mist of boredom. The empty hours so threatened us that it is painful to recall my hunger for things that would interest me or activities that would fill my time. Unlike enterprising adults, who can draw upon their stored-up memories from many years' experience, we had no such wealth on which to reflect. The mysterious power of imagination was not yet sufficiently developed in me to let me construct coherent stories or art-work which would provide doorways leading out from that gruelling avenue of endless present moments.

Perhaps that barren stretch of childhood, when I was starved of stimulation, helped to prepare me to appreciate that I can choose to use each moment. I am still learning that no matter what we may lack in the present moment or how narrow our range of options might have become, we can choose to recognise the assets we do have and to see our surroundings as a cup half-full rather than half-empty. From the stories of Nelson Mandela and others and my own brief experience of police cells I have learned that one can be free even in a prison. No matter what the outward circumstances, to a surprising degree we have the power to determine how our inner life will be played out.

We can be free in any place, content to do without many of the things that people consider essential. We may be in ill health or ageing, or not even able to move our limbs. Persons totally paralysed have written books one letter at a time by whatever small movement they can manage with eye or tongue. In any present moment – until death removes us out of time – our powers to think, to choose and above all to love, open up countless doors, opportunities to reflect on past experiences and explore new directions.

We have enormous power to affect our future by the way we choose in this present moment to react to external things like our physical circumstances and other people's actions; or to internal realities like our emotions and health. We can choose to move towards healing past relationships by forgiving wrongs done to us and asking pardon for the harm we have done to others. For people who are absent or dead we can do this in our heart. Looking ahead to coming events we can resolve to treat others with love and kindness, even when they are unkind to us. All these choices can be made only in the present moment, this fleeting, ever-renewed instant where all our growing takes place.

During my novitiate I was impressed to hear that a Jesuit in the 18th century had described the present moment as a 'sacrament', a sacred event in which we are in touch with God.[49] Each moment, each *now*, is new and unique. There has never been, and never again will be another moment like this one, because the spinning of our planet and the turning of the galaxy ensure that we will never again be at the same place among the components of the universe as we are right now. This uniqueness might suggest that there is little point in preferring one moment or one time over another – everything has its place, everything fits in.

The circumstances around us are unrepeatable and almost infinitely varying. Since our bodies go on changing and our senses and minds continue to explore, we countless human beings alive now resemble the growing leaf-buds at the outer edge of a vast tree of consciousness, drawing life from humanity's roots and trunk that began several million years ago.

↭

The physics lecturer was telling us that time's arrow goes in only one direction: that the second law of thermodynamics dictates that we and our universe are all heading in the direction of maximum entropy, or, in other words, disorder. The lecturer added that it was not understood from physics alone why this should be so, that everything wears out and decays, as the fictitious Murphy's Law humorously puts it: 'whatever can break down, will break down'[50]. The physics lecturer didn't seem to notice that the Earth is populated by billions of living creatures who each, like himself, spend their time fighting against entropy to *increase* the order in their bodies – and in their minds, in the case of creatures which have one. Even physicists should be in awe of this remarkable power that living things possess, to reverse – if only for a time – what this lecturer seemed to be saying is a universal *diktat* with no exceptions. If we living creatures cannot quite turn back the clock, we can hold back the tide of entropy for as long as we live and breathe. When our time is up, our mortal remains resume their place among things that are dissolving towards chaos ... but is that all there is to it?

Human consciousness is the highest level of life that we are familiar with. Leaving aside for the moment the critical question of whether we will live on beyond the time when our body stops breathing, there seem to be other small signs that we are to some degree independent of time's arrow-flight. On several occasions I have listened to persons who sincerely believed they had knowledge of future events before they happened.

One of these was a woman who came seeking help about dreams which were greatly troubling her. She would often dream, she said, about some human disaster such as a plane crash, only to see it announced in the media a day or two later, with details that clearly identified it as the one dreamed of. She was so disturbed by these dreams that she tried hard to ignore and suppress them. Two nights before I met her she had been deeply disturbed by dreaming of a boy suffocating in a collapsed sand-tunnel. On the morning after her dream she had seen in the newspaper – as I had – the report of such an accident. I have only her word for the accuracy of what she told me, but she showed no signs of mental disturbance and had no reason to deceive me. It is not uncommon to hear anecdotes of such predictive dreams and of premonitions which people have when awake. The stories of the separate premonitions of Mike Willesee and Bill Bennett have already been mentioned[51], both fulfilled within moments of being 'heard'.

Once, in a parish group, a woman shared with us that one of her sons, early in his childhood, would often describe something moments before it actually came to pass. For instance, she said, when sitting beside her in the car he would describe in detail a child on a bicycle who was about to emerge from the side-street that they were approaching. The mother was completely befuddled by these predictions, for he could not possibly have seen the cycling child. She did nothing about them, and was relieved that he eventually 'grew out of it'.[52]

During a seminar I attended, its leader, the psychiatrist Dr Elisabeth Kübler-Ross, gave us an instance from her own experience of this kind of prescience. She told how, when travelling with her baby on a long flight, she had temporarily placed the infant in its basket in the aisle beside her seat while she attended to some task. Suddenly she felt a strong but 'irrational' urge to move the child. She picked it up from the basket and was holding it in her lap when shortly afterwards a stewardess walking down the aisle stumbled and tipped scalding coffee into the basket.

Such examples of people glimpsing or being warned of some future event seem to be explicable only if we accept that beyond the time dimension that we are familiar with, there is another territory or dimension where our future is to some degree visible and known. We are naturally surprised by this, just as first-time travellers are surprised to find in foreign countries that the climate, architecture and customs are quite unlike their own, which until then they had assumed were the only norm.

We do not have to accept that there are 'other universes', as some propose as an attempt to solve the paradox of uncertainty in quantum physics. The premonitions of which we are speaking seem generally to warn of approaching dangers, so it would seem sufficient to postulate that in a dimension outside the time which we inhabit, there are minds – or a Mind – which on occasion 'nudges' us with a helpful warning about some event that is soon to unfold and against which we need to be warned. In our age so shaped by rationalism these premonitions make for strange and somewhat eerie narratives, but the strength of evidence seems to leave us no option but to accept them. They seem to convey the solid warning that our understanding of time is seriously incomplete.

12
'I Am Not What I Am'
Deceivers and hypocrites

A central paradox in the four gospels is that to become our true self, we need to 'lose our self'. I once thought I might have prematurely attained this state when I looked into a mirror and did not see my face reflected there. It happened in a convent in Karachi, whose Sisters spend their lives caring for children with extreme physical and mental disabilities. We were introduced to the residents, who in many cases had been abandoned as infants because of some deformity. Some of them could do no more than lie on their beds; some were blind, but they were all left in no doubt that they were greatly loved and had a real home here. The sister who showed us around had worked for decades at the arduous tasks of feeding and cleaning these less able human beings – and loving them. She and her community members obviously saw them as their own sisters and brothers and it was just as evident that they appreciated her help and friendship. One child who could not move from her cot responded with a joyful, beatific smile when Sister merely touched her and spoke a word in Urdu.

I was greatly challenged by what I was seeing, and the words of Jesus rang in my head: 'when you did it to the least of these you did it to me' (Matt 25:40). The one whom Christians believe to be Son of God said that these creatures, some of them physically repulsive and far from the 'normal' that we typically expect in people if we are to feel comfortable in their presence, *are* the beautiful Christ. How can persons who may seem to lack full humanity be identified with the Infinite One? Listening in that ordinary room to a woman who loved in an extraordinary way, I began to ask more deeply: if I were stripped of my superficial layers – education, intelligence, membership of my

'I AM NOT WHAT I AM'

family and of the Dominican friars – what would remain? Who, in essence, *am* I?

As the Sister talked, I sat facing the top of the stairs leading down to the ground floor. I could see the pinkish cement walls of the stairwell and a bare light-bulb hanging above the landing, all reflected in a mirrored wall. When it was time to leave we moved towards these stairs, and as we commenced our descent I felt a sudden shock. At first I was puzzled to know why I was feeling alarmed, then realised that in the mirror facing us there was no-one on the stairs: my image was not there!

I felt like one who had opened a door in some high building, thinking it led to the next room, but found nothing but a sheer drop to the ground far below. For a fraction of a second I groped for an explanation, but found only blank incomprehension, almost real despair. Relief came only when I saw that I was not looking into a mirror at all, but across a space into *another* stairwell identical to ours and divided from it by a wall about waist high. There was no glass in the opening, and the twin of our landing was also lit by an identical hanging light-bulb. It was an unusual piece of architecture, the like of which I had never seen before.

My apparent absence from what I had thought was a mirror stirred me to ask: do I depend so much on my image in a mirror to know who I am? Have I been using mirrors all these years to maintain an illusion of myself, as I quickly checked my image in glass to see that my clothes and hair were tidy before walking out to meet people? What do I really know about myself?

The shock of that moment on the stairs helped to free me. In a vast, strange city, where so many people barely cling onto life (that selfless old Sister and the disabled people she helped every day) the sudden loss of my 'self-image' showed me a little more of the wisdom in the ancient Buddhist and Christian truth, that to find my real self, I must let go of who I think I am.

At the end of the sixteenth century, in that time that we have come to call the Renaissance or rebirth, should it surprise us that the genius Shakespeare was fascinated by identity: by the mysterious something that makes a person to be *this* person? In the first scene of his tragedy *Othello* he introduces Iago, the conniving assistant to General Othello, who is so deeply entangled in jealousy that he will eventually destroy his employer, along with many others. Did Shakespeare have in mind, as he was shaping this character Iago (who emerges as totally evil) that he was forming something like the obverse of the Infinite Goodness of God? When Infinite Goodness introduced itself to Moses from the burning bush it said 'I am that I am'. (Exodus 3:14, King James Version). Did Shakespeare smile as he let Iago, the negation of goodness, sum up his double-dealing in the taut phrase 'I am not what I am'?[53]

As the tragedy unfolds, Iago makes Othello so madly jealous by hinting that his wife Desdemona is unfaithful, that in a rage Othello murders her. In the last scene of the play, someone calls out asking where Othello has got to. Othello himself replies: 'That's he that *was* Othello. Here *I* am.' Having destroyed the woman he loves, his main reason for living, he seems no longer to consider himself to be the same person.

Shakespeare needed actors as indispensable agents to embody and express his thoughts. While it was a pleasant extra that they made him wealthy from ticket sales, he seems to have loved manipulating human puppets on the stage to unearth life's ambiguities. At many levels, his actors were not what they seemed.

⁌

By definition, actors are dissimulators. From their Greek name we get the word *hypocrite*. But when they portray Iago, Othello, Cassius or Lear, is it all pretence? I was once greatly impressed by a radio interview with Dame Judith Anderson, renowned for her portrayals of Medea and Lady Macbeth. When the interviewer asked the elderly actress how she could so successfully pretend to be these violent characters, Dame Judith rounded on her: 'I do not *pretend!* I *become* Medea.' She went on to explain how for each performance she needed to probe deep into her heart to find those real emotions which are in all of us and which in certain circumstances can drive a person to kill for political power, or slay her own children to take revenge on an unfaithful husband.

This seasoned actress taught me a basic truth about the entire universe of make-believe which the proscenium opens up for us, whether in live theatre or its many equivalents in cinema, television and radio. When through these windows we are shown make-believe images of the villains and heroes who populate our mythologies, we are offered privileged glimpses into our own hearts, although we may not recognise these fragments of our own self, or be ready to acknowledge them when we do.

In our earliest days we seem to be at one with the world around us, unable to distinguish our self from our surroundings. Bit by bit we master that distinction, and learn also to distinguish the objects outside us from the 'pictures in our head', while recognising that there is some correspondence between the two realms. We also learn that the various things we perceive 'out there' bring about diverse feelings in our body, but we may still be inclined to believe that these feelings *are* our self, or at least so close to our identity that when people challenge or dismiss our thoughts and feelings it is our whole self that is hurt.

What would happen if we were temporarily to separate ourselves from all those physical or mental objects that normally preoccupy us, and even let go of our feelings about them? In many cultures, people have learned to do this through various forms of meditation. In 1997, in a village north of Auckland with the picturesque Maori name of

Kaukapakapa, I was introduced to the ancient Buddhist meditation method known as *vipassana*. For the first few days of a nine-day silent retreat, we sat for ten hours each day, apart from breaks for meals and toileting, focusing calmly on whatever physical sensations we could notice in the philtrum on our upper lip, the small groove just beneath our nose. When we had developed sufficient sensitivity in observing that area, for the remaining days we observed in turn every part of our body, starting from the crown of the head and sweeping systematically downwards to the soles of our feet, then back up again.

For hour after hour, during these repeated scans of our body we were advised merely to *observe* each sensation, 'without craving or aversion'. No matter how pleasurable or painful they might be – and back muscles can become very uncomfortable! – all sensations are temporary and soon pass. To describe them we were invited to use the Pali word *anicca*,[54] meaning 'it is passing'. By focusing solely on each limited physical sensation, this process of meditation seemed designed to help us to see that our 'self' is something other than the contents of our senses and thoughts, and possibly other than the faculties that bring them to us. Those days of stillness brought a degree of detachment and freedom from the complex pattern of preoccupations that normally fills our consciousness. When we grasp this distinction between our self and its activities, the subsequent detachment brings a great peace, enabling us to manage our lives more effectively. Such meditation, if repeated daily, reinforces the discovery: we learn, increasingly, to let go of our shallower *ego*, which is inclined to be overloaded with self-concern and busyness and to lose direction. Stillness equips us to become more aware of some deeper part, a central core or pure self that normally lies hidden.

That we have such a deeper self is a common teaching among those who have set out to explore the human interior. Before Buddha or Jesus, the ancient Hindu tradition spoke of *atman*, literally *essence, breath, soul*, which is the real self of the individual, the innermost essence, deeper even than the mind or consciousness. This was considered to be identical with *Brahman*, the essence of the Divinity, which created the universe. When they used the phrase: *tat tvam asi*, – 'Thou art That' – the Hindu sages were saying that we have within us, beneath our selfish attributes, a deeper True Self, identical to the Divine Being. The Hebrew-Christian tradition likewise saw the human person as made in the likeness of God[55], but this tradition maintained that there is a clear difference between the human and the divine: that likeness to God is not identity with God.

It is commonly understood among the faith traditions that our best humanness can emerge only after much struggle – by passing through many doorways. Time after time on our singular journey we need to stop and re-focus beyond the near-at-hand to take in the bigger picture, a wider and deeper vision. The gospels call this *metanoia*, changing our mind, conversion, to discover a fuller but never final view of the world. In the Christian tradition, the need to search does not diminish the dignity of the human person who is shaped and loved by God and who contributes to his or her own destiny, being progressively joined to the Divine. The ultimate result of that mystery is that humanity is raised to the level of God: '… on that day you will know that I am in my Father, and you in me, and I in you' (John 14:20).

This distinction between our superficial and deeper self played an important part in the psychology of Sigmund Freud and Carl Jung. Is it this distinction that is emerging when we find ourselves admitting that 'I was ashamed of myself', or when we are just silently reflecting to ourselves before making a big decision? Who are the dialogue partners here? Are we simply playing, as children play, with an imaginary partner? Or are we showing that in this one person there are different powers at several depths, one of which is able to judge the others?

Is the deeper one the 'second me' that Alphonse Daudet was aware of from the age of fourteen, and more than a little afraid of?

> ... at the death of my brother Henry, when my father cried out so dramatically: 'He is dead! He is dead!', while my first self wept, my second self thought: '... how fine [that cry] would be at the theatre'.

I was then fourteen years old. This horrible duality has often given me matter for reflection. O, this terrible *second me*, always seated, while the other was on foot acting, living, suffering, bestirring itself. This *second me*, that I have never been able to intoxicate, to make shed tears, to put to sleep. How it sees into things, and how it mocks.'[56]

Does the deeper 'me' include what we know as our conscience, a power to pre-judge our own decisions before we make them, and later re-examine them so as to re-assess and modify the path we have taken? Those who are inclined to see the world and the human as purely material must explain these levels of self-awareness in us, which enable us to evaluate the consequences of passing through life's many archways before we enter them, as a truck driver judges the height of a bridge before driving under it. How is it that before we choose among several courses of action we can measure them against the values we have been taught and evaluated for ourselves, then after an internal debate, choose which way to move forward?

⌇

It would seem to be a significant stage of our maturing to discover these different forces existing at different levels within us, and bring them into some degree of harmony. This ability is obviously not easy to attain, nor does every person succeed in attaining it.

Other writers besides Shakespeare have been fascinated by the drama of our dividedness. Charles Dickens once told Fyodor Dostoevsky that there were two people in him,

> one who feels as he ought to feel and one who feels the opposite. From the one who feels the opposite I make my evil

characters, from the one who feels as a man ought to feel I try to live my life.

Dickens was echoing Saint Paul, who wrote in some desperation: 'I can will what is right, but I cannot do it. For I do not do the good I want, but the evil I do not want …' (Rom 7:18-19). Paul does not give us details of what he had to struggle against, but from Dickens' life it is evident that he had no better than average success in uniting the two halves of his personality. At the age of forty-six, after twenty-two years of marriage, he abandoned his wife and ten children for the eighteen-year-old actress Ellen Ternan, who remained his mistress for the remaining thirteen years of his life.

Perhaps I was not alone in my fascination with this question. Two other nineteenth-century writers wrote of the schism within us, our struggle to reconcile the two or more facets that make up our character. Robert Louis Stevenson in 1886 examined them in *Dr Jekyll and Mr. Hyde* and four years later Oscar Wilde wrote a similar reflection in *The Picture of Dorian Gray*. Stevenson's character Dr. Jekyll had in his youth lived a self-indulgent life, but concealed his dissipation. He found himself 'committed to a profound duplicity of life'[57], but convinced himself that he was no less himself when he laid aside restraint and plunged into shame, than when he laboured to advance medical knowledge and relieve sorrow and suffering. He came to the questionable conclusion that 'man is not truly one, but truly two' and might even contain other 'multifarious … and independent denizens'.[58] By experimenting, he found that certain drugs would change his body, transforming him into the purely evil side of his character who took the name Mr. Hyde, while a repeated dose would transform him back to Dr. Jekyll, with ordinary human tendencies, including a conscience. Jekyll wrestled with the decision to keep returning to the character of Hyde in whose identity he could indulge his passions without risk of being found out or punished. He hoped that 'if each could be housed in separate identities' his life would be relieved of its struggle'. Eventually his better half resolved to give up detouring into his darker self, but the evil half had begun to dominate. He found himself becoming Mr. Hyde spontaneously, and to his horror, the drug was failing to bring Jekyll back. He had failed spectacularly in the normal human struggle to unite the differing elements of personality.

Oscar Wilde's character Dorian Gray was a singularly handsome young man. The painter Basil Hallward was infatuated by him, and the portrait he painted excelled all his other work. Feeling that he had exposed too much of his own soul in the painting, Hallward would not exhibit it publicly but gave it to Dorian, who fancifully expressed the wish that he could preserve his youth and beauty by letting the painting absorb all the changes that life's ravages might bring.

The cynical Lord Henry Wotton was also attracted by Dorian, and gradually corrupted him, encouraging him to indulge himself without restraint. When Dorian jilted a beautiful young actress who had loved him and killed herself when he rejected her, he noticed a first subtle change in the portrait's expression. His wish was being granted, and throughout the following stages of his dissolute life the painting successively showed all the ruin that was happening to his inner self. Dorian Gray wonders '... at the shallow psychology of those who conceive the ego ... as a thing simple, permanent, reliable and of one essence'. To him, man was 'a being with a myriad of lives ... complex, multiform, creative.'[59]

Stevenson and Wilde were not imagining the quandary which they described in their fictional characters. It can happen in real persons that the 'self' appears to become severely divided. Such persons are not only aware of two diverse internal tendencies: they suffer from a strange disorder of the psyche which we unwisely try to categorise by such labels as 'schizophrenia', while knowing little about it. Their several inner elements are so seriously out of balance that they become convinced that a voice or voices within them are issuing commands. The contemporary author Lily Baily continues to master this affliction and has written convincingly about it.[60] Is this the silent voice that most of us refer to as conscience? In these unfortunate people, what causes it to become audible, even irrational, and to begin to trouble them from a young age? In Lily's case the voice convinced her that she was 'bad', and that her very thoughts were causing specific harm to others. She felt compelled to build elaborate and bizarre patterns of thought and behaviour in her desperate attempt to contain the evil that she feared she might cause.

We are naturally proud of our identity, but if one person is mistaken for another it can be a source of great amusement. Many comedies-of-error have been based on this concept. Little Elizabeth, a three-year-old girl of my acquaintance, was famous in her own family for making embarrassing comments in public. The priest from their local church, a rather pompous man, came to dinner one evening, and on the following Sunday she recognised him at Mass, where he enjoyed presiding: a tall, imposing figure in flowing chasuble. Elizabeth, in that wonderfully clear voice young children use when we wish they wouldn't speak at all, told all around her: 'Look, there's Fr. William, pretending to be God!'

One major school of Hinduism identifies the mysterious deeper part of our self with Brahman, the highest Divinity. Christians believe that we share in the life of Jesus of Nazareth, whom his followers increasingly came to see as divine and, having passed through death, as present throughout the universe as the Cosmic Christ. In the Eucharist, the thanksgiving ritual central to Christian communities, the leader blesses bread and wine in the words that Jesus used at the Last Supper, believing that Christ becomes more deeply present in those elements and in the praying community. The simple ritual meal becomes a doorway into the transcendent, for Catholics perhaps the most profound of all. Without at all understanding this mystery I had accepted its reality since childhood, relying on the evidence of the ancient Scripture-based tradition. It was central to my choosing to offer myself for ordination as a priest, and still inspires me more than half a century later.

At the central climactic moment of the Mass the celebrant lifts the consecrated bread and wine to show them to all present, announcing that we are doing this: 'Through Him [Christ], with Him and in Him, in the unity of the Holy Spirit,' [we give glory to God] '... forever and ever.' To this the community responds with a strong 'Amen'. Sometimes, when saying this prayer, I feel a strong sense of integration, such as several professional dancers have told me they feel at the height of their dance. It seems that energy passes down through my body and feet, through the building, grounding me to the bed-rock of the Earth from which we are formed. This feeling of integration and rootedness reminds me of the archetypal symbol of the Tree of Life which is prevalent in various mythologies and mentioned at the beginning of the Bible and at its end.[61] In Christian mythology it has been linked with the cross on which Jesus died, metaphorically uniting heaven and Earth.

This feeling of being 'grounded' or whole has occurred on other occasions, notably when I have tried to take a stand on some matter about which I was convinced, but about which others differed. Physical feelings are hardly a sufficient foundation on which to judge issues or make key decisions, but it would seem important to listen to them, as an integral part of our self. When Iraq was invaded in 2003, a companion and I made a strong protest with our own blood in the Auckland office of the US Consul. Two years later I again protested by exposing an antenna of the Waihopai Valley spy-base which was assisting that illegal invasion.[62] Much thought went into the planning of each action, but it was a strong gut-conviction of the rightness of those protests that eventually enabled me to go ahead with them.

While I take full responsibility for my part in those unusual, even outrageous decisions to break, with symbolic intent, the laws protecting property, to some degree it felt as if the actions were prompted by some other source beyond myself. At one point in our early discussions about how we might symbolically oppose the enormous might of Empire by attacking its spy-base it suddenly became clear to me that despite my then sixty-seven years, and notwithstanding public opinion, it was permissible and right for *me* to take the step we were planning. Moreover, I somehow felt confident that at no point in the process would we suffer any serious harm from our action. This conviction persisted even during our trial, when our lawyers felt that we were losing the case, and at its conclusion, when the foreman of the jury was about to announce the verdict which could have put us in jail.

In 2004, to a lesser degree, when pondering how to celebrate the 40th anniversary of my ordination as a priest, I felt impelled to commit to a long bicycle pilgrimage from Canberra to Uluru. The choice appears to have been confirmed by many small synchronicities during the ride and by a much more important one at its conclusion.[63]

Again, in 2015, when my appendix became gangrenous and burst, causing severe peritonitis, I felt calmly confident that this often-fatal condition would not cause my death. This conviction remained with me through the difficult weeks following the abdominal operation and then, despite setbacks, through the following long months of recovery. From what part of us do such convictions come?

This feeling of integrity, perhaps connected with influence from some source from outside our self, is perhaps not so uncommon. While the instances mentioned were rather different from the composing of musical works of art, Gustav Mahler was not the only great artist to wonder where his art was coming from. In his own view, his music seemed to be not entirely his own idea, but to be 'given' to him. When composing his Third Symphony he wrote to a friend:

> One becomes, so to speak, only an instrument upon which the universe plays … at certain places in the score, a quite uncanny feeling takes possession of me, and I feel as if I had not created this myself.[64]

Knowing that ideas, impulses and inspiration can come from some part of us deeper than our conscious mind, Jung asked whether this territory is shared with consciousness other than our own. What kinds of boundary might there be between this possibly shared unconscious and our individual conscious self? Noel Ginn, who was jailed in New Zealand as a conscientious objector during World War II, seems to have felt this barrier dissolving at times, during his stay in prison which the authorities strove to make as cruel as possible:

> Without warning, a wave of generosity – that is the nearest word – rushes in and takes over. It comes from an unknown source, it washes in from an unknown sea. It is something other than me, but so completely adaptable and congenial that I am perfectly at ease with it. It is no use trying to portray it, for it contains all dimensions and gives the feeling that nothing is left out. I just pause quiescent, in an indescribable embrace. I feel that, as scientists have got inside the atom, those who have experiences like this have got inside time. It is as if time is porous and between one moment and the next are other worlds.
>
> What is it then? It is the golden moment that dances before us like a firefly. Who can seize it and who can ravish it? We all can, but it chooses the time and it does the ravishing. It is unfathomably deep but is as accessible as our mother tongue.[65]

Ginn also calls it 'the place where authenticity resides … where the mind makes its original discoveries; and when we know it and relocate there, we can survive any bewilderment or adversity without too much dismay', for it is, as Ginn says, 'the place of ultimate approval'.

13
You Are Not Like Us
Opening towards others

I was staying as guest in a room in a priory where I had lived many years ago. Late one night I was at the desk, about to switch off the computer and prepare for bed when the telephone rang. It was not my business to answer it, nor did I know how to transfer calls, but I picked it up, annoyed that I may have to leave my room to go looking for whoever the call was intended for. But the doorway I was about to pass through was of quite a different kind.

The caller sounded drunk. This at once annoyed me, and my irritation increased when instead of asking for anyone by name, he began to berate the Dominican friars in general. When I began to ask him as calmly as I could why he was angry, he blurted out the horrible accusation: 'Father Wilfrid raped me!'[66] I well knew the priest he had named, but gently asked who the caller was, and heard a name that I had once known, long ago. Gradually I remembered in dim outline a young man who had been a friar for only a few years but had left our community. Because of the antiquated rule that demanded 'separation' between priests, students and lay brothers – as they were then called – I hardly ever spoke to him except at rare feast-day recreations and picnic outings.

Father Wilfrid was an affable, presentable, gentleman; cultured and well spoken. He was fond of music and art, and put his talents to good use with choirs and creative magazine production. It would have been easy to deny to this angry caller and to myself that the crime he was claiming could ever have happened, and then hang up … but something stopped me. A vague memory lurked at the edge of my mind. I had once overheard a senior priest remarking to someone that Wilfrid was still resentful, years after he was moved from working at our school because of some trouble involving boys. The comment had puzzled me then: now I continued to listen.

The caller calmed down when I told him that I remembered him and that it was important for him to tell his story, but I did not expect the shivers down my spine when I realised that the crimes he was describing took place in the room where I sat listening. Wilfrid had lived in it – I tried to calculate – almost fifty years ago. Scraps of memory whirled in my mind: Wilfrid's sense of humour; his civility when entertaining guests, and affability when among students. On an important occasion he had given me some significant help when I asked him. But there were also occasional outbursts of great impatience and anger. The man on the phone – I will call him Terry – barely managed to contain his own anger in relating how Wilfrid had used his seniority to demand that Terry call at his room one evening to collect an item that the brothers needed for their work in the kitchen. There followed a strange mixture of promises to protect Terry and to speak on his behalf when the community came to vote on his application to make vows. Then came affectionate words; then demands followed by force; then rape. It happened again on several occasions.

Terry had come to us as a prayerful teenager full of youthful piety. After the priest had grossly misused his power and seniority, Terry left within months, his faith shattered. He stopped attending Mass and avoided church altogether. Later he threw himself into study and gained several degrees in theology. He remained hungry to discover and connect with the realm of the Sacred, the Transcendent, yet later his hunger had to contend with the alcohol and drugs he used to assuage the enormous pain that continually haunted him after the traumatic injustice he had suffered.

When at last he hung up, my head spun with questions which gradually solidified into one: how could a priest put aside his years of training for dedicated service; his hours in community prayers and shared Eucharist; his prudence and common sense; his humanity?

How could he lay plans to seduce a young and vulnerable member of his community, tricking him to come to his room, with an abominably selfish intent? How had he allowed himself to make the decision: you are not worth as much as I am; you are disposable; you are not like me?

~

Soon after our birth we looked out from an archway, peering from below rudimentary eyebrows at the blurred patches of colour that moved before us. Without knowing it, we were on the first step of an endless road towards enlightenment that had already been trodden by countless millions before us. We had no idea of the journey we were beginning, where it would lead us or what amazing things we might discover in the days and nights that would unroll before the unknown hour of our death. Neither did we yet know that some of the coloured patches of light moving before us were centres of consciousness like ourselves; much less, among all of their kind whom we would later see, did we know which ones would be kind to us and which hostile. The portals of our eyes, ears, nostrils and skin began to bring in information about them and their world, and we began hungrily to devour it, instinctively trying to escape from our isolation.

Each morning when we wake, we look out yet again through the archways below our forehead and re-emerge into consciousness and light like a hibernating creature leaving its cave. We look cautiously around us for any danger, even if the only threat may be a few aches in our body or the grumpiness of another at breakfast. Our precautions are justified, for we have learned that most of the dangers that could threaten us come from the words and actions of others.

It was on an ordinary morning, November 2nd 1989, that the young Ursuline Sister Dianna Ortiz left the breakfast table at a retreat house in Antigua, outside Guatemala City, and went to sit in the garden. Within an hour her life had become worse than any nightmare.

The torture-room is filled with screaming and the moans of those who can no longer scream. Sister Dianna has been blindfolded and waits in terror for what the soldiers might be about to do to her. Three of them have just brought her here after seizing her from the garden of the convent where she had been relaxing in a week of prayer. It is only a few years since she has come down from the United States to teach the children of peasants and workers on the banana plantations.[67]

Dianna well knows that Guatemala's military government constantly terrorises its own people: that anyone who dares to organise for better working conditions in the plantations or speak out for better wages will be labelled 'communist' and either killed in a raid or disappear to be tortured. Their body may later be found by a roadside, or tipped from an aircraft into the sea. But Dianna is not at all involved in politics. She does not even know that it is the *Central Intelligence Agency* (CIA) in her own country that since the mid-1950s has been supporting the regime of terror that will ultimately kill 40,000 Guatemalans – just to protect the USA's business interests. Her arrest could have been a mistake, or might be intended to show that not even a nun teaching children is beyond the military's control.

Sister Dianna is soon stripped naked and horribly tortured throughout the day. She is repeatedly gang-raped and a dog is used to further humiliate her sexually. The torturers play with lighted cigarettes on her body, burning her more than a hundred times. She is mockingly told that her God has no power to help her now, and is forced to hold a machete and take part in torturing another woman. Her tormentors now taunt her for having become a torturer herself, telling her that she can never escape this horrible stigma. Indeed, this last will become the worst memory that lurks in her mind and constantly flashes back to haunt her. But Dianna did manage to escape, at least physically. When I met her in Auckland more than ten years later she was still suffering severe after-effects of the trauma.

During her ordeal in the torture room she wondered who the man with a North American accent might be. He was instructing her torturers, and eventually ordered them to release her. He was driving her to some unknown destination when she leapt from the car at the traffic lights and escaped through the crowds. After many difficulties she got back to the USA and during years of painful recovery laboured to gather scraps of information from government departments until at last she found that man's name. He was a United States citizen and an agent of the CIA.

⌇

Why did reading Dianna's book shock me so deeply? Was it because atrocities distressingly block us from entering doorways and following paths that will lead us to the infinite in the human person? Does the ugliness of acts that demean people drag us backwards, away from understanding, from enlightenment? From Dianna I learned how successive United States governments had abandoned morality in colluding to 'protect our interests' in Guatemala. By the 1950s the USA was rapidly increasing its efforts to protect particularly the interests of *The United Fruit Company*. It was the early days of the Cold War, when the USA saw every political rival as a Communist, even plantation workers asking for better working conditions.

One member of the Dulles family owned the fruit company and another was head of the CIA. Quite soon that agency was helping the Guatemalan government to crush any attempt by the workers to improve their conditions. The US military trained Guatemalan troops in 'counter-insurgency'. To keep the populace submissive, in the following decades they tortured, murdered or 'disappeared' people without discriminating, as Sr Dianna Ortiz learned. When the soldiers took her through the fearful portal of the *Politécnica* torture centre in Guatemala City, she entered a world where ordinary people were processed like cattle in an abattoir, treated as less than human, 'not like us.' The United States are far from being the only empire to have acted in this way. It seems to be of the essence of Empire – with a capital E – to do so, as will be discussed later.[68]

The soldiers who tortured Sr Dianna in 1989 and those who abused prisoners in the Abu Ghraib and Bagram prisons in Iraq and Afghanistan after 2003 were not going beyond their orders, but obeying them. The men and women who abused those wretched victims were not 'a few bad apples' in lower ranks who went against official regulations: they were encouraged and guided to torture – at least by clear hints, suggestions and the absence of rebuke – in a chain of command reaching at least as high as Secretary of Defence Donald Rumsfeld and Vice-President Dick Cheney.[69] Within the USA, lawyers were being pressured to misinterpret or re-write the law so that torture could be used without restraint, while in various complicit countries the CIA maintained a number of 'Black Sites' to which prisoners were secretly flown to be tortured so that the US government could distance itself from the cruel and illegal activity.

The torturers had handbooks to guide them. In 1997 the *Baltimore Sun* used the Freedom of Information Act to obtain copies of the KUBARK Manuals[70] that the CIA had published in 1963 and revised in 1983. Despite many passages that were blacked out before they were released, the *Manuals* leave no doubt that at least since the Vietnam war the CIA has routinely used torture, including electric shocks and near-drowning, to obtain information from prisoners. It is chilling to read how scientific ingenuity has been applied to cause pain more effectively in fellow human beings.

> ... whereas pain inflicted on a person from outside himself may actually focus or intensify his will to resist, his resistance is likelier to be sapped by pain which he seems to inflict upon himself. In the simple torture situation, the contest is one between the individual and his tormentor ... and he can frequently endure [but when] the individual is told to stand at

attention for long periods ... The immediate source of pain is not the interrogator but the victim himself. The motivational strength of the individual is likely to exhaust itself in this internal encounter.[71]

When I read of the horrors perpetrated in Guatemala in the 1980s or Abu Ghraib in 2003 I was bewildered that people could do such things to their victims. I could dimly understand how one person could become a psychopath if they had been severely brutalised as a child and their sensitivities were deformed or even destroyed; but how could ordinary soldiers, young men and women with spouses and children, take part in such atrocities?

⁓

Back there, on that day we were born, gentle hands held and took care of us. The hearts that guided those hands felt deep compassion for the newborn and responded to our needs. They saw that this little creature newly separated from its mother was obviously different from themselves in size and weakness, yet essentially and profoundly similar. The empathy that others felt for us when we first emerged into daylight is such a deep instinct that we must wonder how any person can ever hold back from giving compassion and help to another. Yet if we watch children playing together we begin to comprehend how disagreements arise between us: we will quarrel over trivial possessions that we have set our heart on, and react savagely to small hurts. We soon start along paths that lead some persons eventually to pursue their own desires to the extent that they choose their own gain even when it inflicts extreme suffering on others, or kills them.

As a child I was never much attracted by overt rivalry. Whenever my older brother proposed that we race around the house to see who was the faster, I co-operated reluctantly. Not just, I think, because he would almost inevitably win, but because such ranking of ability did not interest me. Nor did I share his enthusiasm about the games he invented in which rolling marbles represented racing horses. He loved to note how only one of their number could emerge as the winner, tossed from the jostling mob by intricate forces, which in the case of real horses included its own courage and its rider's skill.

No doubt I harboured rivalries of a more interior kind, perhaps even fiercer than my brother's. I wonder, do most of us cherish a sense of superiority over others even if we never voice it aloud, and despite ample evidence that we are not better than them. We can catch ourselves judging as inferior in various ways even those we love: wanting them to adopt our ways of seeing and acting.

Even in reading schoolbook history, it seemed to me that at most periods some powerful groups, like schoolyard bullies, had succeeded in stripping whole classes of 'the other', of their human dignity so as to exploit them. I had always found it extremely sad to read about African slavery. In the seventeenth century, the growers of sugar and cotton in the New World saw that Indigenous Africans would make a convenient cheap workforce, so wove a network of words, a pseudo-theology pretending to 'prove' from the Bible that black people were meant to be slaves. The argument was that among Noah's descendants, the black children of Ham were to be punished for their ancestor's sin by being slaves of the descendants of his other sons (Gen 9:18-27). Africans were transported like cattle to the New World, them, exposed naked in the public slave market and housed in squalid conditions. They were further demeaned by an abundance of insulting names: *Niggers, Nigras, Jigaboos, Coons, Spades*. Before this deception was unmasked, is it estimated that twelve million Africans were exported to the Americas, and perhaps a similar number born there into slavery.

Taking sides against others is relatively harmless when we are cheering our favourite sports teams, but once we begin to forget the truth that our rivals are people like ourselves we can become capable of unbelievable horrors. This is easiest to comprehend when we look objectively at armies, which surround themselves with ancient traditions and parade with flags and stirring music to disguise the truth that they train young men, and now women, to kill their fellow human beings as efficiently as possible. To persuade people who are otherwise civilised to do such things, one must first tell them the terrible lie that their victims are lesser beings who are a threat to us and so must be attacked with violence.

This is the exact opposite of the best ways that we teach children to deal with arguments and quarrels: that the person opposing them is basically a good person, with the same rights as ourselves. If they are behaving badly just now, their behaviour is not the same thing as the good person that they are.

We start to travel the road that can lead us to destroy another person when we step through the portal of demeaning names and labels. In times of war insulting nicknames are invented for 'the other' and given to soldiers to train them to kill, and fed to the public through the mass media to teach them to hate. *Huns, Krauts, Gerries; Frogs, Limeys, Argies, Dagos, Wogs; Nips, Japs, Tojos; Slopes, Gooks* and *Slant-eyes; Round-eyes; Commies, Rag-heads, Towel-heads, Goatfuckers, Camelfuckers, Kaffirs* and *Hajis* are probably only the start of the list.

Words and nicknames lead to racist attitudes and may end in total cruelty. A veteran of the 2003 Iraq war explained:

> Racism within the military has long been an important tool to justify the destruction and occupation of another country ... the killing, subjugation and torture of another people. Racism is a vital weapon employed by this [USA] government. It's a more important weapon than a rifle, a tank, a bomber or a battleship. It's more destructive than an artillery shell or a bunker buster, or a Tomahawk Missile.[72]

Racist language, accompanied by fictitious stories of atrocities committed by 'the enemy', leads Governments to commit resources against those who have become the enemy, and in a few more steps to persuade the populace to condone amoral actions like the carpet bombing of whole populations, the incineration of Dresden and most of the cities of Japan, then the obliteration of Hiroshima and Nagasaki.

It was Ben Griffin, former soldier of the British Special Air Service (the SAS), who showed me more clearly how we can be led into this other perverted world, the obverse of humane sensitivity and compassion.[73] He explained how he was conditioned by harsh training to kill without question. SAS trainees are drilled repeatedly in tactical movements until they can perform them mechanically, automatically. If an individual fails in a task, the whole group is punished with physical violence, so that strong peer pressure makes each member conform unthinkingly. These elite soldiers are taught, Griffen revealed, to despise as 'inferior' everyone outside their select group; even the civilians of their own country. How much more readily do they dehumanise the people in a foreign country where they are sent to use their violent skills.

The soldiers' inhumane tasks are made easier, Griffin reflected, by being separated into sections so that each one sees only the small part allocated to him or her. One group will raid a family home to arrest 'suspects'. These are handed over to another unit which trucks them to a prison. Prison guards are assured by superior officers that their victims – who may later be found innocent – are a serious threat. Meanwhile, each group who has 'processed' them is encouraged to 'roughen up' the captives, so that by the time they reach the torture squad they look squalid and disreputable. It is easier to torture those who seem hardly human. As it was in the extermination camps of World War II, all these small decisions and tasks add up to the total tragedy, whose full extent no single participant can grasp. In this way an institution can form ordinary people into obedient units, trained to obey every order without question and to kill on demand in wars whose purpose they do not understand. The ordinary soldiers who tortured people every day in the *Politécnica* in Guatemala were mostly family men. They were preconditioned to commit such atrocities by being told that the people delivered to them were 'enemies of the nation', and then forced to continue in their ghastly work because they were under military discipline, and afraid of what would happen to them or their families if they dared to refuse to take part.

Many war veterans deeply regret what they were told to do to their fellow human beings and most are left traumatised by it. One summed up the insidious process that transformed him:

> To kill for pure enjoyment [as notorious murderers do] is most contemptible, but to do it because Bush II, Tojo, Bin Laden, or Netanyahu commands it – this is virtue at its highest. Killing for your own reasons is criminal. Killing someone you have never seen for the benefit of a politician you have never met is a source of medals.[74]

Institutions are not persons, and so lack a conscience in their dealings with the 'other'. These include national governments, churches, financial institutions and military forces, all of which stand exposed as notorious for making decisions which callously hurt individuals, and for concealing their actions by self-deceit and lies of monumental proportions. Their topmost members have often dodged responsibility by claiming that their actions were necessary for the good of the whole institution – such as 'national security' – and lower ranks have used the excuse that they are carrying out their superior's orders. These lesser members derive their livelihood from the institution, so government employees, even principled lawyers, judges and priests can find themselves administering rules that result in inhuman cruelty. Lawful refugees are imprisoned and tortured; poor folk lose their life savings; the nation's resources are squandered.

Large numbers of weaker 'others' are ruthlessly sacrificed: soldiers sent to war and neglected on their return; the victims of chemicals like Agent Orange, or of nuclear fallout and depleted uranium; countless abused children and their parents. Behind each mis-step lies the profound error that 'You are not like us.'

14
The Narrow Gate
Journey into darkness

... the gate is narrow and the road is hard that leads to life
(Matt 7:13)

During a seminar on the Jungian interpretation of drawings, the tutor inspected an abstract picture I had just completed in coloured crayons. He enquired whether I had recently passed through any kind of crisis. He was asking, he said, because the dominant shape in my abstract resembled a butterfly, the insect that can symbolise the emergence of new life from darkness. The shape in question consisted of two great parabolic curves whose apexes were almost touching. I had thought it resembled an hour glass lying on its side, but could accept his interpretation. Its spreading 'wings' did suggest a stylised sketch of the adult butterfly, the natural symbol and promise of resurrection because its larva seems to die in the cocoon it has woven around itself, but in fact is transformed there to burst forth and move freely in a totally new dimension. What I had unintentionally produced was a convincing demonstration that what is deep within our unconscious tends to produce effects in our external actions: not only in what we draw, but in the stories we write, and even in the look on our face and the way we walk or stand. Nineteenth-century psychologists, studying the drawings made by children in hospital, began to find symbols of their inner life and even hints of bodily conditions of which neither the children nor their doctors were yet aware. Our drawings, like dreams, can reflect the otherwise unknown depths of our mind.

My teacher was right. Not many months before that seminar I had sat in Doctor Brian Hurley's office in a Canberra hospital. As

I glanced out of his window at a view of Black Mountain, I heard him tell me that the lung blockage that for three months had kept me weak and feverish was an oat-cell carcinoma. This deadly cancer, he reluctantly told me, might respond enough to chemotherapy to allow me to live for another year or two, but without that treatment I would be dead within six months. As I walked out of his office and took the lift down to the busy hospital foyer, I felt that I had suddenly entered a world entirely different from the one I had been living in just half an hour before. Although there were people all around me, I was in a new and different framework of reality, quite disconnected from them as they came and went across the lobby. In this new dimension of my life, the tasks and concerns that had filled my life before I walked into the doctor's office now seemed completely irrelevant.

Through the hours and days to come I began to digest the harsh truth that had been given me. Oddly, I felt quite healthy. This was because the exploratory tube of a bronchoscope several days before had drained the fluid that for weeks had filled my lung and deprived me of oxygen and energy. Although still confined to hospital while awaiting treatment, I would often walk in the nearby park and try to reconcile my feeling of wellness with the implications of the doctor's statement: that these hands and my whole body would soon rot from within, and in the not-too-distant future be buried in the ground and disintegrate altogether.

In the weeks that followed, these thoughts would often come back to me, although I did not dwell for long on the horrible reality. Friends and acquaintances visiting me in hospital did much to sustain me, as did many more who sent their love and good wishes in letters and cards. From all that was happening to me I was able to distil a conclusion, which I shared with a doctor friend. Despite all the fuss, I told him I was really no different from him or any other person, for we were all on the way to our death: I merely happened to know with a little more accuracy when mine was going to happen.

In the event, the doctors' predictions were to prove quite wrong. The morning came when I was scheduled to commence the severe chemotherapy treatment, which would poison my body in the hope of killing some of the cancerous cells in my lung. I was still feeling quite healthy, and as I was being prepared for the treatment the doctor directing my treatment came into the ward and declared that 'the committee' had decided that the tumour might not be the lethal oat-cell carcinoma they had at first diagnosed, but a carcinoid tumour, a less invasive kind. Under the microscope, the two kinds of cancer cells look quite similar. It was possible that I was the victim of a pathologist's error. If so, the alternative was much more acceptable: a carcinoid tumour could be cut out by surgery. They had decided to operate on my lung. This was a huge relief, even though lung surgery was no light matter. I had always suspected the original diagnosis, and inwardly doubted that I needed chemotherapy. Within ten minutes I had thrown on some clothes and, leaving my bag in the bedside locker, walked out of the hospital into the open air, to share the news with a friend who lived a few kilometres away.

Several weeks later I returned to the hospital for the ordeal of having my rib-cage cut from front to back and most of one lung removed. I submitted to the rituals of preparation, and lay back to feel darkness suddenly wipe out all awareness. The next moment, it seemed, light and noise rushed over me and flooded into me as I woke from the anaesthetic. Despite pain from the forty centimetre wound and from several drainage tubes projecting from my torso, I heard with relief the surgeon's words that their decision to operate had been correct. From now on I should be free of the cancer.

That time of crisis had brought months of discomfort and occasional fear. I had not stared fully into the face of the destruction that had threatened me, but only glanced at it sideways. Despite the pain and uncertainty, the whole experience had been most helpful. Looking back from successive vantage points in the following years, I saw that passing through that narrow archway had freed me from almost all fear of dying, and much of my fear of what people thought or said about me. It took me to depths in myself that I had not previously known. Passing through tunnels of pain can close us in on ourselves and push us to become quite selfish, at least for a time, but I was learning that this narrow passage can also lead to a different place. It helped me, at the age of forty-one, to understand myself better and be more aware of the pain that others suffer. I began to see the experience as a gift.

Thirty-four years after the tumour was removed from my lung I was again privileged to pass through a proscenium of pain. Again, it led to new insights that once more changed my life. At age 71 I had volunteered to work in the Solomon Islands. In tropical environments bacteria can be a serious threat, as my experience was to prove. Four times I had a cellulitis infection in my leg; then a virulent *pseudomona* lodged in my lung, imitating the symptoms of tuberculosis, and eventually – when I was back in Australia on leave – my appendix died and burst, filling my gut with dangerous poison. This happened when I was travelling from Melbourne towards Canberra by train and bus. I was admitted to Calvary Hospital, and when I awoke from the operation the surgeon warned me that at my age I would take 'a long time' to recover. He was right. I spent a week hugely swollen with fluid, which caused my heart to pump at twice its normal speed. This was eventually corrected by the same technique used on defective computers: under anaesthetic my heart was briefly stopped, then restarted. After a month in hospital I returned home, my wound still open to prevent internal infection, with a small pump to drain it until it healed.

As I continued to heal I sought out a quiet rural parish where my only duties were to celebrate weekend Masses so that I could spend the rest of my time writing. The Ballarat diocese was very accommodating, and I spent a total of five months in two such places, but when ten months had passed I needed a second operation to repair the abdominal hernia that had developed after the first. What should have been a simple repair became something of a nightmare when the synthetic mesh used to reinforce the wound became infected. This eventually meant two more operations, the last one reinforcing the wound with a patch derived from pig tissue, and then a second cardiac reversion to get my heart back to nearly-normal behaviour.

In the midst of this sequence of medical failure and success, I found myself telling friends, seriously, that I was having the best two years of my life so far. What did I mean? Beneath the surface troubles I had been surprised to discover I was living with a new and deeper sense of freedom and joy. Pondering what had happened, I concluded that this came from the fact that twice during those months I had reason to wonder whether I would still be alive the following morning. The stark limits of these situations seemed to give my mind sharper focus and somehow freed my heart to be deeply grateful that I was alive.

There must be a reason for this. Many people have told me that although they do not belong to any religion, they believe that 'there is something out there', responsible for the vast and wonderful universe. Over many years I have come to see – like other people through the centuries – that the 'something' responsible for the universe, which my family and primary school had introduced to me as 'God', is a Mystery which must have at least the same perfections as those things it has brought into being. Most of all, it must have all the qualities that make us to be persons: 'It' must be aware, intelligent and affectionate, but in ways beyond anything we can imagine. I have sometimes imagined it as a furnace, like the stars it has given rise to, but an infinite furnace, of love. This means that we can relate to 'It' in the way the Jewish philosopher Martin Buber neatly condensed in the title of his book: *I and Thou*.[75]

It was this 'Thou' that I came closer to at the times when my body's condition made me wonder whether I would be alive for much longer. I did not see any visions of light, but simply became more aware that this concept is unquestionably true, and that even when we are in the deepest hole the Thou is still with us. I am reluctant even to call it God, for the word has been used so often to describe a being that is much too human-shaped. In many of our descriptions, especially some found in the Old Testament, it seems neither godly nor good. During my slow recovery, this Being was with me as Friend, as guarantor that 'all will be well', no matter what 'all' might contain. But more of this later.[76]

In moving to the Solomon Islands four years previously I had found it necessary to leave behind many things: books and other surplus possessions that I had previously thought necessary to carry with me at every move. I used a back-pack and two smaller bags to carry what I claimed were all my possessions, ignoring the fact that in moving from one Dominican community to another I had the use of a furnished bedroom, kitchen, laundry and chapel, and sometimes the use of a car. Perhaps I was learning at a deeper level that we tend to *define* ourselves – or try to – by merely exterior things: our possessions and lifestyle. But to define anything is to *limit* it. That is why, when we let go of things, as many as possible, we feel immediately free. We have taken a step through an archway towards the un-defined, the infinite.

This letting-go had already given me an increased sense of freedom, and the later sequence of serious illness enhanced this. What seemed on the surface to be horribly negative, gave me a hugely positive experience. In the darkest, most solitary moments, when I felt that I might soon be forced to let go even of the life in my body, I was able to reflect, speaking honestly to the Mystery on which my being completely depends:

> Those who love me will grieve at my death. I'm sad about that, but I place them in Your care. Their grieving will eventually diminish. Just now, *You* are all I have. I look forward, eagerly, to our meeting.

I was grateful that in the most difficult moments my mind was still clear enough to ponder what lay beyond the boundary that I seemed about to reach. Would my mind still operate when my body had stopped? I had always assumed that this would be so. In addition to the rich, mythical stories in my Christian heritage,[77] the many reports of Near-Death Experiences that I had heard and read had strengthened my hope[78]. I presumed that I would find myself in the living presence of others: my ancestors and closer relatives, my parents and younger brother, my beloved T and other departed friends. In those days, was it only in my imagination that I was more aware than usual of their silent presence? I spoke often to the Transcendent Mystery itself and was confident that I was heard, although there was no concrete evidence that I could point to. This many-sided awareness came not from any fevered delirium, but in moments when my mind was completely clear, often in the prosaic setting of a hospital toilet during the long week when my hugely bloated body had to learn again how to let fluids pass through it; when it was learning again the basic processes of living.

Thanks to the dedicated men and women who cared for me professionally, I found myself recovering, although long days of pain and discomfort were still to come, when sitting up or getting out of bed was painful, walking difficult and eating unattractive. I had never imagined that my normally lean body could bloat to the size of a barrel, or my scrotum to the size of a medium-sized rock melon. It seemed that I might never recover my former physical strength, although I persistently walked small distances to try to retain some of it. I was learning by direct experience how fragile is the life-force that keeps my heart beating and my body upright, and valued it more deeply for its fragility.

※

I was not entirely surprised that this new health crisis brought with it the breakthrough that I am trying to describe. I was taught in childhood that we can grow strong in body and character only at the price of physical discomfort, even pain. I fear for the children whose parents give in to their every whim and protect them from all discomfort. Every would-be athlete knows that to develop stronger muscles they need to push themselves past the pain limit. I used to hate cycling up hills because of the pain they caused my child-thin legs, but later appreciated that it was precisely by riding up hills that I was later able to ride, day after day, for thousands of kilometres. What I was learning now seemed only a natural extension of the truth that crises, even severe ones, give us access to some kind of opening into a different level of our being where we make new discoveries about ourselves and find new insights that are of more value than the cost of any physical discomfort.

In their ancient cultures Indigenous peoples would often celebrate the stages of a person's development with rites of passage. At some of these milestones the initiate would be compelled to endure discomfort and even serious pain. Our own contemporary cultures retain mild echoes of these practices: Baptism, fully celebrated, is a ritual imitation of death and burial; candidates at Confirmation are given a slight slap on the cheek as a reminder that they are now strengthened to face opposition to their faith; similar relics may still exist in celebration of *bar mitzvahs*, weddings, or when we extinguish the fires on a birthday cake. We retain, but only just, reminders that the growth-stages that we pass through are, in a sense, natural crises in our physical and mental health, and need to become doorways from which we emerge, transformed, into a wider dimension, a new stage of our existence. That such crises invigorate and increase, rather than diminish us, is a truth that seriously challenges those who would maintain that our world and humanity consist of nothing more than physical matter.

For eight years Caroline Jones hosted an ABC radio programme called *The Search for Meaning*.[79] Using a gentle, less aggressive interview technique than most news interviewers, she listened sympathetically, giving her people space to share the meaning they had found in life.

One of these, Stan Arneill, had been a soldier in the second world war. In 1942 he had been captured at the fall of Singapore and with thousands of other prisoners was taken by his Japanese captors to work as a slave building the infamous Thailand-Burma Railway. He survived the brutality, starvation, dysentery, typhoid and malaria that killed many of his comrades and at the end of the war returned to Australia in a skeletal condition. He slowly regained his health, and later married and raised a large family. When Caroline Jones asked how he might summarise his horrendous experience as a prisoner of war, Stan gave the surprising reply that he considered it 'a privilege'.

When questioned further, he explained that as much as he appreciated his restored health, his loving wife and large family, back then amid the inhuman sufferings of the prison camps he had 'learned more about love' than he had experienced even in twenty-five years of good married life in peace-time. As a slave he had had almost no possessions, and often nursed friends through grave sickness or held them in his arms as they died. He had learned how generous human beings can be; how deeply they can trust and love each other. This self-giving love let him discover and cherish the sublime dignity at the depth of the human spirit. Stan's suffering had taken him across some kind of threshold of human understanding, so he could declare that gaining this had far outweighed the inhuman horrors he had been forced to endure.

Stan Arneill was not unique. I later read another account by a survivor of the Burma railroad, who summed up his years of suffering a little less articulately but with the similar, surprising statement that although it was indeed ugly and horrific, he 'wouldn't have missed it for quids'.[80]

15
The Emptiness of the Roadside Beggar
A hitchhiker's guide

When the tabloid press urges us everyday to fear this or that evil group, and by implication to mistrust every stranger, it becomes quite counter-cultural to stand beside the road with your thumb extended, begging a ride from anyone who chooses to stop. Hitch-hiking challenges the materialism that is choking the generosity out of us: 'I paid big money for this car. It's for my use only. How dare you ask to sit in it!' As soon as a driver sees 'one of them' in the distance, he or she is forced to judge how generous they can be; to decide whether to share part of the journey with this unknown mendicant. In a lifetime of hitching I have learned that those who drive expensive cars tend to whiz past the hitcher almost every time, avoiding eye contact. They seem determined always to say 'No!' Notoriously, most drivers who do stop to pick up a hitchhiker are in vehicles that are older, battered, even partly dysfunctional.

Our very presence there by the roadside challenges drivers to reconsider their choice, every time. If one day they feel a momentary urge 'just this once' to pick up some stranger they may be surprised what they gain from the experiment. We white-line beggars are saying: 'I invite you to share your vehicle and part of your journey with me. Let down your guard just a little. Amazing things can happen when people trust each other enough to share their life-journey.'

On our long walks home as children attending Mepunga East school, local farmers would occasionally stop, unasked, to offer my brothers and me a ride, but I cannot recall actively hitching until a school friend and I cooked up a plan to make a long trip during the term holidays in our last year at school. Our mothers especially must have been gravely concerned about us, but in 1958 there was less reason to be. Without even a tent, sleeping in whatever shelter we could find, in three weeks we hitched from Melbourne to Brisbane up the two-lane coastal road, the Princes Highway and then back on the more-frequented New England and Hume. Surviving on school-boy pocket money, we managed to live for the three weeks spending less than ten pounds each of the old currency to buy food; travel on the the occasional suburban train or bus; and a ticket to see the newly-released *Bridge on the River Kwai*.

⌒

During more than seven years as Dominican students preparing to become priests we did not mix openly in society, so opportunities to hitch were limited to a few occasions each summer during community holidays at the beach. In 1965, when eventually I was ordained, a priest was seen as an honoured leader in the Catholic world, so it took me some time to decide whether in my newfound dignity I could again stoop to this kind of roadside begging. But eventually there came occasions when there was no vehicle available for a long trip, so I dared to take to the roadside again, and found it fitted closely with what I believed the real work of a priest and itinerant friar to be.

Hitchhiking creates meeting points, opportunities, doorways where lives can touch and overlap. To travel by begging for a ride would seem quite appropriate for Dominican friars who in the first decades of our existence in the 13th century never travelled on horseback, as the wealthy did, but walked across Europe, systematically begging even for their daily food. Our communities were founded to share with people at all social levels the truth as we knew it, the reality of God and the adventure of searching into that Mystery of love and forgiveness. The more I thought about it, the more puzzled I became as to why priests, particularly Dominicans, did not hitchhike frequently, for in more than fifty years of intermittent thumbing I have noticed very few others on the roads. Not that I open the conversation with the stranger who has kindly picked me up with: 'Been to any good church services lately?' Healthy people rightly despise 'Bible bashing'; but that is not what happens. It is about getting to know a new companion who has just now kindly shared their vehicle with a stranger. In the relaxed and friendly atmosphere of a long journey, listening to part of each other's unique story will often deepen the understanding of both.

Some of my Dominican brothers tried to discourage me from hitching, stressing its dangers. It is true that hitchhikers have at times been robbed or even murdered by those who have picked them up, but this risk must be much less common than being killed in an accident in one's own vehicle, or in a 'home invasion'. I did have to admit that their argument gained strength when between 1989 and 1993 no fewer than seven backpackers disappeared around Belanglo State Forest, south of Sydney. The notorious 'Backpacker Murders' were eventually traced to Ivan Milat – now jailed for life – who perhaps had an unknown accomplice.

Despite the spread of motorways and the increased speed of vehicles, acts of trust of the kind that hitchhiking demands are still important if society is not to become paralysed with selfishness. Hitching remains easier in smaller countries like New Zealand or Ireland which are less urbanised or industrialised. Success is more likely on rural roads rather than freeways, but even on these it is still practical to wait for rides at the on-ramp. Notwithstanding the occasional psychopath, backpackers exploring a new country still find that asking for rides is one of the best ways to meet local people. Only recently I stopped to pick up a young Japanese immigrant farm worker who stood hopefully waiting by the roadside outside a village in Western Victoria. In the next hour we shared a fascinating discussion of our common spiritual search.

In support of my practice I used to remind critics that in *The Acts of the Apostles* Philip hitched a ride in the chariot of an Ethiopian official, whom he then helped to understand the meaning of the prophecies of Isaiah that the man had been reading (Acts 8:26-39). I used also to point out that hitching coincides closely with Jesus' own lifestyle. Although he never rode in a motor vehicle, perhaps not even on a camel, the gospels often describe him as listening to and teaching people while walking on his journeys. John's gospel describes him on one journey entering into a deep discussion with a stranger, the woman at the well in Samaria. It began when he begged from her the simple gift of a drink of water (John 4: 1-26).

I never sought such dramatic successes or even considered myself a missionary. In fact, through all my time as a priest I do not know that I have ever been instrumental in bringing anyone to undergo a 'conversion'. Recently however, a friend in New Zealand sent me a copy of a story from the front page of *The Wellington Post*, which reminded me of one enjoyable encounter with a stranger. The page displayed a photograph I recognised and an interview with a lawyer, a leading public servant. Towards the end of the interview he was questioned about his family life and what, if any, were his religious beliefs. He said that he used to be an atheist, but once, when travelling, he had picked up a Dominican friar who was hitchhiking and had an interesting discussion … so now he is an agnostic.

One frosty morning, needing to get to Melbourne, I arranged for a friend to drop me on the edge of the Canberra suburbs at about 10am. Only as I stood there 'unwinding' after my hectic preparations to get away, did I remember that it was midwinter and I had only seven hours before sunset for a journey of more than 650 km, and hitching after dark is usually fruitless. I refrained from panicking, for I was beginning to learn to be patient, and not create false expectations. As I was reflecting on these things, a young man stopped: an art dealer, travelling through to Melbourne. Through the hours of travel we got to know each other, and although he made some detours regarding prospective purchases, we reached Melbourne just after dark and he volunteered to take me to the address where I was to stay.

Another time, when in Sydney, I had to go to Deniliquin to begin a week of retreat for a community of Sisters which was scheduled to begin at 7.30pm the following evening. Checking the map, I was alarmed to discover that Deniliquin was 730 km away, much further than I had thought. The next morning I took a suburban train to Liverpool, at the edge of the city, and began hitching. To my delighted surprise I began to get almost non-stop lifts that landed me in Deniliquin half an hour before my appointment. Through the long day of depending on others' generosity my average speed had been an impressive 73 km/hr.

⌇

During my time in New Zealand I once needed to attend a country wedding but couldn't leave central Auckland until 5pm on the preceding day, Friday. The little church was about six hours' drive away, but our only community car was not free that weekend and there were no buses. Besides, a main reason for hitching is to cut back the amount of petrol we burn: 'Share the car, spare the planet', so at 5pm I waited, thumb-out, by the motorway on-ramp. Hundreds of new looking sedans and SUVs crept past in the queue, and it was perhaps fifteen minutes before two young Maori men in a battered van stopped to ask where I was headed. No matter that they could take me about ten slow kilometres on their way home from a heavy day delivering building materials: they were happy to meet and help me. As we crept along amid four lanes of near-stationary traffic, they asked if I played any music. When I admitted to being half-competent on the recorder, they asked whether I carried it with me. Finding that I did, they insisted on a few tunes, and even turned off their heavy-metal cacophony to listen. They found the few Irish folk songs that I know, 'awesome', and even clapped and cheered a bit of classical

– though I didn't try to explain 'Handel'. Before dropping me off at Penrose nearly twenty minutes later – still not fully realising that not all music is electronic – they urged me: 'You've gotta get an amp, Bro'.

A couple of rides later, just before sunset, I was two hours beyond Auckland's din and traffic fumes, standing among green hills and enjoying the clean air and rural silence – between the infrequent swish of cars. I began to wonder where I might have to spend the night. Hitchhiking is closely related to meditation, and by many roadsides I have learned to enter a state best described as 'emptiness'. It is important to admit that maybe no one will stop; that I might spend the night on the outskirts of a city I am trying to leave, or worse, be caught in some remote spot without shelter and a storm approaching. I have learned to try to have no expectations, and find that I am usually provided for.

This was well proven when I was hitching from Bendigo to Canberra in the 1980s. By late afternoon I found myself at the monument known as The Dog on the Tuckerbox, 'five miles from Gundagai'. After thumbing unsuccessfully for a while I looked with alarm at an ominous black storm-front approaching from the south. I had no tent, but what use would a tent be in such a storm? Nor, I concluded, would it be wise to shelter in the culvert under the road. All I could do was admit my absolute helplessness. I said as much, to the Mystery that runs the universe.

Although I was trying to trust, at the same time I was beginning to feel a bit scared and actually rather stupid, when an approaching car slowed and stopped. Unusually, it was a woman, driving alone. She said: 'sometimes I know I can trust a person'. I felt honoured, even while I glanced out the back window at the spectacular storm about to burst over us. Within minutes we were pushing through pelting rain, the kind that makes windscreen wipers useless. It was to last for the rest of the journey. 'It just happened' that the woman was going all the way to Canberra. On a normal day the trip would take four hours but

THE EMPTINESS OF THE ROADSIDE BEGGAR

it took at least five in this storm, which continued all night and closed the airports in Canberra and Sydney.

Years of hitch-hiking have made me almost comfortable with this 'prayer of emptiness'. It seems singularly appropriate to use when hitchhiking, for the activity is a miniature model of our whole life. Although we can work in solidarity with others to make perhaps a significant impact in changing society, as individuals we can feel completely helpless. We may be very gifted, but our strength and health must eventually run out, and we are, in the end, completely powerless in the face of our death. So likewise, when hitching, we can make choices about the details of when and where, or in some places we can give up and take the train; but we cannot change the weather, or dictate people's freedom whether or not to stop for us.

When waiting for the next ride I have learned repeatedly that whatever the weather or the hour of day, it is mature and rational *not* to expect a ride. After all, you have no *right* to presume that others will be generous. In general, when we build expectations on our own wishes or prejudices we create desires that only add to our misery when they are frustrated, as they often are. It seems far more rational – and spiritually mature – to expect *nothing*, but to accept with gratitude all that is given.

Persons who have an exaggerated view of their own importance expect everyone, and everything, to bend to their needs, and are often miserable when this does not happen. In a paradoxical way, it is when we *let go* of our own needs and desires, and 'go with the flow', that we see the benefit in everything that comes our way, and in a sense *do* become a centre of the world, not to exploit it for ourselves, but to enter into it more fully. This attitude is rather Buddhist, in that it simply observes the situation without clinging to its joys or fleeing from its pains. It is also deeply Christian, striving to accept as 'the will of God' the things I cannot change, which applies in fact to a large part of my life. The hitchhiker who has perfected it can happily say: 'If I get continuous rides, or none at all, either is good.'

But on the road to that wedding (which I have not forgotten) I was a bit surprised when a BMW stopped. Craig, the driver, was one of those people who have been run over by life itself in such a way that they have learned to be more deeply human. A motor accident had deprived him of one leg and left him with a serious back injury. When he met me, he was also grieving for his recently broken marriage and afraid he might lose custody of his young son. People like Craig are glad to help someone needing a ride. Thanks to him, by 9.15pm I was in Taupo, 240 km from my starting point and sleeping soundly in a backpackers hostel. Next morning I had other friendly lifts from people who, again, had faced big difficulties in their lives. My last ride, which took me to the little church at Whirinaki, somewhere north of Napier, was from Tom, a carefree young English tourist travelling around the North Island in his dubious red van. Knowing that the bridegroom and bride were more *Zen* than I, and wouldn't hesitate to welcome an extra guest, as we neared our destination I asked Tom if he would like to come to the wedding. He was delighted to be welcomed into the social life of his host country. He enjoyed the wedding, the guests and the feast that followed, then the groom's family invited him to visit them on his journey further north.[81]

His meandering journey took him through Auckland. A week later, in that city of well over a million people, I was cycling through its sprawling suburbs when I 'just happened' to come upon Tom's red van pulled over at the kerb. Tom was consulting a map, and I was able to guide him to the motorway he needed to continue his journey towards the north. Both of us were astonished at this 'synchronicity', but did we need to be? Hitching teaches us that such surprises, such gifts in life, are almost a rule of thumb.

My life took a surprising turn in 1975, when I was asked to take up the task of directing our novices in their year of preparation before

THE EMPTINESS OF THE ROADSIDE BEGGAR

their first vows. In order to learn a little of how novices were prepared in other parts of the Dominican order, I asked to visit novitiate houses in some other provinces. I went first to Oakland, California, where there was a vigorous group of novices and students, and before moving further eastwards to novitiates in the Mid-West and Boston, my round-the-world ticket allowed a side-trip down to Mexico. After putting my rudimentary Spanish to the test among the friars in Mexico City, I planned to see more of the country by returning by bus to Texas, then Chicago. I was at that time young, with the love of adventure that I hope never to lose, but was soon to meet with an experience that would test my enthusiasm to the limit.

The bus journey from Mexico City to the US border at Laredo was around 1100 kilometres and would take eighteen hours. It began pleasantly enough. The bus was full and the man beside me, a hypnotherapist, spoke English so we enjoyed an interesting conversation. The highway took us through long stretches of arid country covered in low scrub, not unlike parts of outback Australia. When consulting the driver on some matter I had noticed we were travelling through it at a steady 60 miles per hour. Towns were far between, but as noon approached we cruised into San Luis Potosi, which I had read about as a silver-mining area in colonial times. The driver pulled into a bus terminal and clearly announced *viente minutos* – twenty minutes – for a lunch break.

I collected my shoulder-bag, which contained my passport wallet, but as I followed the crowd into the terminal I left my other small case on the luggage rack. I quickly bought a sandwich and a can of soft-drink and stood in the crowded lounge to eat my snack. I was still amazed to be making this journey, joyfully astonished that I was in central Mexico. My happy calm was not even ruffled when a child of the poor quietly stole the drink-can that I had placed down beside me. Having seen the living conditions of some of the vast legions of Mexico's poor, I cheerfully bought myself another drink, then with five minutes to spare went back to the bus. But the bus had gone.

On a few occasions when I have had to deal with serious emergencies, I have managed with reasonable competence, but at that moment my heart was definitely sinking as I began to assess what possibilities were open to me. Laredo was more than 700 kilometres further on as we had not even come half-way. I did not think there would be a useful air service from here, but even if there was, it would be hugely expensive. Perhaps I could catch up with the bus? It could not have left more than five minutes ago. There was a row of taxis at the nearby kerb.

A man was leaning against the first cab talking lazily with the driver. I was reminded of the spirit of *mañana*, said to be characteristic of Latin Americans generally, and recalled the song *Tihuana Taxi*, which described a vehicle that was broken-down and unreliable. These thoughts rapidly led to me deciding to approach the second car, looking into my wallet as I did so to see what cash I had. What I saw was sickening: I had just enough Mexican pesos for a couple more meals, and only US$10 that I kept for emergencies. To safeguard against theft, all my other money was in travelers cheques. That normally made me feel secure, but I caught my breath when I discovered that by some stupid oversight they were packed among my clothes in the other case, on the bus.

Quickly I approached the second taxi, preparing a question in my inadequate Spanish. I asked him to take me on the road to Laredo to see if he could catch up with the bus, but explained that I had only US$10, so to please let me know when we had reached that limit. He looked quite puzzled, but cheerfully agreed, and off we set. We were soon out of the city and travelling through semi-desert landscape such as we had passed through before we entered the town. I checked from the sun that we were actually heading north, and sat back, knowing that I could do no more for the moment. It was a small satisfaction that I was doing my best to remedy the crisis, whose cause I still could not understand. I was far from relaxed, but felt a great emptiness. How would this work out?

THE EMPTINESS OF THE ROADSIDE BEGGAR

A moment later, any remaining security I had was completely shattered when I glanced across at the speedometer of the labouring taxi. The needle was waving around 50mph, and I recalled that the bus was easily doing 60. My emptiness deepened and became a bottomless gulf. Not many more minutes passed when I realised that time was almost up: my money would run out quite soon, and I must be careful not to exploit the poor taxi-driver. I began to look around and ahead at the arid, semi-desert landscape, but saw nothing to suggest any relief. Wait! There *was* something! Ahead, on the right side of the two-lane highway, was a solitary road-house. It immediately reminded me of the movie cartoon called *The Roadrunner*, that we used to enjoy in childhood at matinee sessions. That fast running land bird used to patrol empty desert highways, whose loneliness was emphasised by a solitary building like the one we were now approaching. I could expect no help from the building or its occupants: it did not even have a verandah for shade. What had caught my eye was that out in front, parked near the fuel pump, was a large black car.

Quickly telling the taxi-driver to drop me right here, I gave him my sole $10 and walked across to the building. The car was empty, so I stood in the narrow shade of the wall to wait for its driver to emerge. He was probably having lunch, and my future would be determined by whether he was going north or south. After a considerable time a whole family emerged and began to climb into the car, but before it could drive off I made my approach to the driver. *Por favor* ... To my huge relief, he not only said that he was going north, but kindly made room for me in the back seat among his children.

Doctor Calles – he was a paediatrician – and his family amicably included me in their conversation for the next few hours. It was a providential meeting, because not only did he take me rapidly northwards, he also used his general knowledge to drop me, after dark, at the bus terminal in the northern city of Monterey, assuring me that the bus, which we still had not seen – must eventually arrive here. I waited, hanging on to a rather tenuous thread of trust in a stranger's word, but about an hour later it did arrive. The look on the face of the driver as I came aboard almost made the whole trauma worthwhile. He spoke too rapidly for me to understand his explanation, but it seemed to include refuelling. Could it be that if I had I waited another five minutes at San Luis Potosi the bus would have returned to where I was? I was sure that I had been in the right place, but recalled that there had been no other passengers waiting nearby. My English-speaking seat-mate had now gone, but my case with the travellers cheques was still up on the rack. To this day I do not know how the bus and myself had come to be parted, nor how I had managed to arrive ahead of it, to continue my journey as planned.

16
Fruitful Exile
Hunger for justice

On a day in late summer, 1975, I stood in a green field near Kilmallock in County Limerick. Fluffy clouds moved slowly across the clear blue sky, occasionally passing their shadows over the grey ruins in front of me. I was standing before the roofless church of the Dominican friars who founded their priory here in 1291. The people seem to have welcomed them, I had read, for within forty years they were enlarging their buildings and adding the square tower to the church.

It was not a large church, seating hardly more than two hundred people. Henry VIII's soldiers had seized these buildings from the friars when all Irish monasteries and priories were dissolved in 1541. The friars had returned in 1622, but a quarter-century later Cromwell's forces sacked their buildings again, murdering two friars in front of the altar. Even then a few friars had stayed in the district, living in secret with a price on their heads during the long, harsh penal times.[82] Much later the Dominican friars, nuns and sisters returned to Ireland, and from there eventually sent nineteenth-century offshoots to Australia.

By the time I visited Kilmallock I had been a friar for sixteen years and had lived in five different Australian priories. As I walked under the Gothic archway into the abandoned church, I could almost hear the friars singing the psalms of the night prayer, Compline, with which they ended every day. I could easily imagine them in their white habits, or with the extra black cloak during the freezing winter months, coming in procession down the aisle singing the *Salve Regina* in the Latin words we still used. As I passed thoughtfully and sadly through that doorway, I did more than step across the threshold into an old ruin: I entered the lives of generations of my Dominican brothers. Elaborate stone tracery still adorned some of the windows now filled only with sky. With what glowing colours had their panes once filtered the flooding sunlight? I imagined how the local peasants would have studied the illustrated biblical stories, and how their children gazed at them as they sat here, fidgeting through the Mass.

Out in the cloister I was surprised to see a staircase had been restored, so climbed up to see what remained of the friars' sleeping quarters. When passing back into the church I noticed the square bolt-hole into which a stout wooden bar would have slid to secure the door. In the lower surface of the aperture a groove perhaps seven centimetres wide had been worn down into the hard limestone. More than anything else in the ruins, that simple sight moved me deeply. The groove had been worn over more than three hundred years of use – despite two invasions and forced evacuations from their home – when each night a brother slid the bar across to lock the cloister and secure the community's privacy.

In far-off Melbourne I was finding life as a Dominican friar fulfilling and challenging. It had given me precious gifts of friendship and supported me as I matured into a life centred on the eternal God, among men who showed the full spectrum of wisdom, goodness, immaturity, eccentricity and sinfulness. Our ancient institution had staying power, and if some of the anachronistic customs in our daily life may have somewhat hindered our human growth, they did not destroy the benefits that come with being part of a dependable, praying community. I had often puzzled over why I had committed my life to this particular order, which I had not even heard of until just a year before I joined it. I had been impressed by the friars' focus on study as a basis for sharing the transcendent truth of the gospel, and a few years later, when I saw some of them making justice issues a priority in their mission, I felt even more that I was in the right place.

The ancient priory at Kilmallock was beginning to suggest an answer to my puzzle. I had come to south-west Ireland to seek possible connections with my father's ancestors, who had come from the Limerick-Tipperary borderlands. Although there are almost no written church records from before 1836, the death certificates of several brothers of my great-great-grandfather indicated that they were born in the district around Kilmallock. As I wandered around these Dominican ruins I found myself wondering what kind of desperate circumstances might my ancestors have endured during the various invasions. What encounter might have taken place long ago between a friar and a worried mother or grandmother who had come asking for prayers? What desperate father had uttered, perhaps with embarrassment, a blunt masculine prayer for help? When persons pray with all their being, who knows what kind of archways in time might open up, making possible links to people in future generations. Although I had not expected to find this Dominican presence in my father's ancestral district, I already knew of events far back in our family history that must have involved depths of pain and desperate prayer whose impact would have echoed for centuries to come, and may well have shaped my own life.

Leaving the priory at Kilmallock, after a number of back-road detours I found the hamlet of Ballybricken. It would have been a substantial village before the Irish population was reduced by Cromwell's wars and nineteenth century famine. Now it is just a church and a few houses strung along a narrow country road. I knew it to be the birthplace of several brothers of my great-great-grandfather. Three of these had come to Australia in 1836, much earlier than their older brother's emigration in mid-century. Why had they come so early? Only after considerable research did we solve the mystery, when we found them together in a register of convict arrivals. The three brothers had been convicted and sentenced on the same day to be exiled for life to New South Wales. Later still we found a version of the story of their trial in the 1836 *Clonmel Herald*.

In the little church at Ballybricken I celebrated the Eucharist to pray for these victims of the empire's cruelty to its colonised populations. I then visited Clonmel and found the jail and courthouse where the three Murnane brothers had been held and tried. The jail had been partly demolished not long before my visit, but the high external wall and the great seven-metre archway of the main gate were still standing. I walked through into the vacant, weedy area, where on the brickwork of the surviving walls I could see the outlines of stairs and vaulted cells. I could almost hear the clanging of doors, the shouts of guards and the glowering, cursing prisoners whose lives, once they were sentenced, started out on new, unknown journeys of catastrophic grief and fear.

Just up the street was the grey facade of the courthouse. As in every major town of the British Empire it is one of the most imposing structures, built to impress upon citizens the inescapable power of the Law. Even now its heavy classical architecture was imposing and menacing. Today no chain gang shuffled along the street, but I had to negotiate a string of Volkswagens and Ford Escorts that lined the kerb, before I could enter the heavy arched doors into the courtroom. It looked as if it had not been altered in the hundred and forty years since Michael, John and Thomas Murnane stood in the dock. The room's high ceiling and dark wood panelling would have overwhelmed people used to the dim, smoky interiors of turf huts. Upper galleries for the public stretched around the walls, except at the back, where a massive, red-draped canopy towered high over the judge's chair.

The three brothers were accused of a serious crime against John Day, landlord of their friend John Walshe. It is important to recall that Irish landlords in the early nineteenth century had almost the power of life and death over their tenants. They could, for instance, evict them from their tiny rented holdings by destroying the turf-sod cottages that were their homes. The court was not told what grievance John Walshe had against William Day, but his three friends went with him to try to redress it, on a moonlit New-Year's eve. In their angry state they broke down his door and tried to injure him: Michael tried to hit him with a scythe; John Murnane had a stick and John Walshe a pitchfork. The youngest brother, Thomas, was unarmed. William Day bravely claimed in court that he knocked down Michael and John, then fled to the police barracks, as he had done on a previous occasion to seek help against the Murnanes.

We do not hear anything about the substance of that prior grievance, but British law classed their present attack as 'assaulting a habitation'. By the Empire's standards it deserved the second harshest penalty in the book: exile for life to the other side of the world, even if this meant that the two who had wives and young children would never see them again. The brothers were quickly found guilty and sentenced to that harsh and dreaded penalty. Even so they were relatively fortunate, for at those same *Summer Assizes* Chief Justice Doherty sentenced fourteen to be hanged on the same day that they were sentenced, despite their pleas for delay.

The reason given for these harsh sentences was that those parts of the country were 'always disturbed', and 'in uproar' at that time. This was the assessment of the landlords who were trying to hold on to the spoils they had inherited from centuries of invasion, occupation and land-theft, and whose peers had written the laws to protect themselves and their gains. The same laws protected a distribution of resources so unequal that before ten more years had passed, when the potato crop failed, wealthy landowners could continue to export food in abundance while more than a million of the Irish poor starved to death, and another million fled their homeland in their attempt to survive.

The three brothers, unlettered agricultural workers Michael, John and Thomas, would in other times and places be honoured as fighters for their freedom. In the British colony of Ireland in 1836 they set out on an 80 kilometre journey along the road to the port of Cork. Did they shamble in chains, or were they piled into wagons? For a few weeks they waited in prison hulks in Cork harbour, ill fed and no doubt wretched and grieving, until picked up by the prison ship *Earl Grey* and taken on their journey of 23,000 kilometres to Sydney. *The*

Fields of Athenry, Pete St John's heart-wrenching song of the 1970s, might have been written precisely to describe their story.

When the *Earl Grey* arrived in Sydney four and a half months later, among the 297 male convicts who had set out, about thirty had suffered from the dreaded disease of scurvy and nine had died *en route*.[83] By 1836 convicts had been transported to New South Wales for almost half a century, and the private contractors who made profit from the business were now better inspected and controlled. The Empire's bureaucracy had brought efficiency into what was still a cruel system. Surgeons were appointed to prevent the barbarous practice of cutting the convicts rations so severely that many died on the voyage. The whole vast system was still an elaborate machine that the British Empire had evolved to control the poor. No doubt some of the people serving within it were compassionate and strove for reform, but it achieved its goals essentially by the systematic use of torture (flogging and solitary confinement) and by tearing families apart.

When I first discovered Michael, John and Thomas in the convict records, it struck me as remarkable that no one in my 20th century family even knew about their story. To be arrested and transported must have been so shameful that my father's family had effectively buried it in silence so that after only three generations the memory had been quite erased.

And yet in the long term, remarkably, the three brothers' cruel exile proved fruitful. Even the worst human suffering can be transformed by courage and patiently clinging to whatever faith one has in the Transcendent. No record can be found of what happened to Michael, but John and Thomas gradually regained their freedom, as the system intended convicts to do. We do not know whether the wives of John and Michael died in the famine of the 1840's, but John remarried in Australia. Forbidden from ever returning to Ireland, within a few years of serving their time John and Thomas – now also married – had obtained small parcels of land near Warrnambool and invited their older brother Cornelius, my great-great-grandfather, to emigrate.

Cornelius eventually brought the rest of his family to find prosperity that they could never have found in their tormented homeland.

※

In 1940, fifty-six years after Cornelius Murnane's death, I was born in Cobden, not far from where he acquired his first parcel of land. By the 1950s my family had moved back to Melbourne and lived in the suburb of Huntingdale, about twenty kilometres south-east of the city. Our house was a kilometre from a railway station, on the edge of a large tract of tea-tree scrub in what was known as the Sand Belt, a popular location for golf courses. Our own street, once you had passed the dozen or so houses, dwindled to a sandy lane lined with scrub. In my mid-teens I loved to explore it, wondering what I might find if I followed it far enough south through the tea-tree.

One day in the school holidays, around my fifteenth year, I prepared to set out alone, with my pockets full of provisions, to follow and explore the sand track as far as I could. My younger brother Denis saw me preparing and asked if he could come too. I was mildly annoyed, but could not refuse for we often shared such activities, and he was a good companion to go exploring with. Although at school I was embarrassed by his mental slowness, it did not matter when we were alone. He could not share what I thought were my deeper ideas, but loved to talk about practical things: animals, birds, ants and snakes, and had a life-long fascination with trains.

I was still annoyed when we set out, for I had been looking forward to hours of solitude on my big adventure. I became more annoyed when he dropped behind as he sometimes did when he got tired or wanted to look at small things of interest beside the track, so I thought I would play a trick on him. We came to a point just past the end of the golf course land, where the track ran beside a kind of dry swamp. Through the fence it looked like a magical place. The ground was covered with close-cropped grass, almost like lawn, and there were frequent clumps of tall bulrushes. Looking back, I made sure that my brother saw me climbing through the tumbledown fence into this park-like place, then quickly ran ahead to hide behind one of the clumps of rushes.

He soon came through the fence, but could not see where I had gone. Spying on him through the rushes, I could easily run to another clump when he was not looking in my direction so that he would never come near my shifting hiding place. For a while I enjoyed the game, but like any one-sided contest it soon began to pall. While I was deciding how to end it, my brother began to call my name. There was a pathos in his voice that touched me deeply. I could hear in it a note of despair, as if he might never find me again. It seemed also to be telling me how helpless he felt, imprisoned in his own deficiencies, believing he was inferior to me and perhaps to everyone else. Before I could decide how to act, he called my name again and again and I seemed to hear the voice of all lonely people such as I had read about in books or newspapers: exiles from their homes; trapped or abandoned in helpless suffering, seeing no way out of their distress. His plaintive call, his distress, opened for me a window that enlarged my world. Almost crying, I walked from behind the rushes and called to him, for in his search he had wandered some distance off.

One of our strongest instincts is to avoid pain, so it is not surprising that we feel reluctant to watch or even hear about the pain of others. Many people don't want to know that 800 million people – about every ninth person on Earth – are constantly hungry. A much larger number have such limited resources that any illness or sudden expense is a disaster for their family. Their sufferings challenge us – or at least they challenge me – with the knowledge that to a large extent their poverty and hunger is caused by structures of finance and trade which my country uses to stay prosperous; structures from which I am profiting every day.

In my twelfth year I was given as a Christmas gift the glossy *Empire Youth Annual.* It enthralled me. I admired the extent and variety of the British Empire, in the very years in which it had already begun to decline and be rapidly dismembered, and was awed by the success of empire-builders like Robert Clive and Cecil Rhodes. I had no idea that the Empire in which I was growing up and which I was being taught to admire had been built by repeated invasions, land theft from Indigenous peoples, and the continuous exploitation of colonial populations. The map of the world has greatly changed since then, but the club of the wealthier nations, and now cliques of corporations, use wars and financial controls to keep the balance of resources and debt heavily stacked against peoples of the Majority World. We who share in the profits of this hugely unjust deal must admit that some of the guilt *is* ours, but our media and our own uneasiness so carefully avoid examining the underlying structures of the system that we can feel almost innocent. Most of us are not callous, but ignorant of how the imbalance of wealth and privilege is maintained by invading and killing, for the media industry twists the crimes to make them look like necessary steps against *others* who are evil. To name only one of the controlling powers, the USA as early as 1898 brutally seized control of the richly-resourced Philippines. In 1918, immediately after the Soviet revolution and long before the evils of Stalinism had emerged, the USA joined with other nations to send troops to try to smash the embryonic socialist regime. Why were the lords of Capital so fearful of that untried ideology whose aim was to share the world's resources more equitably?

Since World War II the USA, 'to protect our interests' has invaded or helped to overthrow the legitimate governments of more than fifty other nations, including many in Latin America, like Guatemala, where Sr Dianna Ortiz was one of its many victims.[84] All of these unjust conquests have been presented to the public in the USA and elsewhere as if they were innocent philanthropy.[85] Whenever greed dominates and commits atrocities, the culprits callously push their victims to the margins or remove them altogether so that they can pretend that the Market is a 'level playing field'. It saddens me that only in my seventies did I learn more fully how this process worked in the district where I was born. Quite close to my birthplace, soon after the first squatters began running sheep on land that they did not own, their workmen massacred at least thirty-five Aboriginal people, including women and children, in a cowardly night raid on their sleeping camp.[86] Those who lived in the path of what the more powerful call 'prosperity' and 'progress' were little by little killed, enslaved, or made extinct, while the perpetrators and their descendants continue to conceal it or deny that it even happened. In 2017 former Prime Minister John Howard continued to condemn what he insultingly called a 'black armband' view of history, refusing to accept that there were in fact systematic 'Frontier Wars' against Australia's Indigenous Peoples. From the ensuing prosperity of those who first appropriated their land subsequent generations of Australians, including his family and mine, have lived in comfort.

In Australia for almost a century the callousness of white people allowed and promoted the mass removal of mixed-race children from their Aboriginal parents. The ultimate goal was to 'breed out' their black identity and so eliminate the Aboriginal Problem. I was shocked to learn that this was partly driven by the new 'science' of eugenics, which in the early decades of the twentieth century was popular in Britain, Europe and particularly the USA. A policy of legalised sterilisation of people deemed 'unfit' was practiced in thirty states in the USA. The policy was praised and then imitated by the Nazi party in Germany.[87]

Not through my own merit – for I can be as callous as the average person – I have been taught to be aware of injustice and at least try to move towards compassion. I thank mainly my parents, who advised or admonished me in this direction. In adult life, friends chide me for choosing books and films with themes of grim injustice rather than lightweight entertainment. Even though such works stir me to anger, I would prefer thoughtful movies like *Twelve Years a Slave* or *In the Name of The Father*, which relates how in 1974 British police forced confessions from the Guildford Four and jailed them, though innocent, for sixteen years.[88] With the Indian writer Arundhati Roy, who is tireless in advocating for those who suffer injustice, I believe that we need:

> ... to never get used to the unspeakable violence and the vulgar disparity of life around you. To seek joy in the saddest places. To pursue beauty to its lair ... To respect strength, never power. Above all, to watch. To try and understand. To never look away. And never, never to forget.[89]

༄

I have come to see that the courage of individuals, supported by networks of 'people power', can survive against empires, transcending the worst injustices that they have produced and even turn them to advantage. Two of the Murnane exiles, John and Thomas, by their individual endurance brought great benefit to their descendants and relatives in later generations. We cannot easily learn to what extent they were sustained by their faith in the Transcendent, but some power greater than the ordinary enabled those impoverished minor outlaws to pass through the archway of exile to transform their lives and our futures.

Like hundreds of thousands of other convicts, despite chains and other degradations they found the strength to persist through each plodding step of their journey. By each hammer blow breaking rocks for road building; in every axe- and saw-stroke converting virgin forest into planks for houses, sheds and fences; through each frosty night tending sheep on the Monaro plains, their spirit triumphed over the cruel machinery of the colonial system and the government that used them as a means to its ends. Although they were pushed to extremes of endurance, some mysterious spirit in them reshaped their world and brought benefits to many others, which gratefully I still enjoy.

17
Pilgrimage of Reconciliation
Bike ride to Uluru

Monday 29th August 2005.

The wind plays my bike wheels like a harpist. They're hardly turning, but I can't push any faster. It howls past my ears: that whistling note tells me it must be more than sixty kilometres per hour. Pushing against it, I can't even manage ten. It's been getting stronger all day.

I left Morgan around 8am ... an hour after the others. Just as they were setting off I found a thorn in my back tyre. Pulling it out, that ominous hiss of air told me I had my first puncture in 1000 kilometres. The rear wheel takes longer to change because of its chain and gears, but when I'd fitted the new tube and pumped it up, it forced the tyre off the rim! I was angry at the junior shop-assistant back in Auckland for selling me a tube too big for my wheel, but the fault was mine for not checking my own gear. I had to go through the whole process again: remove the wheel, let out the air, lever off the tyre, find a tube that fitted ... then repeat all those steps in reverse order. I didn't catch up with the other four, or Phil with the car, until they were setting off again at the end of their morning tea-break. It was much the same at lunch. And they're still somewhere ahead, out of sight.

As if the wind isn't enough, the road is climbing slowly towards the Flinders Ranges. At Morgan, where we camped last night, the big Murray River was less than fifty metres above the sea, although it still had hundreds of kilometres to meander before reaching it. Tonight, in the hill-town of Burra, we will be 580 metres up. That's if we survive these eighty-seven kilometres of salt-bush and a few gum trees, without a town or roadhouse. Some farmers still try to grow wheat here, but somewhere nearby the map showed World's End Creek. I'm not surprised.

Struggling to the top of a rise I look forward to easier riding down the other side, but these ridges are like stairs: they go up but not down. Anyway, the wind stops me from going downhill any faster. Those mounds of crumpled khaki in the far distance are the Flinders Ranges, our improbable goal.

No relief in sight. I ache for the comfort of a break in the wind, but it never slackens. Like someone in chronic pain I start to feel sorry for myself. The road surface is new, but that's poor compensation; it has a white rumble strip at the side, meant to wake up straying drivers. Again and again the wind forces me onto it and the juddering makes riding even harder. It infuriates me.

Far ahead, there's a dark patch of trees to the right of the road. They will give me some shelter from the wind, even for the short time it takes to ride past them. I grab at the least consolation. It takes me an age to struggle towards the trees, but when I get near my heart sinks: they are no shelter at all: just thin scrub, with wind howling through their miserable trunks as it does through the spokes of my wheels.

Hours pass. The road gets steeper. It can't be far now. We got across the Hay Plains in head winds; we'll get to Burra too. A bend coming up: the slight change of direction will mean the wind is not directly in my face. But when I struggle around the bend the wind seems to adjust itself: still in my face and stronger than before. I brood on this. It's more than I should have to put up with! I lose patience: why doesn't it do what I *want?*

But suddenly I see: the wind isn't trying *to oppose me, much less insult me; it has no interest in me at all. I'm not* that *important. Why* shouldn't *the wind batter me? Wasn't it* my *choice to come here? Isn't it me who's doing the pushing?*

At the limit of my strength and patience, I'm being offered insight! When a moment ago I felt only my aching limbs, now I find I'm beginning to recall people who are feeling more pain than I have ever felt or probably ever will: people being tortured, right now, in remote prisons; sick people in Majority World slums with no hope of being cured. Why am I complaining about aches that I'm causing myself?

The thought comes from somewhere: I don't deserve anything at all: not a gentler wind, nor to reach Burra soon; not success in this pilgrimage nor even to be alive in this straining flesh and pumping blood and the breath coming dryly in and out. I might never have been. Everything is gift. As I continue pumping the pedals, left, right – push breath out, again – I wonder: 'Who is giving me all this? Are You here? Now?'

'Tout est grâce', said Bernanos' country priest in that famous last line of his Diary … everything is gift. The ache in my muscles stops mattering. Strangely, I feel free. Nothing matters! It's all right to be here, just like this, in the wind, even if the struggle gets worse or goes on for hours. I'm exhausted but feel detached, almost comfortable. If we enter into The Mystery, even a little, does our world turn inside out, opposite to what it seemed just a moment ago?

Around five o'clock my battle with the wind is over. A left turn leads towards the town, a kilometre or two off the highway. The road is up a steep hill, but where before I would have groaned and complained, now I almost cruise up, joyfully. It's that ferocious wind – almost at my back now – pushing me. I pass several of our team whom I had not seen for hours. We don't even pause. What comments could describe the day we've been through? A shared grunt of recognition is enough.

It wasn't quite over. Phil had driven on ahead of us as usual, but missed the Burra turnoff and carried on some distance down the highway. He waited loyally on a hilltop, wondering when we would appear. Meanwhile we five had gathered at the edge of Burra and together found the camping ground, but we had no food or gear. While some watched out for Phil, others found a fish shop and as night closed in we discovered near-ecstasy in steaming, golden, crunchy fish 'n' chips. When at last he arrived, Phil's only punishment was that he had to eat them cold.

꘡

Why ride a bike from Morgan to Burra at the age of sixty-five? This was in fact day fifteen of a pilgrimage from Canberra to Uluru in central Australia that would take us thirty-three days. It was my odd way of celebrating the forty years since I was ordained a priest in 1965.

What connection is there between a triumphalist ordination ceremony in a Gothic cathedral and an old man pushing a bike across a windswept plain? The contrast itself might symbolise the changes that forty years had made. During those years both I and the Church that gave me this ministry had evolved beyond imagining from what we once were. Those who can remember the 1960s speak with awe about the changes in technology that have occurred since then. The telephone is a homely example. In the early '60s it was a weighty black pyramid of bakelite with a circular, spring-driven dial on its front and a heavy receiver cradled on top. It had been possible only recently to dial Melbourne numbers automatically, without the help of an operator; but long-distance calls still went through a human agent. Those phones have evolved step by step into wondrous little screens which almost everyone carries, incorporating a radio, cameras to capture still and moving pictures; a sound recorder, calculator, alarm clock, stopwatch, notepad, diary, multiple dictionaries, language translator, flashlight and much more. Because they can access the internet – which had not yet been dreamed of in the 1960s – these instruments can download an endless variety of apps to perform almost limitless other functions. Almost incidentally they are telephones, by which we can talk, make video calls, send text, photos, documents or movies to persons in almost any part of the world.

Since the 1960s the transistor, which had just then replaced the radio valve, has evolved into the microchip, increasing its power exponentially. The long-playing record gave way to the cassette tape, which begat the video cassette, then the CD and DVD, and now the flash drive. Jet airliners had just begun to carry people between continents: the supersonic Concorde came and went, but the jumbo came and stayed. On the ground, car ownership increased more than tenfold; television spread to almost every home; the contraceptive pill revolutionised sexual behaviour; the personal computer came, then shrank in size and grew in its power to 'process' words, sounds and pictures until it gave us undreamed-of access to most of the stored knowledge of the human race.

The explosion of technology since the '60s let people sail around the moon, then walk on it; send machines to peer at the planets and launch orbiting telescopes to find billions more galaxies. At the same time, we discovered new universes within living cells, and by altering genes virtually created new species. But more than technology was changing: human hearts too, began to experience new awakenings.

In former colonies, independence movements were throwing off the yokes of empires and radically changing the world map. In the southern states of USA – and in South Africa and Australia – the struggle for civil rights for black people rose to a crescendo. In Australia we had a referendum and voted overwhelmingly to recognise Aborigines as human beings, even if we did not yet give them the right to own land or control their own lives. In the countries that were busily destroying Vietnam, anti-war movements blossomed and eventually ended that war. Radical changes in our social behaviour seemed to come from nowhere. Young people began to put aside cultural norms, adopting strange new styles of hair, clothing and music. Older folk were bemused and concerned as the young demanded a say in the running of schools and universities; began living together before their marriage or dispensed with that ceremony altogether.

In the seemingly unchanging Catholic Church, remarkable things began to happen. An old pope unexpectedly called all the world's bishops into one place, enabling the Spirit within them to begin renewing the church. This mysterious creative force in all people, which the Church knew as the Holy Spirit and its leaders thought had been tamed and sidelined, began to disturb congregations, convents and monasteries and awaken emotion and freedom in Christians. The Mass was everywhere restored to the language of the people taking part in it, and as in earliest days the presiding priest again faced across the table to those he was leading in the meal that recalled the self-giving death of Jesus two millennia before.

In his book *The Structure of Scientific Revolutions* Thomas Kuhn used the term *paradigm shift* to describe fundamental changes in science – radically new patterns of perceiving and acting.[90] Whatever we called them, similar shifts were now affecting the lives of almost every person on the planet and the changes within the Church had enormous impact on the role of priests in the forty years since I began to work as one. Perhaps I chose this long bike ride because I needed to explore and reflect on what these changes had done to my life, heading for the centre of my land as a way of looking into my own heart.

But what *is* a pilgrimage? Is this ancient custom just another way of trying to escape from the everyday: the prototype of the holiday cruise? Or are pilgrims pursuing some further goal? Their physical destination is usually a place where some holy person has lived or died: someone who stood out among ordinary self-centred lives. We suspect that the exceptional goodness of this prophet, saint or seer showed that they were more in touch with the Transcendent than we are.

Jerusalem was the original goal for Christian pilgrims, where Jesus of Nazareth was crucified and – as they believed – passed through death into new life and was again seen by his friends. When politics made Jerusalem inaccessible, pilgrims settled for holy places nearer to home. The pilgrims in *The Canterbury Tales* were heading for the tomb of Thomas A'Beckett, the *holy blisful martir*, hardly a hundred kilometres from the Southwark inn where Chaucer describes them gathering. Many other pilgrims have trekked across Europe to Santiago in Spain, which claims the bones of St James the Apostle. Poorer folk had to settle for walking around a maze set in the floor of their local cathedral.

Followers of the Buddha make pilgrimage to the various places in India where he received enlightenment, taught, then passed into *nirvana* five centuries before Jesus was born. Seven centuries after Jesus, the *haj* to Mecca became one of the five pillars of Islam, and now each year millions of the Prophet's followers journey to his birthplace and to Medina where he died.

Any journey can broaden our horizons, but these ancient journeys through sacred thresholds add the promise of access to the Transcendent dimension that perpetually lures us but seems always beyond our reach. The pilgrim shares something of the artist's creative task, setting out on a journey that also leads inwards. Pilgrims don't paint with pigment or carve wood and stone, but by their own journeying they link together particular places and times. They hope that their road, like the artist's work, may open up vistas showing what 'ordinary' life is about. Their voyage is a miniature model of the whole of life; a manageable slice from that larger span of years whose turnings are mostly unpredictable and whose terminus is beyond our control.

The present moment, say the wisest guides, is all we have to work with: 'The past is gone; the future is not yet ...'[91] If we focus sufficiently in the present, on the here and now, this step we are now taking can paradoxically take us out of ourselves. If this is what the pilgrim is seeking, he or she may try to make every step, every turn of the bike's pedal crank into a kind of prayer, an attempt to connect with the Transcendent Mystery that lies behind every day we live and every path we take.

The pilgrim's search for personal growth may be somewhat selfish. Most pilgrims are comfortably off, whereas the majority of the world's population are so lacking food and resources that every day is a struggle, and funds or leisure for *any* journey are beyond their dreams. Thoughtful pilgrims recognise that they have a responsibility towards the majority of human beings who will never have their privileges.

If the pilgrimage has elements of a holiday, the road to the holy shrine, like the making of art, can be long, onerous and lonely. Some pilgrims choose, or even vow, to travel in a specially difficult manner: on foot, barefoot, fasting. In colloquial speech to 'roll' can mean to cruise or take it easy, but not for those Hindu pilgrims who choose literally to roll their hunched body along the road to Varanasi, sometimes for hundreds of kilometres. Uluru was a daunting 2,700 kilometres from our starting point at Parliament House, Canberra; easy enough on a rolling bike if we carried no extra burdens, so in deference to our age we used a vehicle to carry our tents, water, and heavier gear.

The best preparation that the artist or pilgrim can make is to get out of the way; to become, themselves, a kind of empty archway or pipe through which some new creation, or at least new insight, may emerge. Once under way, the artwork or the pilgrim's journey may partly take over the person who thought it was *their* original idea. Inexplicable hints and forces seem to guide the paintbrush, chisel, pen or bicycle wheel in unexpected ways. Something greater than a human agent appears to speak to those who will listen. The Transcendent seems to want to be found.

About a year before that significant anniversary I had begun to look for an appropriate way of celebrating four decades of working as a priest. Always eager to travel, I thought of a pilgrimage, but ruled out the places which I had already visited: south-west Ireland from which my father's family had come; the roots of my Dominican family in southern France, and of Christianity in Rome and Jerusalem. I turned instead towards Australia, where I had not lived for fourteen years, and wondered how I might explore its heartland as well as connect in some way with its original inhabitants.

Uluru, the great red sandstone monolith at the heart of the Australian continent, had been returned to its ancient custodians, the Anangu people, twenty years before.[92] By making that our goal I hoped in a small way to add my voice to those who were speaking the truth about my own people's theft of Aboriginal land and to share in the growing national movement towards apology and reconciliation. At another level, the pilgrimage that I planned to make was also about the longer, slower journey that we make towards the centre of our self. As we move daily nearer to the end of our physical life we are sometimes moved to ask questions that we normally avoid: what am I, really? Who is this person bearing the name that I use? How am I related to all other people? … How am I related to The Mystery?

In all relationships, the idea of healing and reconciliation will arise. There are always things that need to be mended. When we – particularly white Australians – dig into the truth about our takeover of the continent, we find much that is discordant, much that is criminal in what we have done. Our story is far from finished. Unlike the long road from Canberra to Uluru, the route of our inner journey towards the centre is not paved with tar nor marked with white lines. It doesn't have a specific terminus but is open-ended. It often runs through desert, but although there are no maps or GPS to show the way, we can find almost instinctively the things that will bring us nearer to our unseen goal.

I do not recall ever seeing in my first twenty years of life an Aboriginal person, and certainly did not meet one. As a child my ideas were being formed by racist cartoons and advertisements like 'Pelaco Bill', the

Aboriginal man shown in magazine advertisements and on railway hoardings, dressed in nothing but a white business-shirt, exclaiming 'Mine tinkit they fit!' Only slowly did I come to realise that the now invisible Aborigines had once occupied every part of the rich farming land of the Western District of Victoria, where some of my family had become prosperous and many more had eked out a living as farm labourers, road makers, railway navvies and heroically as pioneer housewives. I knew the stories of how, over a century and a half, European settlers had cleared the forests and 'developed' the district for their own purposes, but only slowly did I realise that in the district where I was born, as in every part of the Australian continent, the original inhabitants had been forced from the homelands where they had thrived since time immemorial and now had to live, out of sight, on reservations.

Not long ago I was shocked to hear some Indigenous people from West Papua telling how Indonesia is not only exploiting their land and its resources but is flooding their country with hundreds of thousands of immigrants from Java. The colonial power aims eventually to outnumber the Indigenous Papuans, take their land and overwhelm their culture. I felt deep anger that such exploitation should be allowed to continue and was affronted to hear the Indonesian government objecting to us 'outsiders' criticising what they do with lands they claim as 'theirs'.

Then I realised, and it shocked me even more, that Indonesia is now doing no more than what we have already done. Starting in 1788 our forebears treated Indigenous Australians in the same way. Wave after wave of white immigrants and their livestock flooded into every part of the continent, displacing Aborigines who had enjoyed free possession for untold millennia. Our people uprooted them from their home places and came close to completely destroying their rich cultures and most of their two hundred languages.

Soon after the white people arrived with their hundreds of thousands of sheep and cattle, the Aborigines saw their water sources polluted and their rich variety of food plants destroyed. Simply to feed themselves they began to kill some of the strange new animals. They often tried to resist the white men's violence or the rape or kidnap of their women, but the invaders then retaliated, ferociously, with superior weapons: rifle bullets, stockwhips, stirrup-irons swung from horseback; poisoned food and water.

Historians now recognise that this pattern of first encounter, clash and slaughter occurred in every part of Australia from 1788 to the mid-20th century. It passed like a slow, tragic wave across the whole continent. Step by step we waged war against the Indigenous people of Australia as we occupied their fertile river valleys, waterholes and sacred sites. More than 25,000 Aborigines were killed directly, and countless others died through disease and privation. The total who died in the Frontier Wars has been estimated at well over 60,000; more than the Australian soldiers who died in World War I. We European-Australians have been able to pretend that this takeover was legal because Captain Cook planted a flag at Botany Bay on 29th April 1770 and claimed the east coast of *Terra Australis* for the British Empire. The British Government subsequently ruled that the land was *terra nullius* – that it did not belong to anybody.

In recent years I had been reading history as written by Aborigines themselves. The first-hand reminiscences of films like *A Lousy Sixpence* or *Rabbit-Proof Fence* had opened many eyes and greatly saddened our hearts. The dry prose of the Deaths in Custody report introduced me to horrors that still happen in Australian jails and the harrowing pages of *Bringing Them Home* revealed the systematic abuse by successive governments in stealing from their parents many Aboriginal children through eight generations. I began to understand more clearly the persistent racism that lives deep within us White Australians. I saw that I cannot come to know fully who I am unless with complete honesty I face my people's culpability, and therefore my own culpability, in the Dispossession of these people who have lived for at least 40,000 years in the land that gave me birth.

Our people have spilled blood on the wattle more often than most Australians know.[93] As a member of the third Australian-born generation in my European-Australian family I was slow to recognise that we need to seek reconciliation with the people we had so cruelly dispossessed. Now, in 2005, through a striking instance of synchronicity, I was to encounter at close quarters one of the last instances of this genocide. Although I had been living abroad for fourteen years, I felt urged to do something towards sharing in the nationwide 'Journey of Healing' that began in May 1999 and which was growing stronger each year, so I pondered a Pilgrimage of Reconciliation to the centre of the land. The Aboriginal Tent Embassy[94] and Parliament House in Canberra seemed appropriate places to begin our ride, the latter being the present seat of governments which since 1901 have passed laws that have ignored the rights of Aboriginal people and even directly harmed them.

Others had made pilgrimages to Uluru, but no one, as far as I knew, had made the pilgrimage by bike. Nor was I confident that I could. But it seemed that travelling this more arduous way would add emphasis when I – a member of the oppressing race – tried to begin to say 'Sorry'. I could have no idea that our journey would bring me to an archway revealing a deep encounter with of one of the last massacres of the Frontier Wars, and showing me that no white Australian family can say with certainty: it had nothing to do with us.

⁓

Some instinct deeper than reason was drawing me towards Uluru: something *felt*, like a need for water. It would have been madness to follow such a feeling without doing some basic research: was I able, at sixty-five, to ride a bike so far? With some training it might be possible. I was astonished to find that in 1897, before there was even a road, Jerome Murif had ridden from Adelaide to Darwin, almost twice the distance that I was proposing.[95] In 1997, to mark the centenary of Murif's epic journey, Bob Moore and Trevor Briggs rode the length of the Stuart Highway. It was their account that first showed me that my journey might be feasible.

Was the whole idea mad? I asked a few friends for their opinion. None said outright that I was crazy and some actually helped me with contacts, so I took heart and set about calculating when winds and temperatures might be most favourable. My Dominican community readily granted my request for leave and funding for the journey. We chose to leave in mid-August so as to arrive in the Centre before the temperatures rose to impossible levels.

As word got around, a few other long-distance riders began asking to join me: from Bendigo, Ray Wilson and Franciscan Sister Suzanne Fairbairn FMDM; from Canberra, John and Julia Widdup who had already ridden around Europe. A classmate from my school-days Leon Daphne, who had become CEO of a major car company kindly arranged the loan of a vehicle to carry our heavier gear. Best of all, Philip Yubbagurri Brown, an Aboriginal man from a Canberra Reconciliation group, asked if he could help. Besides being an excellent driver for our support vehicle, he linked us with many Aboriginal communities on the way. His didgeridoo playing helpfully announced our presence at lunch breaks and campsites, and he played and spoke at the schools we visited.

Despite all these practical preparations I still did not know the deeper reason for my pilgrimage. During the months of planning and then riding towards the heart of my country, I had thought I was engaging in a pleasant if challenging bike ride. In the event, I found I was drawing back the curtain of the past to watch part of the drama of history that tragically linked my own family to Aboriginal people. I was to uncover a story that continues to challenge us in the journey of reconciliation, but I would know none of this until the long journey had been completed. The discovery would be one of the strangest examples of synchronicity I have encountered.

After our small group of riders had at last reached Uluru, we met with local people at Mutitjulu, in the shadow of the rock, and in a simple ceremony mingled with the ashes of their campfire the ashes we had carried from the fire at the Tent Embassy in Canberra. We then dispersed to go our different ways. I rode with the car into Alice Springs and during a week there spent many hours in the local library. It was only in my last hours in the library, on the afternoon before I was to take the train down to Adelaide, that I came across a booklet titled *The Hidden History of Australia* by Bill Hornadge,[96] a collection of essays by little-known authors. One chapter caught my eye: an account of one of the last massacres of Aborigines, in 1926 at Forrest River, near Wyndham, Western Australia.

Skimming through the text, I learned that the massacre had occurred in revenge for the fatal spearing of the cattleman William Hay. He had a reputation for violence against Aborigines and for sexually exploiting Aboriginal women. A certain Lumbia, whose wife he had kidnapped, speared him to death. The attitudes among whites in frontier communities made it almost inevitable that in retaliation for the action of one man who had been seeking reparation, many Aborigines would be killed in revenge, so in June 1926 a heavily armed posse rode out from Wyndham to 'punish the Blacks'.

Sometime after the ensuing massacre, Ernest Gribble, a strong-willed Anglican missionary, protested so strongly about the mass murders that eventually a Royal Commission was established to enquire into them. As I read the account of that Commission, I was shocked to see listed among the accused my own family name. One of the defendants was Daniel Murnane, a fourth cousin. I had never met Daniel, who died at seventy-five years of age in 1973. A veterinary surgeon, he was at the time one of the few members of our extended family to have gained a university degree, which was why he had sometimes been held up to my brother and me as an example of what we might achieve if we applied ourselves to study. Later I found that at the age of eighteen, armed with an inky note giving the permission of his schoolteacher father, he had volunteered for the army and overseas service. It was 1915. He was assigned to a stores unit, and before the year was out had arrived at Gallipoli just one week before the evacuation. Daniel's unit was then shipped to France and spent the rest of the war behind various front lines supplying food, coal and equipment to the fighting troops.

It is possible that he never fired a shot at any person during the entire war, but he would have seen and heard enough of the horrific results of trench warfare. When he returned to Australia in 1919, he may have been undamaged in body, but like most others he no doubt carried some terrible memories, and would have found it difficult and monotonous to settle into life as a student on a returned servicemen's scholarship. After gaining his degree as a veterinary surgeon, when the Commonwealth Scientific and Industrial Research organisation needed researchers into buffalo fly in the far north of Western Australia, Daniel no doubt saw it as an attractive opportunity for adventure, without the horrors of war.

It was his misfortune to have as his host William Hay, the womanising cattleman who was speared to death about a month after Daniel's arrival. Like most cattlemen in the area Hay was an ex-army man. He had treated Daniel with generous bush hospitality, so when he was killed, and every white man around Wyndham gathered to form a posse, it would have taken a superhuman degree of independence and courage from Daniel to refuse to join them. Yet he does not seem to have been unwilling, for he later defended himself before the Royal Commission: [William Hay] *made me thoroughly welcome* [at Nulla Nulla, his 790,000 acre station] *for a period of four weeks; placed his motor launch at the disposal of my department, as well as plant, horses and everything on the station.* When Hay's speared body was found swollen and half-eaten by maggots and dingoes, Daniel considered it the least he could do: *if ... I endeavoured to catch the man who had killed him.*

The hastily-formed posse rode out on June 1st, with the people of Wyndham encouraging them to take no prisoners. The group included two police; two 'Special Constables' – a cattleman and an unemployed wharf labourer sworn in for the occasion; five black police assistants; two Aboriginal 'boys' – i.e. stockmen – and the wife of one of these.

Daniel Murnane and another cattleman came as extras who had no legal right to be in the party. It was not a small group: thirteen men, and one woman, with forty-two horses and mules. Its members were armed with rifles, shotguns and side-arms and carried four or five hundred rounds of ammunition. They kept no record of how many shots they fired nor has it ever been accurately discovered how many Aboriginal people they killed in the following days. After Daniel had been with the posse for more than three weeks, and many blacks had been rounded up, on one fateful night Daniel and two white men left their camp, accompanied by nine Aboriginal prisoners. Dismissing the trackers Frank and Charlie, they went up a ravine, but the next morning only the three whites returned. It may be to Daniel's credit that he left the posse soon after this and set out alone on the difficult overland trip of more than sixty kilometres back to Wyndham, through the red sandstone hills and then by dinghy along the Cambridge gulf. His CSIR employers in Melbourne instructed him to return by the next coastal vessel.[97]

That these killings did not remain hidden was due mainly to the Reverend Ernest Gribble, the colourful, eccentric and domineering superintendent of the Anglican Forrest River mission. Described as 'a terribly wild man', he was no paragon of virtue, having earlier been dismissed from a Queensland mission. He ran the Forrest River mission in the autocratic, even brutal way that was common through more than a century of mission enterprise.[98] But in his own tormented way Ernest Gribble laboured for the welfare of Aborigines and often defended them. He began to realise the extent of the destruction wrought by the Wyndham posse when a traumatised brother and sister, Numbunnung (Kangaloo) and Loorabane, escaped from the killers and fled to the Mission, where they told of the murder of many children and women. Gribble was determined to take the matter further, despite strong opposition from the people of Wyndham and from his bishop and the Church Mission Board.

Gribble was sure of his evidence. He had taken *Aborigines Inspector* Ernest Mitchell to Mowerie and Gotegotemerrie, two of the sites where blacks had been killed. Mitchell was sickened by gruesome discoveries of human teeth and bone fragments where the killers had tried hard to burn the bodies and crush remaining bones. Later Sulieman, another tracker who had been with the posse, guided Police Inspector Douglas to other places where prisoners' bodies had been burned in large fires. The Inspector was moved to declare 'I am not a praying man but I will now pray to God to bring the fiends that did this to justice.' Douglas followed the horse tracks in and out of the ravine into which Daniel had ridden with the other two. He saw the remains of the fire, to which timber had been dragged from all around, and thousands of pieces of bone.

The Royal Commission was restricted by its terms of enquiry: for instance, it was authorised to examine only a few, not *all* of the alleged massacre sites. After several years of investigation, it recognised only sixteen killings, but there might have been many dozens. Nothing was admitted. The judge regretfully stated that whereas he had hoped that Daniel, as an outsider, might have given helpful evidence, he had in fact 'lied like the rest of them'. The evidence is clear, despite modern attempts to whitewash the crimes, but in the absence of any admissions, it is left to our imaginations to penetrate the darkness concealing that tragedy: a night scene of horror, where the light of a bonfire played on the barrels of rifles and on the sweating red faces of men labouring at their grisly task, leaving for later investigators only an abundance of ashes and countless fragments of human bones.

18
Resisting Empire
When we need to break the law

In March 2003, when the USA and its allies invaded Iraq for the second time, I was still living in Aotearoa New Zealand. The invaders named the initial bombing of Baghdad *Operation Shock and Awe*, unintentionally admitting that it was a supreme act of terrorism against a population that had in no way harmed the invading US or its allies. As an excuse for the invasion they used the false claim that Iraq was ruled by a dictator who had 'weapons of mass destruction' and was an immediate threat to the world. Ignorant of that Muslim country's history and its culture, they also claimed that by violent invasion they could make it 'free' and 'democratic'. To gain popular support for the invasion, US leaders also stated that they were seeking retaliation for the recent destruction of the World Trade Centre, although they could show no connection between Iraq and that crime.

This last claim was the most outrageous among the lies by which they tried to justify the invasion. In fact, the young men alleged to have flown the aeroplanes into the twin towers were not from Iraq but from Saudi Arabia, a country that was and still is a close ally and trading partner of the USA and Britain. As for the tragic devastation at the World Trade Centre, lots of questions remain unanswered about whether the US government knew in advance, and whether it was in some way complicit. The timing was suspiciously opportune as an excuse for attacks on Afghanistan and Iraq, which the 'neo-cons' had long been planning.[99]

As has often happened to other countries, Iraq was invaded and its people devastated for spurious reasons. About a million Iraqis were killed; millions more became refugees, and Iraqi mothers far into the future will fear lest their unborn children are horribly deformed by the depleted uranium in weapons used by the invaders, which continue to emit radiation that has already increased the rate of birth defects and cancers.[100] The whole tragic affair was based on the lies of politicians vainly trying to conceal their greed for control of the resources of the Middle East, the spoils of that tragic war.

Not long before the invasion I had taken part in a massive march to protest against it, as had millions of people in every major city around the world. I had spoken with Dominican Sisters in Iraq who were serving a people already stricken by the war of 1991, then by twelve years of sanctions. With the Sisters I had been horrified that those sanctions had caused the deaths of about half a million children, and angered by the hypocritical claims that Saddam Hussein had to be removed because of his treatment of the Iraqi people. Evil as his actions might be, the governments calling for his removal had often supported dictators who had done worse things: Shah Pahlavi in Iran; Sukarno in Indonesia; Pinochet in Chile and dictators in other Latin American countries. When it served their own purposes, the countries invading Iraq had tolerated or assisted in the massacre of populations in Indonesia, Guatemala, East Timor and elsewhere. When Indonesia invaded East Timor in 1975, Australia and its allies had approved the atrocity, then for twenty-five years ignored Timorese cries for help while a quarter of their population were killed.

I was deeply moved and angry at these lies and injustices, and so looked for a way to protest this new invasion. With a friend from the Catholic Worker community I planned a symbolic protest in the Auckland office of the US consul, whom we visited by appointment on 24th March 2003. Only later did I realise that this was the anniversary of Archbishop Romero's murder in 1980 by the US-backed dictator of El Salvador. The Consul, Mr. Young, received us courteously and listened as we challenged him to resign over the huge injustice his country was committing against the people of Iraq.[101] In his youth, he said, he had criticised his government and sometimes took part in protests. On this occasion he had considered resigning in protest but could not or would not do so. At that point we made our gesture of protest. From beneath our shirts we each took a small plastic bag containing our own blood, previously extracted by a doctor. Ignoring his complaints, we poured it out, making a large cross on the carpet. We were prepared to be arrested, but the Consul, probably hoping to minimise publicity, continued to chat for a little longer before asking us to leave. Mildly astonished, we found ourselves out on the street, free to depart and release our prepared media statement, which was reported locally and internationally. A great many people affirmed our act of resistance, for it underlined the massive protests against the war that millions of people had recently made in every major city.

Some, including the local Catholic bishop, disapproved of our action. The Catholic Church professes to follow Jesus, who taught that the Reign of God can fully arrive only when people shun violence and war and genuinely love those we call 'enemies'. But within a few centuries of Jesus' time the Church began to collaborate with the Roman empire, which like all empires was based on ruthless violence. Since then Church leaders have often found it difficult to criticise or challenge what can be called Empire – with a capital E – because they implicitly condone its politics and have become to some degree enfolded into its structure.

Empire, in its various mutations, is any organisation that wields supreme authority. Formerly Empire ruled mainly by military conquest, but in more recent times its domination tends to be more in the economic, cultural and even religious spheres. Ruled by a small minority who assume the right to increase their power and wealth at the expense of the majority who do most to produce it, Empire ruthlessly crushes those who resist it. It thrives on conflict and typically selects an 'enemy' whom it brands as 'evil' – Jews, heretics, communists, 'terrorists', Muslims – in order to unite its own people through fear and hostility. In radical contrast, Jesus announced that the Reign of God, whenever it is realised, means the ending of conflict, with consequent freedom and peace for everyone. It was and is my conviction that each of us can choose to resist Empire in various creative ways, not least by forgiving and loving those who seem to be our 'enemies', even as we take action to resist the evil that they commit.

I had been awakened to Empires' cruelties when I learned that the appalling punishment of crucifixion was not inflicted only on Jesus, as some Christians might think, but was an extremely common way by which that empire controlled conquered populations. Before killing Jesus, Pontius Pilate had already crucified thousands of people to maintain the 'Roman Peace' in Judaea.

Empire always seems to run on corporate murder and by laying waste to the Earth's resources for the benefit of the powerful few. I had learned that the main concentration of Empire in our era is the United States of America, as was evident from its war in Vietnam; its connivance in overthrowing the Allende government in Chile in 1973 and many other governments; its role in Guatemala where Sister Dianna Ortiz was fearfully tortured[102] and other examples. It was ever ready to use its unique military power to destroy even ordinary, non-political people who stand in the way of its concern to protect its 'interests'.

Like many others, my fellow-protester and I recognised that the Empire's invasion of Iraq was an evil of enormous magnitude. We grieved for those millions who would soon be killed in the invasion, see their homes destroyed or be forced to flee as refugees. We hoped that in a small way we spoke for the Iraqi people whose country was being devastated. This hope was confirmed for me when I was sent an email that moved me as much as any message I had ever received. A young Iraqi woman whom I hardly knew wrote: 'Thank you for sharing your blood with my people.'

Our protest made an impressive impact, but of course the war went on. It was painful to watch daily hints – albeit heavily censored – of the Iraqi people's sufferings. The following year came the revelations of widespread torture at Abu Ghraib prison. 'Our side' was doing exactly what we claimed as the reason for removing Saddam Hussein. Yet again, the lies of Empire were exposed. The gospels had taught me that our neighbour's distress is our concern: we cannot look the other way. I often asked myself whether by remaining silent I was tacitly accepting the evils being committed: was my inaction a kind of collaboration? 'Someone should do something! ... If not me, then who?' But in what other practical way could *I* resist?

Long before I was ordained, I had determined not to become a priest whose whole life was centred on the sacristy, or who conformed to the generally middle-class attitudes and standard of living in the average Australian or New Zealand parish. This intention, and my choices to give time to matters other than ceremonies, ritual and parish administration, may have hindered my effectiveness as curate or pastor, but I believed that the Dominican friars were founded to contemplate and preach the Word of God not just from the viewpoint of the Church as institution, but also in the much wider world context. Dominic Guzman, our founder, had radically changed and extended the institution of monastic life, making it more democratic and mobile. He had centred his men in the newly growing cities and universities to influence society towards the truth as he knew it. In today's world, how could I pretend to be speaking truth if I did not turn my attention and compassion towards the majority of the people who are pushed to the margins and exploited by the powerful few who use the instruments of war and financial manipulation? Jesus declared himself to have come 'to bring good news to the poor ... to proclaim release to the captives ... to let the oppressed go free' (Luke 4:18). Shouldn't the priest's voice be drawing attention to this, even by prophetic action when possible?

Later I would find myself agreeing wholeheartedly with a statement by Professor John Maloney, a former priest from Ballarat:

> The hand of death lies heavily on any society where the sacred voice of protest is stifled. The voice of the priest must be raised

in protest, even though he may be a sad and lonely voice. This is the role of the priest, and therein lies his glorious challenge.[103]

I had studied the nonviolence of Jesus whose last command to his followers was to reject violence: 'Put your sword back into its place; for all who take the sword will perish by the sword' (Matt 26:52). When he angrily threw the money-changers out of the temple,[104] Jesus was not just attacking a few stall-holders but was symbolically opposing as 'a den of robbers' the whole *system* of the temple economy. He was also challenging the Roman Empire, which appointed the high priest who administered the temple and its taxation. This is why he was charged with sedition and condemned to be murdered on a cross, the usual way that Rome terrorised the poor into submission: 'We found this man perverting our nation, forbidding us to pay taxes to the emperor, and saying that he himself is the Messiah, a king' (Luke 23:2).

I had long been impressed by Gandhi's insight – which he learned partly from Jesus' teaching – that the power of truth, *satyagraha*, is much stronger than the physical force wielded by Empire, and I found new inspiration from the writing of James Douglass, a member of a Catholic Worker community, who suggests that we are all involved in humanity's liberation.[105]

As the war in Iraq went on through 2004, news emerged of more war crimes. In defiance of international law Iraq's essential infrastructures had been destroyed yet again, leaving people without electric power, clean water and sewage treatment. Depleted uranium weapons were still being used. This all increased my desire to resist. Some friends in a Catholic Worker community had been taking part in annual protests against the Waihopai Valley spy base near Blenheim, which we knew was contributing to the war in Iraq, so several of us considered making a more substantial protest there. We set out to learn as much as we could about it, especially from the book *Secret Power* by investigative journalist Nicky Hager.[106]

When built in 1986 the Waihopai Valley base was the latest tool of the worldwide network known as the Five Eyes, which since the 1940s had linked New Zealand with the USA, UK, Canada and Australia in collaborative spying on international radio traffic. With the coming of satellite communications, the Waihopai base provided the essential Pacific link in the group's worldwide listening network. Operated by the Government Communications Security Bureau (GCSB), it continuously shares its espionage with the National Security Agency (NSA) in Washington DC. We found that through its listening at the Waihopai base the NSA was gathering information needed for the Iraq war and the so-called 'war on terrorism'. It could locate people for the CIA to capture and send to be tortured at secret 'black sites' outside the USA, or to target and kill them – and often their families as well – by missiles launched from drones. Few people in New Zealand knew that the Waihopai base existed, let alone that it was New Zealand's link with the Pentagon, collaborating closely in the illegal Iraq war in which 'neutral' Aotearoa New Zealand had no official part.

A group of us began discussing whether we could conduct a Ploughshares Action at the base, in the tradition of previous protests in the USA, Ireland and the UK. These actions had symbolically disarmed weapons of war such as nuclear submarines, nuclear missile silos and the military aircraft that refuelled in neutral Ireland on their way to war in Iraq. Ploughshares protesters quote the text of Isaiah (Isa 2:4) in which the prophet dreams that humanity will 'turn their swords into ploughshares and their spears into pruning hooks ... neither shall they learn war any more.' After symbolically disarming a facility, Ploughshares protesters wait to be arrested, intending to use their subsequent trial and even their imprisonment to bear witness against the illegitimacy and folly of war.

A group of us discussed a possible protest, and three of us felt free enough to take an active part: Sam Land, 24 and as yet unmarried; Adi Leason, 44, who supported his wife and six children from an organic garden and part-time teaching; and myself, an ageing friar of 67. Although Sam and I were relatively free, if Adi were jailed, his family could suffer serious consequences. Sam and Adi belonged to *Catholic Worker* communities, whose members in several parts of the world had also inspired me by their radical way of living the challenge of the gospels. For my part, I had indicated to our Provincial Prior that I was intending to make a protest which might lead to my arrest. He generously saw that it might be prophetic.

For some months we discussed our plans for a non-violent action, and decided to unveil one of the base's huge antennae which are each concealed under a 30-metre inflated plastic dome. By deflating one of these with a sickle, we hoped symbolically to expose to the New Zealand people how their government was secretly supporting the Empire's terrorism. We were determined that our action would place no person in danger, but we knew that by damaging property we would be risking a term in jail. The Common Law allows that some more important obligation, such as saving life, can override laws protecting property, and we also knew that the higher moral law can sometimes even *oblige* us to break lesser laws. We hoped that a jury would see this, and that our trial might help the populace in general to understand how they were unwittingly complicit in the horrors of Iraq's destruction. We hoped that we might hinder, however briefly, the crimes in which the base was collaborating.

As our planning moved forward, we learned that the base was protected by formidable security: a double fence, four and a half metres high, of which the outer barrier was electrified and the inner protected by infra-red beams. Within the base a third fence surrounded each of the two domes. Cameras were everywhere, and the perimeter was regularly patrolled. Believing that we could not go *through* these barriers we sought a way to go over them, so bought an old truck with a hydraulic crane-arm on the back, and attached a simple wooden device that would support two of us while the third lifted us over.

We planned that in the early hours of April 30th 2008 Sam would place an extra padlock on the main gate of the base to delay the entry of the police if they arrived before we had completed our task. Meanwhile Adi and I would bring the truck through an adjoining vineyard, then up to the outer fence. As midnight passed, we thought our plans were going well. We were pleased that the rain that had been falling for several days was diminishing, but did not realise how difficult it would make our task. The clay track through the vineyard was so slippery that in slowly turning a corner the heavy truck escaped Adi's control and slid into a deep ditch. We tried desperately to extricate it but it was impossibly bogged and we saw that our months of preparation were now made useless. At this point I felt emptied of all resources; hopeless. I had found in the past that at such a point we can reach some deep, silent level in our heart from which can come surprising results. I gave voice to what I felt, and found myself saying aloud, with absolute conviction: 'God, we have nothing!'

By this time Sam had rejoined us, and as we stood in the continuous rain, some impulse led us to decide to continue on foot and try to do what we had already judged could not be done – to break through the fences using the simple tools we had with us. At the first fence, with its alarm and multiple wires carrying 40,000 volts, we seemed somehow to agree that as the oldest, with fewer present commitments or future prospects, I had less reason to be concerned about injury, so I took the wire-cutters. They had rubber hand-grips, but my hands and body were soaked by the rain, so I was prepared for a shock similar to that from a cattle-fence. On cutting the first wire I was delighted to feel no shock at all, so cut five more, enough for us to scramble through. Although sparks leaped around some of the fittings, we felt no electrical shock ourselves. Even more surprising, the alarms failed to work, or at least we could hear none and no guards appeared.

As we prepared to cut the second fence, I assured Sam beside me that the alarms would surely sound when our bodies blocked the infra-red beams. We cut through that fence too, but again, nothing. Inside the base now, we ran joyfully across the grass to the nearest dome which loomed huge in the glare of the floodlights. The circular fence around it was made from vertical rods, about a centimetre thick. Sam produced the bolt cutters which he had been complaining were needlessly large and heavy. He now found that if he had not made that 'mistake' of buying the maximum size we would have got no further. The large cutters bit easily through the bars and at last we could touch the domes that from a distance had so long fascinated us and other protesters. Exulting, Adi and Sam cut and slashed with their sickles, throwing aside all caution as they shouted out the names of groups of victims who had suffered in the war in Iraq.

A strong wind rushed from the deflating dome, making it difficult for me to set up a small shrine from a carton covered by a red cloth and bearing icons and a lighted candle. We hung banners on nearby fences, photographed the scene and knelt to pray for the victims of the Empire's terrorism. We continued our vigil of prayers and hymns while waiting to be arrested, for it was some time before the first guard, a rather frightened woman, found us. She stood back, nervously watching these three wild-looking and muddied intruders but became calmer when we laid our sickles near her, handle-first. Having completed our work, we also gave her the key to our padlock on the front gate. When at last the police arrived we were questioned, then loaded into their van and taken to the Blenheim police cells.

We applied for bail that afternoon, but neither the police nor the judge could grasp what we had done nor fit us into any category among their usual captives, so bail was refused and we had to wait five days before another judge visited Blenheim. The police had confiscated all our outer clothes, so their paper overalls and short prison blanket were poor protection against the frosty nights and the freezing air ducted constantly into our cells. My colleagues chose to fast from all food until our release, but fearing to lose too much strength, at each meal-time I ordered bread and water *a la carte*. We found that even behind bars it is possible to be joyful and profoundly free. We were allowed a few phone calls, and some good local people brought us clothing from the Salvation Army shop, and Bibles. At our second bail hearing – this time nationally televised – we appeared in court in our op-shop clothes, at which we were scorned by a high-salaried media 'personality' for not wearing well-ironed shirts. For him, this was the only criterion by which to measure our credibility. This time we were released, but on strict conditions: not to associate with each other; to report twice weekly to police, and not to approach closer than 100 metres to the spy base or any military installation.

Our excellent lawyers worked hard to have our trial transferred to Wellington, for in the small town of Blenheim many people worked for the spy base or the nearby air force base, and it might be difficult to convince any jury convened there that our action was anything other than vandalism against military property. It was two years before our case was heard in the capital, where judge and jury listened well to evidence about our motives. After eight days the jury acquitted us, but because the media covered only the beginning and end of the trial, many people were displeased that after 'wasting tax-payers' money' we were acquitted. Such critics failed to understand that the New Zealand government, through the base, had been breaking international law by helping the US government to wage war in Iraq, capturing people to be tortured and killing civilians in drone strikes. Nor did they pause to ask whether the base and the GCSB are worth the cost to the taxpayer of more than NZ$40 million each year, of which no detailed account is given.

Seven months after our acquittal the GCSB tried to sue us in a civil case for NZ$1.2 million, which they claimed was the cost of restoring the dome. We appealed twice against this, but were rejected at each level. We then appealed to the Supreme Court, but before we got there the government quietly dropped their case. One reason for this was that they had recently been caught and penalised for spying illegally on private citizens, despite repeatedly denying that they were doing this. Another reason was that they knew, as we knew, that to win their case they would have to refute our accusations of their wrongdoing by revealing in court some details of what the base actually does. This they would never do.

To what extent did we awaken the public to the destruction caused by this instrument of Empire? Who can tell? Part of the public feedback – probably about one third – saw the point of our action and supported us. Another third was openly hostile. Friends said they found that doubters were easily convinced of the value of our action when it was explained to them. We ourselves experienced many unforgettable, joyous moments: when released from prison on bail; when the jury of ordinary people acquitted us because they accepted our beliefs and our right to protest against the government's illegitimate acts; and when at last the government itself dropped the civil suit, thereby implicitly admitting that they habitually conceal illegal activities from the people who elect them.

To protest against the actions of Empire, as we did in the office of the US Consul and at the Waihopai spy base, one has to cross a line or pass through an archway that divides the world of legality and 'respectability' from that of the outlaw. Crossing this line brings more than a surge of adrenalin. At a certain point during planning sessions when we made the decision to go forward with either action, I vividly recall a kind of awed awareness that I was about to step across this boundary line and do what most people would see as socially outrageous. I was choosing to break strong social conventions that divide the 'acceptable' from the disreputable, not to mention that we would be damaging that sacred thing, property. This feeling returned as we walked down the street towards the Consul's office in 2003, and five years later, as we approached the security fence of the spy base an hour before dawn on a chilly autumn morning. Although I knew many would condemn me for what I was about to do, I felt a calm determination. For reasons that were valid in my own judgement I was descending into a new level of my self; entering more deeply towards the centre. I was in a place where I felt that nothing could divert me from what I was about to do, or could harm me after I had done it.

Our action did not cause the base to be closed, but for a time we stopped one of its antennae from functioning. During the fifteen months before it was covered again some colleagues were able to measure the angles of its tilt and so calculate which satellites it was listening to. But the surveillance continues at increasing rates and private citizens are spied on more than ever. Every day the Empire engages in murder and torture; threatens to destroy our human family by the madness of its nuclear weapons and to ruin our planet by its ecological irresponsibility. Despite this, we can resolve – as can any compassionate person – to resist it. The situation of each of us is well described by Albert Camus' challenging words: 'Perhaps we cannot prevent this world from being one in which children are tortured, but we can reduce the number of tortured children.'[107]

19
Beyond the Last Archway
The doorway of death

My older brother and I are standing at the sink, in the kitchen of our home in Bendigo, drying the dishes as our mother washes them. It is 1946 and I am about six years old. She tells us that a telegram came this morning to tell Dad that his aunt has died. I am drying a green eggcup, shaped like a squatting rabbit with a basket strapped to its back. The rabbit is grinning stupidly and showing two buck teeth. There are matching eggcups of red and bright yellow but this is my favourite. Its pale pastel is a deeper pea green in the creases and hollows, and one of these is at the bottom of the eggcup, inside the rabbit's stubby tail. I peer into the dim interior, and see a bright pinpoint of reflected light there. I try to reach it by poking the end of my finger into the green dimple and enjoy the smooth, glassy feeling.

My brother starts to talk about heaven, for as Catholics we know that after you die you go to another place where people never get sick or die any more. We swap ideas about what Dad's auntie is doing now, and what we will do when we go there. I wonder out loud whether there are rabbits in heaven, and think that there are, and all the other animals too, but the rabbits probably don't get killed by dogs, and the wild animals won't hurt you. We wonder whether people in heaven can travel anywhere they like, without having to pay for tickets? My brother, who is now in Grade Four at the Marist Brothers says they only have to think about a place, and they are already there. I am confused by that idea, so I say they can't; but he is already wondering if we will meet famous people, like the ones in his history book. I'm not interested in that, because I don't know any famous people, except a few in the Bible stories.

I know all about dying. We saw a dead dog in the gutter once, on our way to school, and I've seen lots of dead birds. I like watching Dad kill a chook for Sunday dinner or Christmas, chopping its head off with the axe at the wood-heap and hanging it up to drain out the blood. Mum sometimes talks about her own little brother Bert, who was killed by a car a long time ago, when she was a girl. She always tells us about him when she warns us to be careful crossing the road.

It is good to know that all these people are still alive in heaven, but I start to have doubts about the chooks. I'm looking forward to going there, but I don't like to think about the other place, where you go if you die with bad sins on your soul. It's horrible to imagine people being burned in the fire for ever and ever.

Our Mother is listening, but is becoming impatient with our chattering. She is a 'convert'; that means she became a Catholic when she married Dad. I wonder, does she believe yet all the things that Catholics have to believe, or does it take time, like learning to ride a two-wheeler bike?

༄

Was it because I was formed in this solid, too-literal, Catholic belief in life beyond death, that I had a relaxed view of what is involved at our passing out of life? Did this belief also lead me, as a youth, to a too-casual view of risking injury or even death? Each day in my secondary years we rode the suburban trains to school. When it was crowded I liked to stand braced in the open doorway as we rattled along viaducts and soared across bridges, high above the traffic passing below. In the 1950s, doors that closed automatically were only in science fiction stories. With one hand clutching the brass stanchion and the other gripping a gladstone bag heavy with schoolbooks, I loved to feel the wind blowing through my short-cut hair.

In mid-teens I discovered snorkel diving. Since I rarely saw school friends during summer holidays, I would sometimes ride alone the twelve kilometres to the nearest of Melbourne's bayside beaches. I delighted in viewing the underwater world through a glass face mask. I was not a strong swimmer, but the snorkel simplified this: floating belly down, my breath came easily through the tube clenched between my teeth while I could gaze uninterrupted on the scene beneath. Swimming beyond the line where the floor of the bay dropped away suddenly, I would quiver at the green depths where flickering shafts of sunlight disappeared out of sight.

I knew that each summer, somewhere on Australian beaches, it often happened that someone was 'taken by a shark', as the local expression put it. I sometimes wondered if a shark might be gliding up behind me and I would feel a brief shiver of terror, but quickly pushed away the thought. The joy of swimming in the crystal-clear water was too good to give up for a remote risk of death, no matter how horrible.

Even in childhood I loved to climb. During a visit to an uncle's farm, when the adults were busy with the milking I decided to climb the windmill that pumped water for the dairy. It had easy steps and hand holds, and I climbed quickly. Not far above my head I could see the circle of iron blades spinning rapidly in the strong breeze, but I knew not to climb near them. My uncle happened to look up from the cow yard below, and like any wise adult, instantly saw the possibility of a child gruesomely mutilated, but his angry shout commanding me to come down at once hurt much more than any fear of danger.

In our final years at school some of my friends and I would get casual Christmas work on the night shift at the General Post Office. During a break we would sometimes wander up to the roof, seven storeys above the street. We could dimly see the cars parked below or moving beneath the street lights. With the brash confidence of youth I began to walk around the wide parapet and stand with my toes projecting over the edge. Was I driven by youthful energy, not yet controlled by prudence, brash ego wanting to prove itself? Was part of my psyche 'half in love with easeful death'?[108]

On a coastal holiday around the same time, an uncle took us to a promontory not far from the house where he and my father had grown up. We were going to drop baited crayfish pots from the cliffs. In the fading light of dusk I followed my uncle as he walked, upright, across a narrow col carrying the ropes and wire pots. On either side of us scree slopes slanted down to cliffs that dropped sheer to the waves below. My older brother and a cousin watched us, horrified, then immediately sat down, unwilling even to inch their way across on their buttocks.

My teenage mind was intrigued by death. In books and movies about war or gangsters, when someone's smashed body has fallen 'in a hail of bullets' and lies dead on the street or battlefield, did their mind go out like a light, or was it true that it survived and slipped through some last doorway? If so, what mysterious state did they move into? My strong fascination probably matched that stage in my youthful journey when I was trying to establish what and who I was, when even adult life still lay beyond an archway through which I could not yet pass.

In my 21st year this fascination increased when I met a man who was actually approaching his end. I was in hospital for a minor operation, but in the bed beside me was a Christian Brother, an acclaimed teacher, who had been diagnosed in early middle age with a lethal cancer and had only a few months to live. Each day I overheard his conversations with medical staff and visitors, showing that he was well on the way to accepting his imminent death. He spoke of the many tasks and commitments that had filled his busy days, but which he now calmly passed on to others, one by one. His attitude deeply impressed me, more so because at the time I was struggling with difficult philosophical studies presented by dull teachers, and secretly envied him that he would soon pass through to some wonderful state of freedom that, I was now convinced, far outshone this present life. I was learning that although many people greatly fear death and try to keep all thought of it from their minds, others can face it peacefully and even welcome it. In adult years, I have watched a number of people labour towards their last breath and then, when they have taken it, lie quite still. Each time I have felt moved to ask: 'Where is she now?' We know almost nothing about what follows.

Trying to provide a guide to that territory the Egyptians and Tibetans each wrote a *Book of the Dead*, and every culture has developed funeral rites, not only to help the living express their grief, but also definitively to send off their dead so that they will not linger to harm the living. Elaborating on hints in the biblical texts, we have invented many metaphors to speculate about death, from pearly gates to purgatory's fires, but know in our hearts that these archways are all constructed from materials familiar to us, and don't really tell us much about what happens after our last breath. Shakespeare made the simple point that death is a country 'from whose bourn no traveller returns'.[109] Almost two thousand years earlier a biblical poet wistfully warned young people that ahead of them lay deafness, weak muscles and final physical disintegration:

> 'Rejoice in your youth, you who are young ...
> before evil days come ...
> when the sound of the mill is faint,
> when the voice of the bird is silenced...
> when to go uphill is an ordeal
> and a walk is something to dread ...
> before the silver cord has snapped,
> or the golden lamp been broken,
> or the pitcher shattered at the spring,
> or the pulley cracked at the well,
> or before the dust returns to the earth
> as it once came from it ...'
>
> (Eccl 11:9, 12:1, 4-7. New Jerusalem Bible)

Death's doorway is mysterious in many ways. Do we even know exactly the point at which we have passed through it? When is a person is truly dead? The threshold was once thought to be crossed when our heart stopped beating, and no breath fogged a mirror held to our face. Every day now people are revived long after those functions have ceased. So death does not seem to consist in our organs reaching 'flatline' on an oscilloscope. Even the brain – for some persons who have died in extreme cold have revived when warmed up again after many hours. A doctor friend, with long experience in intensive care, told me that it would be dangerous and in fact impossible to try to define the moment of death in legal terms.

It was in the late 1970s when I first heard that many people who been 'clinically dead' but then revived report experiences of a psychic or spiritual nature. I was deeply interested. One cardiologist found that about forty percent of the people he revived have this so-called Near-Death Experience (NDE). He had been sceptical about the phenomenon until he began actively to question and survey his patients. Those who had been 'out of their body' while their brain and heart had ceased to function could often give precise details of what they had 'seen' and 'heard' the doctors and nurses doing during that time, even describing in detail the various instruments used by the medical team. On the other hand, patients who had no such experience during their clinical 'death' could describe only sketchily, if at all, the operating theatre and its procedures, relying on their general knowledge and on guesswork.[110]

This seems to show convincingly that some persons, when clinically 'dead', learn new things they could not possibly have acquired through their senses. One woman undergoing brain surgery had her eyes taped shut and ears plugged and her brain drained of blood to enable surgeons to repair a blood vessel. On waking, she correctly described instruments used by the doctors and conversations between doctors and nurses, which she had observed when 'out of her body'.

Blind people experience NDEs. About 80 per cent of these have shown that they 'saw' their physical surroundings. Vicki Umipeg was one of more than thirty blind persons that Dr Kenneth Ring and Sharon Cooper interviewed.[111] She was born blind, her optic nerve having been destroyed, yet her NDE was similar to those of people whose vision was sound. After a car accident she found herself floating above her body, near the ceiling of the emergency room, watching a doctor and nurse working on her body which she recognised as hers only by her distinctive wedding rings. She found herself going up through the many floors and ceilings of the hospital until she was above the roof of the building and saw a brief panoramic view of her surroundings. She found this ascent exhilarating and tremendously enjoyed the freedom of movement. This was the first time she had 'seen', and known what light is. She admitted, as did some other blind people interviewed, that at first she found it foreign and disorienting, like hearing words in an unknown language.

After rising through and above the hospital, Vicki felt she had been sucked head first into a tube and was being pulled up into it. The enclosure was dark, but she was aware of moving toward light. She then 'rolled out' to find herself lying on grass, surrounded by trees and flowers and a vast number of people in a place of tremendous light which could be felt as well as seen. Everything she saw was made of light, '... and I was made of light'. The light somehow conveyed love. She became aware of five people she knew in life welcoming her. Two of these, Debby and Diane, were blind schoolmates who had died at ages eleven and six. In life they had both been profoundly retarded, but here were bright and beautiful and vitally alive, 'in their prime'.

In this rapture, Vicki felt '... everything made sense ... that ... I would find the answers to all the questions about life ... about the planets ... about God.' Near her she saw a figure far more radiant than any other person. She recognised this to be Jesus, who greeted her tenderly but told her telepathically that she could not stay, but must return to life. Vicki was extremely disappointed. She was reassured that she would come back, but needed to learn and teach more about loving and forgiving, and to have her children. At that time childless, she did want to have children, and later gave birth to three.

The authors Ring and Cooper suggest that a person's awareness during an NDE is 'transcendental' for it involves multisensory knowledge, seeing sometimes from many angles at once. Their findings, and other research, show that in clinical death the person can function at a level quite independent of their senses, but that what they report can later be reinterpreted only in terms of normal sensation.

The Near-Death Experience was known and described in the literature of previous ages. Plato's *Republic* relates the myth of Er, who visited the Afterlife and awoke on his funeral pyre. The myth strongly resembles accounts given by our own contemporaries, and has all the indications of originating in someone's actual Near-Death Experience.

In one of his letters Saint Paul describes in the third person his own out-of-body experience:

> I know a person in Christ who fourteen years ago was caught up to the third heaven – whether in the body or out of the body I do not know; God knows ... such a person ... was caught up into Paradise and heard things that are not to be told, that no mortal is permitted to repeat (2 Cor 12:2-4).

Possibly he had this experience at Lystra, when he was stoned by a mob and left for dead (Acts 14:19).[112] In his *Dialogues* Pope Saint Gregory the Great (c. 540-604) taught the soul's immortality, the reality of post-mortem punishment and the efficacy of Masses and pious works to help the dead. As 'proofs' he used deathbed visions and eyewitness accounts of the other world.[113] Did these originate in some persons' actual Near-Death Experiences? Among the many anecdotes he used, several became favourites of medieval readers. In one a hermit, revived from death, testified that he had been to hell. Just as he was being dragged into the flames, an angel in shining garments came to his rescue and sent him back to life with the words, 'go back, and consider carefully how you live from now on.' After he had returned to life, the hermit's fasts and vigils were popularly taken as evidence that he had indeed been transformed by his otherworld journey.

Bede the Venerable, in his *Ecclesiastical History of England*[114] relates the story of a Northumbrian man who around 696 A.D. had a serious illness and 'died' one evening, but revived at dawn and suddenly sat up. During his hours of apparent death, he was led by one with 'a countenance full of light, and shining raiment'. They came to a broad and deep valley of great length, where the souls of persons who had repented only on their deathbed were tormented by flames and violent hail and snow. They next came to the real hell: a dark pit from which flames were rising, and 'a stench, foul beyond compare'. He saw 'evil spirits' dragging souls into the pit.

He was next led to a place full of brightness and the fragrance of blooming flowers, where innumerable companies of people clothed in white were rejoicing. These were people waiting to go into heaven, a place even more delightful. Reaching this, the man was told by his guide that he must now go back to live again among people. Most unwillingly, he found himself alive, but like persons who have returned in our own time, he changed his life significantly, becoming more helpful to others. He settled his affairs, then lived austerely as a hermit, known as Brother Drythelm, near a monastery on the river Tweed.

There are many similar stories from medieval Christian sources telling of persons who returned from a visit to hell, purgatory and heaven and subsequently lived better lives. No doubt they were developed and used by religious teachers to educate and edify the populace. Possibly they were also used to maintain clerical power over hearers and so strengthen the authority of the Church, but despite these probable dubious motives they are so similar to Near-Death

Experiences recorded today that it is safe to conclude that they are based on some persons' actual experiences, and are not mere literary inventions.[115]

⸻

Reports of Near Death Experiences can be found during the eighteenth century, but not surprisingly there are more frequent references to it in the more abundant publications of the nineteenth. One happened to a Mr. John Brown (b. 1817) who fell ill:

> ... I could not speak ... my eyes could no longer see ... my limbs were useless ... my breath had almost stopped, but I heard and knew all that was said and done ... I heard the doctors say, '... he will not move again; he is dead.' ... In the distance I began to perceive a lighter ... spot in the darkness. ... this light gradually increased in size ... till finally it filled the room ... It was not like the light of our sun [but] more white, more still. It appeared to carry with it a life principle ... I found myself ... above my body ... With no effort ... I moved off ... and stood upon my feet ... I could see [my body] on the bed ... others ... seemed to go right through me ... all at once I was raised by a power, unseen by me ... and seemed to soak back into the body which all had pronounced dead ... I was alive ...[116]

From the late 1960s there was a marked increase in publications about the Near Death Experience, with research and publications by Celia Green in Oxford and later by J-B Delacour and Raymond Moody.[117] With today's more frequent resuscitations the experience is occurring more often and through worldwide communications is becoming more widely known. When I first read about the NDE in the late 1970s I was amazed and fascinated. Here, it seemed, was clear evidence, visible proof of dimensions and life beyond death. Its authenticity is shown by the way an NDE changes the lives of those who encounter it. They generally re-order their lives, becoming more eager to learn and more willing to serve others. They also lose much of their fear of death and look forward to re-entering at the end of their life the state that they have briefly experienced, although they know that suicide is not an option to reach more quickly that much-desired goal.

After recording and studying many thousands of NDEs, researchers have observed that they all include similar elements, of which some people report only one, while others recount up to a total of eight, not always in the same order. Kenneth Ring summarised these stages, by which the person in an NDE:

1. Finds that they are outside their body but fully conscious, peaceful and free.

2. Travels rapidly through a dark tunnel.

3. Sees a light at the tunnel's end.

4. Meets a person(s) who has died earlier, often a family member or even some previously unknown ancestor.

5. Approaches the light and finds that it contains a divine personage.

6. Experiences a universal but non-judgemental review of all the details of their life.

7. Enters into the light.

8. Reaches a boundary or barrier and is told to return so as to complete some task. [118]

In Canberra in the early 1980s I interviewed a woman who had such an experience after childbirth. She had begun to haemorrhage, was fearful and distressed and called out to her husband before falling unconscious. To her surprise she suddenly found herself alone, standing on a bush track and feeling surprisingly at peace. Naturally she decided to follow the track to see where it led, and after a time came to a bridge across a creek. On the far side of the bridge she saw a man who was unmistakably Jesus. She ran joyfully towards him, but he held up a hand commanding her to stop. She did so and received the clear message – without words, as if by telepathy – that she had to return to care for her baby and continue sharing life with her husband. The next thing she knew, she was back in her body, in great pain, being revived and attended to.

This example shows clearly that in such episodes a person perceives something beyond their normal senses and thoughts, something impossible to describe. When her body shut down, the woman moved instantly from pain into peace and joy and encountered 'Jesus'. But there *was* no bush track or bridge over a creek. She had begun to function at some deeper level of her mind or spirit, and in attempting to describe it afterwards she needed to call on pre-existing images of a favourite peaceful environment in the bush, among trees and birds, away from domestic cares. In trying to explain her real encounter with the transcendent Being she automatically chose to use images current in her religious culture: the Jesus of Scripture and of religious art. It is interesting to note that this Christian woman interpreted the Presence she encountered as Christ, but Hindus interpret it as Krishna and Buddhists as the Buddha: a telling reminder that all our dogmatic or artistic attempts to understand or describe the Transcendent are only anthropomorphism, and our efforts to depict the Infinite in dogma or art, mere childish scrawl.

People normally declare their Near-Death Experience to be 'completely indescribable', but then immediately proceed to try to describe it to any willing listener. This should remind us that their extraordinary experience happened when their body was not operating, and that the senses cannot describe it except by the available doorways of metaphor. Like the Canberra woman, they can use only the sensory images stored in their imagination. These they use to try to dress with fitting detail the real encounter they had when they were for a short while on the margins of that land from which, once the body-spirit link has been fully severed, no one can return.

When I talked with Joe Geracci in Hartford, Connecticut, in 1983, it was seven years since his massive physical collapse and profound NDE. When that happened, Joe was a middle-aged father of two teenage sons and manager of a school in Connecticut. He surprised me by saying that in his NDE he did not pass through any of the usual preparatory stages, but found himself immediately 'in the Light.' He went on to describe that there were 'many of us there', yet all seemed linked together in deep bliss and harmony. The memory of it was so powerful that Joe wept as he told me of this most sublime moment in – or beyond – his life. He did not hesitate to say that 'I was in God', but surprised me when he went further to say: 'I *was* God'.

At other times I had met mentally ill persons who made this statement, but I had no reason to judge that Joe Geracci was insane. Even as he spoke I was reaching the conclusion that this normal family man was saying no more than St Paul said when he claimed: 'It is no longer I who live, but it is Christ who lives in me' (Gal 2:20), and more than thirty times throughout his *Letters* described the Christian community as the 'body of Christ'. Jesus, before his death, promised that he and the Father would 'make their home' within the believer, making us intimate sharers of God's own energy and love, even of God's *identity*. Despite reading this in Scripture, we not surprisingly find it difficult to accept, unless, as with Joe Geracci, we have temporarily seen beyond the last archway.

The more accounts I have heard of these 'visions' that occur when the body has temporarily stopped during clinical death, the more they confirm beyond question the ancient traditional belief that we survive beyond death. They radically challenge those who interpret the world and ourselves as consisting only of 'matter'. Not surprisingly, contemporary critics have tried to explain away the NDE as hallucinations, the product of drugs, or of a lack of oxygen to the brain; or as a last desperate effort by the dying brain to 'project' some kind of consoling utopian vision.

All these doubts have been satisfactorily refuted by noting that NDEs often occur when none of the other suggested causes were present. People have experienced them in the *absence* of drugs or anaesthetics. They have experienced NDIs before the body has even been injured, as when a mountaineer was falling from a cliff, or a still uninjured person saw that a traffic collision was imminent. One psychotherapist noted that he had himself experienced dreams, hallucinations and an NDE, and affirmed that the NDE is quite different from the others.[119] Most convincing of all is the evidence – as mentioned earlier – that during an NDE people can gain information that they could not possibly have known otherwise. As well as patients who 'saw' and 'heard' the scene in the operating theatre, others have reported meeting an unknown person during their NDE and only later learned from a photograph that the person was a relative who had died before they were born. Included in this group are the many blind persons – previously mentioned – who learned new information which they 'saw' during their NDEs. It is undeniable that these experiences are true glimpses into a dimension beyond at least the initial stages of death.

There are other kinds of verifiable stories, inexplicable by the physical sciences, which point to our continuing existence on the far side of death. If they do not convince those who are imprisoned in unconquerable scepticism, at least they challenge them to produce alternative explanations. Just as impressive as the NDE are the death-bed visions studied by Haraldsson and Osis, in which dying people in their last moments see persons who have died previously summoning or welcoming them. Sometimes the vision is also witnessed by other persons nearby. These visions too can be shown to be more than subjective hallucinations, for sometimes the dying person did not know that the person appearing before them had already died.[120]

Among many lesser phenomena surrounding death, I will offer here only two from my own experience. In the Brisbane parish where I was pastor around 1990, a little girl about three years old was accustomed to carrying around an old grey T-shirt as her 'security blanket'. Her mother often washed it but felt disappointed she could never make it look clean. One day the child came into the room where her mother and grandmother were chatting as they ironed clothes. Both were surprised, not only that she was wearing the T-shirt on her head, 'like a veil', but that it was shining white, and appeared in fact to be glowing. Both remarked on it then, and much more three days later when the little girl became suddenly ill of a virus that attacked her heart, and soon died. They wondered, with reason, what or who had given them a comforting premonition that there were other dimensions to their tragic loss besides the beautiful child's departure from their household.

Near our priory in Canberra in the mid-1980s an old man lay dying in the home of his daughter-in-law. She had brought him to live with her family during his last weeks, but this generous gesture brought problems: as he lay all day on the living-room sofa his impatience and constant angry complaints made life almost unbearable for her and her family.

When I visited the family shortly before he died, his daughter-in-law was much happier than she had been earlier. She said that a day or two previously he had grumpily asked 'where's that music coming from?' Presuming that he was complaining about some neighbour's loud radio or a student practising music, she promised to investigate and deal with the offender. He grumpily replied that no, it was not a radio, but that it 'sounds like psalms' such as he had heard in Catholic churches during his youth in The Netherlands. From that point he often listened intently to the music that he alone could hear and soon became more peaceful, gentle and affable until he died a short while after.

～

Death often strikes suddenly and with devastating force. When someone we love has died and we can no longer see or touch them, it can feel as if we have lost a vital part of our own body. We urgently need some glimmer of hope, and the small predictive signs such as those mentioned, or inexplicable events surrounding a death, can offer some comfort to grieving people. Even to hear of other people's Near-Death Experience offers significant hope that life goes on, and those who themselves encounter an NDE often say that not only has it removed their fear of death: they now look forward to it. Despite the scepticism of those who have difficulty accepting the evidence, there are ample hints that when our bodily life reaches its inevitable boundary, much more lies beyond.

A prayer composed by English Dominican friar Bede Jarrett, often quoted at Catholic funerals, expresses this consoling hope '... death is only an horizon, and an horizon is nothing save the limit of our sight.' Does it matter whether we gropingly describe this hoped-for life beyond by using the name heaven, nirvana, samsara, or 'resting with our ancestors'? We have no knowledge of what it will be like, so must be content with the many hints that we will pass through into, and be welcomed by, a Transcendent Mystery. Men and women who have shared a mature love with a person who later died have often told me that they continue confidently to 'feel' that they are still at some level in contact with their deceased lover, even after many decades. They are sure that this is more than mere memory, and know by experience that our powers to love and to pray – which appear to be similar if not identical forces – transcend time and death.

In medical practice, where once death was seen as a medical failure and persons nearing their death tended to be abandoned by medical personnel, a broader, hopeful vision is creeping in. Many doctors and nurses now accept evidence that dying patients are preparing for something immeasurable and treat them accordingly. In this they are following the work of pioneers and visionaries, notably of Dr Elisabeth Kübler-Ross, who struggled to convince her colleagues to accommodate the possibility of life beyond death and was persecuted for insisting that they look beyond the material aspects of the dying human being. Galileo was not the last person to feel the prejudice of people who would not accept evidence of a revolutionary truth.

20
Doorway to the Infinite
The ultimate mystery

Where do the archways lead? We call death the last archway, but that is our usual trick of failing to face the question. If life and death are full of scattered doorways, where does this suggest we are going? Are we finite, confined in the circle of the material universe, or is there a final doorway to the infinite?

One hot afternoon in Bendigo, in 1944, I am sitting with my mother and father on the front verandah of our wooden cottage. Three unsteady wooden steps lead down to the short gravel path and the front gate in the dusty cypress hedge. My brother has just returned home from school through that gate. He starts to show us his Bible History book with a picture of Moses up on a mountain, standing in front of someone sitting on a throne among the clouds. Moses is holding two slabs with writing on them. He has a beard and is very old, but the bearded one on the throne looks even older. My brother tells us that this is God.

I listen carefully. Here is something quite new to me. I have been taught that when we say our prayers we are talking to God, but I don't really understand. I have heard many stories about fairies and giants who can do things people can't do, but I know they are only stories. I still believe in Santa Claus, who brings real presents, because when we put out a slice of Christmas cake he left only crumbs and a few white whiskers on the plate. But I feel different about this picture of God in the sky. Is he there all the time, above the world? When did he first sit there? Why doesn't that throne fall through the clouds?

The simple metaphor of that drawing took me through to a region that none of us could see, then or now, but which had enormous influence in all our lives. It introduced me to something that will never be understood by those who think that reality is limited to the world our senses show us. At that moment my mind was opened to *think* about the infinite God. I asked some questions, but don't recall what they were or how I was answered. Sometimes I look back to that spot on Earth, or rather on dilapidated verandah boards, where I thought of this profound question for the first time.

All through childhood I remained untroubled in the belief that God was 'somewhere up there', just as, far away, there was a country called China, but I took no great interest in either God or the Chinese. With a classroom full of children, I would soon be reciting answers to the first questions in the Catechism with: 'God made the world!' and I would be liking the promise of: 'God made me, to know, love and serve Him here on Earth and to be happy with Him forever in heaven!' When I began to ask where I had come from, then who had made my parents and grandparents, I was told that 'God' was at the end of the line. I still had no sense of the limitless. Like any inquisitive child I then wanted to know 'Who made God?' and was puzzled but satisfied to hear that God had no beginning: God was just there, like a giant bookend. Even in my early teens I did not venture further, nor yet try to form a concept of a First Cause, a different kind of being from all the beings it had given rise to.

In adolescence I was fascinated by an ancient carving: a neat, oval head of white, unpolished marble from the Cyclades, carved around 2,700 BC. I saw it illustrated in an art book in the public library. It was clearly a human face, but its only feature was a long, straight nose: an ancient attempt to portray God? I have since learned that archaeologists disagree about what it represents, but it struck me that the artist had found a shrewd way to avoid the problem of showing details of what God might look like.

This narrative began at a speech-night, when I was fourteen, and felt for the first time that I had passed through a proscenium arch to another world, transformed by beauty. In later years I was often fascinated by the power of that archway of theatrical make-believe and the many other doorways of imagination and metaphor which let us penetrate in different ways beyond the apparent limits of reality. Synchronicity is another such archway, far more common than we recognise, but of which we had the leisure to notice many examples during the long bike-ride from Canberra to Uluru in 2005. Towards the end of that ride, yet another example took me by surprise.

After riding for a month at average of 87 kilometres each day, we had crossed into the Northern Territory. Two more nights and we would reach our goal. Turning off the Stuart Highway at Erldunda in calm, sunny weather we pedalled westwards and around 1pm arrived at the Mt Ebenezer roadhouse. This was one of our planned stops, so even though it was early afternoon we pitched our tents in the red dust of the camping ground. For the last few nights we had camped out among the spinifex, so after enjoying our first shower in several days we settled down for a restful afternoon.

I dug out the book that I had received from my brother just before leaving Auckland: his newly-published collection of essays, *Invisible Yet Enduring Lilacs*[121] and lay back gratefully in the tent to enjoy it. The book is a work of fiction, but as I began reading the piece *Stream System* I recognised that the younger brother of the narrator strongly resembles our own younger brother Denis. The literary creation moved me deeply, even to tears. But only when I had read it to the end did it suddenly hit me that today, the 15th of September, was the twentieth anniversary of Denis' death. Not for the first time on this journey, nor would it be the last, I was stunned by the connection. Why had I picked *that* book today from among several in my luggage? Why, among all the stories, had I chosen *that* one from among its middle pages?

Our younger brother Denis had suffered brain damage at his birth. Only in her last years did my mother confide to me that the attending nurses, lacking confidence and possibly competence, had tried to delay his birth until the doctor arrived. His consequent intellectual disability must have been the greatest continuing pain in her difficult life. She was protective towards him and sheltered him as far as possible from life's rougher edges. It was probably wise for him to drop out of primary school at Grade 6, but what then? In the 1950s if there were any 'special schools' where he could develop his abilities, our parents either did not know of them, or did not trust them.

As a teenager, he began work as a labourer for a builder friend of our father, but he was not physically strong enough. Seeing him come home each day sweaty and exhausted, our mother withdrew him from that job too, and for a time he earned a small income doing piecework jobs from home. Denis had a wonderful, simple sense of humour, and entertained himself mainly by reading magazines, and occasionally travelled alone to far parts of Australia. He had no close friends but would frequent a local football club where he was accepted as a kind of mascot. Local people befriended him, like the man who owned a tiger moth aircraft who would occasionally shout him a joyride.

By his thirties Denis was finding life more and more limited and frustrating. Painfully aware that he could not do things that most other people could do, he began to express his frustration in angry outbursts. Living at home with our widowed mother, he often quarrelled with her over trivial matters. These conflicts brought their mutual frustration to such an unbearable pitch that she felt compelled to seek other accommodation for him in one caring community after another. None proved satisfactory, until she finally found a place for him in a government institution in Colac, about a hundred kilometres from her home. Each week she would make a day-return trip by train to visit him. This climax to the steady barrage of suffering that had rained down on her brought her to such a low point that she stopped attending Mass. Intense sadness had driven her to do what she once would have seen as unthinkable – she gave up on God.

In 1985 Denis contracted an infection which turned to septicaemia and he died within a few days, as much from a lack of a will to live as from the bacterial attack. He was 43. Our mother was stricken by his death, but a peculiar synchronicity was to give her some comfort. The bedroom that we three brothers had shared in each of our various childhood homes was dominated by a picture of the dead Jesus which some pious family member had given to our parents. Almost a metre high, it showed Mary holding Jesus' body in her lap after it had been taken down from the cross. The artist's licence had allowed him to show Mary's heart, pierced by seven small daggers as Simeon had prophesied. We knew the tradition listing seven sorrows endured by Mary through her life, which the Roman Catholic calendar recalled on the feast day known as Our Lady of Sorrows.

As boys, we never questioned this unfortunate choice of art. It was an example of the distorted emphases that were not uncommon in Catholic practice before the Second Vatican Council:[122] that human life was a 'vale of tears', and our best choice was to accept suffering, like Mary, as Godsent affliction. The crucifix, prominent in our home and in every Catholic classroom, reminded us constantly of the tortured death of the Son of God, a central mystery which one tradition even tried dubiously to explain as a price paid to God to make up somehow for the evil committed by the human race.

On the day after Denis' death I sat in the room he had occupied before moving out of home, beneath the same too-large oleograph that had hung on his wall through most of his life. While selecting texts for his Requiem Mass, I checked to see whether the day of his death had any particular significance in the church calendar and was amazed to realise that the day he had died, September 15th, was dedicated to Our Lady of Sorrows whom the icon portrayed. When I immediately told this to my mother, she tearfully exclaimed, 'So she [Mary] *was* watching over us after all!'

My mother's simple, anthropomorphic view interpreted in homely, human terms the realm of the Infinite Mystery. I was pleased that she found consolation in the thought that Mary understood her pain and grief, but inwardly smiled at what I imagined was her view of a very physical and motherly Mary watching millions of suffering people from some location which no one ever bothered to specify.

As an educated priest I had come to look indulgently on such pious imaginings: but had I myself come to terms with the mystery from which they had evolved? Had I dealt honestly and satisfactorily with the belief-system that I had been given as a child, and about which, one way or another, I spent my life teaching? Here, in central Australia, a book in my saddle bag and the picture it led me to remember, had become archways into the Christ, the Mystery, Providence, the one who refers to himself as the door.

From my first years of school I began to learn more about 'Baby Jesus' of the Christmas crib. The man whom history knows as Jesus of Nazareth was a unique phenomenon, an enigma, about whom controversy has raged for two millennia and shows no sign of abating. He is one of the most written-about persons in the ancient world, and several communities recorded their treasured memories of him within about seventy years of his death.

The writers of all four gospels report that before beginning his public ministry, when baptised in the Jordan river Jesus had a profound experience of being close to the Infinite One. The writers tell of a 'voice from heaven', calling him 'my beloved son' (Mark 1:10-11). When I first learned of this, I tried to imagine the impact such an announcement would have on the person hearing it.

The writers also describe a similar incident, more strikingly visible and known as his *Transfiguration*, but they are careful to show that he was an ordinary human being who felt the full range of human emotions. Reading this, I began to appreciate that he was exhausted by long hours of teaching and healing; was overjoyed at his own success when people accepted the Good News he was trying to spread, yet wept when his nation as a whole rejected it. In reflection, I tried to empathise with the fear that overcame him in the hours before his torture began and his despair as he died, his mission apparently a failure. Even John's account, which portrays him as equal to God, allows that he was tired after a journey and wept when his friend Lazarus died. As each year went by I found it easier to see Jesus as a person, and thus as someone I could relate to – he wasn't a distant God.

It was an important discovery for me to realise that Jesus often taught with humour. Jokes don't translate easily, and his have been re-rendered through at least three different languages before becoming our modern versions. Nevertheless, I could still see the humour of telling the poor that yes, rich people can enter God's realm … just as easily as a camel can pass through the eye of a needle! The over-critical are warned to notice big things wrong about themselves – like a log in their own eye – before they complain about small things like splinters that could affect others' vision. I saw dozens of such penetrating jests, each surprising us with a truth about everyday life, and each, we can still glimpse vaguely, being absurdly and deeply funny.

I have found the wisdom in Jesus' jokes to be sometimes well hidden, until the point dawns in a flash of realisation: when a Roman soldier conscripts you to carry his heavy pack, you can stop him from exploiting you by offering to carry it a second mile! (Matt 5:41). If he accepts your offer you will get him into trouble, for he will be punished for breaking his own regulations, which forbid him from conscripting peasants for more than one mile.

I could see that the apostles often found themselves trying to describe experiences far beyond anything they could comprehend. They record seeing Jesus' body at times radiant with light; walking on the waves, enabling hungry crowds to enjoy an abundant meal, empowering cripples to walk and persons born blind to see for the first time. On a few occasions he even raised up the recently dead.

Those among whom he walked knew that some other dimension had burst into their lives, and when I read about it centuries later it left me scratching my head in bewilderment.

I asked myself whether such things can be observed in our own era, when 'scientific' observation and analysis have improved, although by no means been perfected. If we enquire, we will find many healings which medical science cannot explain, such as those at Lourdes and in many other places. They usually occur in the context of prayer, especially when large groups unite to pray. Sometimes these healings include the sudden restoration of living tissue.[123]

I even heard first hand reports of the 'multiplication' of food when the poor were being fed. Such phenomena force us to wonder about the context of the mysterious nature of matter itself. Does our most advanced research know what 'atoms' consist of? Is it energy? Photons? Quarks? Electrons? Whatever matter is, and whatever quarks are, we are told that the space that matter appears to occupy is actually 99 per cent empty. How can we claim to know when or by what forces it may be altered?

Similarly, we do not know a great deal about the powers *within* ourselves, but are impressed to see these emerge in exceptional persons who focus on developing them. The gospel stories describe Jesus as able to call on healing power almost at will, and that he often drew attention to the link between healing and the readiness of a person to believe or trust.[124]

⁓

Who was he? I often pondered. While my Catholic tradition had told me that he was the 'Son of God', he most often described *himself* as the *Son of Man*, The Human One, showing that he saw himself as an ordinary person. Yet he would have known that in the vision of the prophet Daniel, a *Son of Man* came to the throne of the Ancient of Days and was given 'dominion and glory and kingship, that all peoples, nations, and languages should serve him,' (Dan 7:13-14). All three synoptic gospels record that at Jesus' trial he claimed that the Jewish leaders would: '... see the Son of Man, seated at the right hand of Power and coming on the clouds of heaven' (Luke 22:69, for example). The leaders took this claim to be blasphemous and used it to justify the death penalty.

These three writers were recalling Jesus' trial about forty years after it happened; were writing about the person they now knew as the Risen One, and trying to interpret his life in terms of his victory over death.

The fourth gospel, written a little later[125], gives us a Jesus who describes himself many times in phrases that begin with *I am*: 'I am the bread of life; ... the light of the world ... the gate for the sheep ... the good shepherd ... the resurrection ... the way, and the truth, and the life ... the true vine;[126]' and most daring of all: 'Before Abraham was, *I Am*' (John 8:58). The author well knew that in the book of Exodus, when Moses approached the bush that burned but was not consumed, The Holy One, the God of Abraham, described Himself with precisely that phrase (Exod 3:14). This gospel was stating that Jesus is *identical* with God: 'the Father and I are one' (John 10:30). This is quite consistent with the author's statement in the opening chapter: that the mysterious *Logos* or *Word* of God, which existed 'from the beginning' and 'was God,' 'became flesh' in Jesus and 'pitched his tent' among human beings (John 1:14).

To different degrees, all four gospel writers seemed on the way towards the same conclusion that theologians and Councils reached after several centuries of pondering and prayer, that Jesus was *identical in nature* to God.

The greatest challenges to me were the scenes that conclude each of the four gospels, telling of a crucified man who has come alive again? After much pondering of this question, I have no doubt that he is alive and present here as I type these words, as he is there, where you are now reading them. But I am equally certain that in that Jerusalem tomb on the first Easter Sunday morning he was not resuscitated like Lazarus. Had there been a security camera installed it would *not* have recorded his glowing corpse getting up from the stone bench and walking – perhaps flying – out past the rolled-back stone door. From the instant that new life was present in his body, he was no longer bound by our four dimensions.

On that Sunday, did Jesus take on the physical form of a stranger to walk beside those two despairing disciples on their way home towards Emmaus? Quite possibly. Is it not also possible that the two of them discovered the truth of his resurrection by meeting some *other* stranger on the road, then recognising that Jesus was actually but invisibly present in *that* person as he walked between them, and later 'broke bread' with them? Whichever way it happened, I think Luke is telling us that Cleopas and his partner had unmistakably experienced the living Christ, and had linked their experience with welcoming a stranger, reading the Scriptures and breaking bread together, and their community. This and the other resurrection stories are also parables about *our own* awakening to the real depths of human relationship, which itself touches upon mystery and infinity. Post-resurrection writers were dealing with the unprecedented; trying to describe the indescribable: how ordinary men and women became convinced that a man whom they knew was dead was now showing them that he had passed through death and was alive.

Like those who have been through a Near-Death Experience, whatever the witnesses 'saw' as a deep conviction of their spirit cannot be put into words, but they felt compelled to try, so we have realistic-seeming accounts of Jesus on the Emmaus road, materialising in a locked supper room, declaring himself not to be a ghost then seeming to eat, inviting them to touch him. They had found a practical way to describe that this human being has passed through death and is now present in every part of the universe.

Are there indications of his transcendence in the texts themselves? '... she saw Jesus standing there, but she *did not know* that it was Jesus'

(John 20:14), '... their eyes were *kept from recognising him*' (Luke 24:16), '... but the disciples *did not know* that it was Jesus' (John 21:4). He was not as he was before, nor could they relate to him in the same ways. On each occasion they eventually recognise him, as do some people during their Near-Death Experience, but their glimpses of him are brief. If we claim to know how his resurrection happened, or what he is like now, we will find ourselves worshipping an image of our own making. Not for the first time, we are offered archways of metaphor and confronted with a choice of whether or not to respond.

When I first read this possible explanation of the resurrection stories, in Edouard Schillebeeckx, my heart took a leap. I understood that the early witnesses first had the *experience* of the resurrection and then, sometime later, came the stories. This is the essence of how we use metaphor in the Scriptures. The understanding freed me from literal, dualistic belief in stories that could never be reconciled with each other or with our own modern lives.

Interested as I was in archways leading elsewhere, one claim of Jesus in John's text caught my attention: 'I am the door [or gate]. Whoever enters by me will be saved' (John 10:7, 9). I heard Catholics and other Christians using this metaphor in their efforts to 'prove' that anyone who did not believe in Jesus had no chance of being 'saved'. I thought the arguments rather stupid, that something had gone radically wrong somewhere, but I struggled to find what it was. Perhaps the absurdity lay in making a universal principle out of a here-and-now warning to those deciding whether to accept or reject Jesus during his lifetime.

I could hear Jesus telling us that his message was essential to our wider life. Those who did not come in to hear it were 'lost' – for now. Jesus' teaching invites everyone. In fact, soon after this text John reported that 'some Greeks' came asking to see him. This might have seemed to promise an opening for him to share his Good News in the Jewish *diaspora* and even in pagan lands, but he simply told them that they could become his followers and 'serve' him like anyone else (John 12:20-26), if they kept his 'law' and chose love as their principle: dying to themselves in service of others, like wheat grains, and so being 'glorified' as he was about to be. In the unlikely event of a group of Chinese or Hindus arriving at that time, surely he would have received them just as cordially. Jesus welcomed all who came to him and died for all God's children without exception.

It is reasonable to ask how, in Northern India 500 years before Jesus of Nazareth, the Buddha acquired his remarkable wisdom; and how, millennia before that, Indigenous Peoples around the world had been shaping their understanding of a right Way to live in harmony with each other and the earth. Is there any reason to doubt that it was the same Spirit of the Transcendent that Jesus promised and sent to his disciples? (E.g. John 14:16-17, 25.)

I concluded that if we begin to quarrel over what might be the 'right way' to follow him who is The Way, but whose infinity we do not begin to comprehend, we are choosing the road that leads to wars of religion, a concept more absurd than anything we can imagine.

As a young adult, I considered that having faith meant that I accepted, with not too much questioning, the stories that were given to us. I saw with a little sadness that many of my generation of Catholic students 'left the faith' either quietly or with some flair, a process that has continued for many generations before and since my own. I don't pretend to understand the reasons for their choice, except that I myself was greatly helped in continuing to believe when I learned that the language of the stories on which our faith-culture was based needed to be interpreted in metaphorical and analogical ways.

I have come to see that faith consists not only in *accepting* stories and the creeds based on them, but on finding that their Author is personal, though more than human, and beckons us. There were rare moments when, when reading the scriptures in private, or sometimes when hearing them read aloud in church, when they would sharply awaken me.

It was as if I were standing before some grand façade, like those in the ancient city of Petra, admiring the awesome architecture and pondering its history, when suddenly a door opened which I had not previously seen, and a friendly hand beckoned me to enter and learn more about the building from a person who had lived there 2,500 years before. Such a bizarre time warp would be a pale comparison to the actual experience that sometimes came from a text I had read many times before, but only now saw its link with the Risen One. My heart 'burned within me', as was said of the two grieving disciples walking back towards Emmaus when they first glimpsed the possibility that their recently crucified leader might still be alive (Luke 24:32). I was struck as if by lightening by such phrases as: 'I am the bread of life. Whoever comes to me will never be hungry ... They will live forever' (John 6:36, 40, 47; 11:27), or Jesus' intimate words: 'I have called you friends ...' (John 15:14).

Sometimes I made similar discoveries during the long hours when as friars we gathered in choir each day to chant psalms and hear the reading of texts. Occasionally a verse or a fragment of a verse would reveal to me something of its deeper meaning, even piercing my heart with the conviction of the poet who wrote nearly three thousand years ago:

> [O God] you have searched me and known me.
> You know when I sit down and when I rise up;
> you discern my thoughts from far away (Ps 139:1-2).

I was awed that the ancient poet saw that space or time could not limit God's knowledge: 'In your book were written ... all the days that were formed for me, when none of them as yet existed' (Ps 139:16).

It gradually dawned on me that I was being impressed not only by the intellectual content of the lines ... learning something more about 'God', but I was touched, deeply, by meeting the *reality* which they imperfectly described.

If love is the most intense experience that a human being can encounter, then to discover that the Ultimate Mystery has 'seen' and known me intimately during every moment of my existence, and that I can relate to it directly, is to be offered an indescribable privilege.

I began to understand that knowledge, even carefully presented in layers of metaphor, is not the only way we can grasp God. After I had joined the Dominican friars and began to learn a little theology, one lecturer told us that although our finite minds cannot form anything like an adequate *concept* of God, our will seeks union with God and 'with our heart' we can meet God's self. He compared it to being hungry or to loving someone: our desires are not content with just an *idea* of food, or a photo of the person. We are only fulfilled by uniting with real food or being with the beloved themselves.

This made me think back a few short years to when I began to take interest in some of the girls on the train and at Saturday night dances. Although my heart was not yet much involved, there was something new here. Reflecting on one budding relationship in particular; and also on my love for family and my friendship with a few good mates, I could agree that love *does* seem to join us to people in a different way than our mind does. I didn't understand what love was, but it was clear that loving people as subjects was different from knowing them as objects. The more I thought about it, the more clearly I saw that such a two-way exchange with God changes our life.

The Infinite One seems to know a lot more about this than we do. Do we have an urge within *ourselves* to draw closer to the doorway leading there? After all, our very existence must have emerged from God's 'thought', from God's own being. I recalled St Augustine's often-quoted line, his anguished cry in the *Confessions* that: 'our hearts are restless until they rest in You'. Later I was pleased to see the poet-artist William Blake saying that spirituality, our search for God, is not an attempt to block or extinguish our desires, but to fulfil them. This agreed with what I was learning in Aquinas. Around this time I was moved by Francis Thompson's poem *The Hound of Heaven*, in which he has God tell him that when he betrayed God, whom he was made for, everything else necessarily failed him:

'All things betray thee, who betrayest Me!'
... but despite all his betrayals he learned that his unknown pursuer was God, 'hounding' him with great love:
... Ah, fondest, blindest, weakest,
I am He Whom thou seekest!

Thompson knew what he was talking about, for his opium addiction had reduced him to living in utter poverty, homeless among the prostitutes and criminals of London's slums until Wilfrid and Alice Meynell recognised his genius, published his work and helped him back to health.

In my bare student's room, during long days filled with a round of prayer in choir and dull classes, I began to understand that the ancient psalmist, Augustine, Francis Thompson and so many others had been moved to write as they did not by their belief in statements about God, or their membership of a Church – conditions that may have prepared them – but by intimate personal *experience*. We were warned that it was not part of Catholic tradition to seek 'religious experience'. I had even heard senior priests preaching that we should beware of 'mysticism', for such inner experiences happened only to people who were a bit suspect. The weak pun was bandied about: 'Mysticism begins in mist and ends in schism'. I later suspected that this advice came from clerical leaders trying to protect their control over people's access to God.

Great saints like Teresa of Avila, John of the Cross, Catherine of Siena and Meister Eckhart spoke of their experiences beyond the ordinary scope of the senses, but they also warned that these are not essential, for everyone can communicate with God, with or without them. St Thomas Aquinas too, taught that we can all be intimate friends of God. He dared to call charity, or love, 'friendship with God', a tradition echoed by the Vatican Council declaring that everyone possesses the Holy Spirit and is called to have an intimate and vital link with God.

I began to see that my simple insights into a few texts might be, at a much lower level, something like the 'experience' that the saints were referring to, but also accepted that what was required was simply to love God in the daily life I had to lead, for at least in part I had chosen it for myself.

I continued to be fascinated by other people's strange experiences. The experience of Noel Ginn during World War II – already mentioned – seemed to be of this kind. Confined in a prison camp for refusing to take part in the war, he described being overtaken more than once by an inexpressible experience which he attempted to describe as:

> ... a wave of generosity ... a golden moment ... unfathomably deep, timeless ... [containing] all dimensions ... like an indescribable embrace ... the place where we ourselves fill with light, and in that light we can see through the form.

He felt as if he was being told:

> All must return to me, into my light, for I come to you through time, but am myself the timeless present. All that occurs takes place in me. Come ... I am expecting you.

Ginn knew that this experience did not come from the world his senses could see around him, nor from his own imagining, but that it was offering him some kind of relationship with 'beyond', transcending all that he knew. Perhaps he was disposed for such experiences by the harsh conditions of his prison, resulting directly from his selfless opposition to the evils of war.

If God is the pursuer, as the Psalmist, Augustine, and Thompson all claim, perhaps our ability to respond to this friendship enables us to pass through archways to the infinite where we may 'experience' deeper levels of Being. Countless people have reported experiences resembling ecstasy of different degrees, often in less cruel surroundings than Ginn's. Were they experiencing something of God? The poet Tennyson related that from boyhood he frequently had an experience in which:

> ... all at once ... individuality itself seemed to dissolve and fade away into boundless being ... not a confused state, but the clearest... surest ... utterly beyond words, where death was an almost laughable impossibility... the loss of personality (if so it were) seeming no extinction but the only true life. I am ashamed of my feeble description; have I not said the state is utterly beyond words ...?[127]

This powerful feeling has often been recounted by mystics through the centuries: *that in a radical sense all is one;* that we are all linked together and that our destiny is to be intimately and totally united with all other people, the rest of the cosmos and with its source.

In the early 20th century William James collected accounts of many such experiences from a wide range of people. He called the experiences 'religious' but pointed out that they happen independently of whether or not a person belongs to any formal religion or has any specific belief about God. People often have these mystical experiences either during long years waiting on God in prayer; being surprised by them as Noel Ginn was; or during a Near Death Experience. They know them to be encounters which radically alter their lives for the better, but which take place at some level beyond their senses.

Through these experiences they know an indescribable peace and joy that appears to come from a Power beyond the human. Many take the natural step of calling it divine.

⁓

Faith seems to be a gift, and to depend only partly on our co-operation. Sometimes people have said to me, usually when we were mourning someone who had just died and reflecting on what might follow: 'I wish I had your faith'. I accepted this as a compliment but could take no credit for its origins. Faith, with its blend of belief and trust, seems like a gift which may be improved by practice, like a talent for playing the piano or being good at tennis.

As a teenager I often used the short prayer: 'Lord, increase my faith', based on the cry of the desperate father of a sick boy in Mark's gospel: 'I believe; help my unbelief!' (Mark 9:24). It seemed sensible to ask God to strengthen the link between us, so I used this blunt and simple challenge: if God wanted me to believe more strongly, this prayer handed back the initiative.

But in those same years, arrogantly proud of my Catholic identity I tended to look down on those who 'did not have The Faith': those who belonged to other Churches, like the Anglicans, the Orthodox or the Presbyterians. I had hardly heard of faiths beyond the Christian sphere. Lowest of all were those who had 'lost The Faith' and no longer came to church or even believed in God. Only after many years of listening to these people's stories did I concede that faith takes diverse forms and is largely independent of religious practice or church attendance. I met many Catholics who could no longer 'find God' at Mass or in a church, usually for the valid reason that people representing the Church had failed to show them compassion, or its laws had prevented them from more participation in local church communities.

Many others, especially the young, were simply not satisfied by the dullness of the liturgy as they saw it, or because clerical leadership excluded them from real participation. They went their own way, perhaps putting on hold the question of faith, their spiritual search unfinished.

While some people 'drop out' for more personal reasons, the valid reasons have escalated enormously since the worldwide revelations of sexual abuse. It is my understanding that these crimes do not show Catholic clergy or religious to be worse in this matter than other clergy, or than parents. What they *do* show is that as the Church became an institution of such magnitude and privilege, demanding so much unnecessary secrecy and obedience from its officials, that abuse of 'lesser people' became inevitable, and was seen as less important than the need to protect the 'image' and property of the Organisation. Church laws – meant to support our faith – have actually helped to conceal crimes.

Catholics who no longer attend church may well outnumber those who stay. Listening to them I saw that such persons may have a deeper faith-relationship with God than many who go to church. From their pain, and their reasoned choices, I saw the hopeful fact emerging: that even for people who have survived the worst rejection and abuse, the Transcendent can later break through, unexpectedly awakening faith at new levels and in quite different forms.

⸙

Finding faith and developing it can be difficult for young people. They may struggle to decide whether they can accept literally the always-metaphorical stories; and find it difficult to respond with their will to the invitation that these contain. I read *Portrait of the Artist as a Young Man* when I was twenty-two, the age of James Joyce when he wrote it. I was deeply interested in the struggle for faith of Stephen Dedalus, the central figure. A budding poet and artist, he saw his Catholic faith as conflicting with his urge to be free to create beauty. Reading it, I seemed to hear Joyce describing his *own* conflict, which tragically set him apart from his family, friends and Church.

Trapped for a time by his youthful sensuality, Dedalus is frightened into repentance by the famous sermon on Hell, and then becomes an ultra-pious young Catholic trying to earn God's approval and love. His Jesuit mentors, impressed by his piety, invite him to join their Society, but he sees that the Jesuit cleric's life would not satisfy him. Dedalus perceives that as an artist he will have something in common with the Creator, or the priest, using 'the eternal imagination to transmute the daily bread of experience into the radiant body of everliving life'. He is determined to express himself authentically and struggles in 'the cold silence of intellectual revolt'. When his mother asks him to make his Easter duty he cannot comply but says – to a friend – 'I will not serve'. He wrestles himself free of 'the fetters of the reformed conscience', mistakenly thinking that to be free he must become independent of the Creator who gave him his artistic gifts. Although he espouses Aquinas' theory of beauty, he does not reach Aquinas' understanding that when creatures serve the Source of their being they are not diminished but fulfilled. He succumbs to our natural reluctance – not confined to youth – to give ourselves in serving another, but does not grasp that the Other is the source of our existence and its purpose.

Where others struggle with doubts *before* believing, Dedalus/Joyce has doubts about *dis*believing. He remains drawn to The Transcendent:

> I am not at all sure ... Jesus is more like a son of God than a son of Mary ... The [Communion] host, too, may be the body and blood of the son of God and not a wafer of bread. I feel that and I also fear it.

Another obstacle is eternal damnation, with which he had been threatened in horrendous detail, but he heroically puts aside his fear: 'I am not afraid to make a mistake, even ... a lifelong mistake, and perhaps as long as eternity too ...' Stephen Dedalus, like his author, felt obliged to shake off the constraints of the clerical-controlled Irish Church which had poisoned his faith by – among other things – with the false teaching of a harsh God who would allow us to be tortured in hell forever. But faith has many depths, and Joyce may not have totally abandoned it. The last words of his story seem to be a prayer to the Creator, beyond Church and all categories: 'Old father, old artificer, stand me now and ever in good stead.'

Leaving Auckland on the last day of 2011 further confirmed what I was gradually learning about faith: how much it involves 'letting go'. It was twenty years since I had arrived in New Zealand, where I had been involved in pastoral work in parishes and universities and in working for social justice. Now, at seventy-one, I was volunteering to work in the formation of young Dominican friars in the Solomon Islands.

I had cut down my possessions to about 35 kg of clothing and books. Despite the regrets of many farewells, I was surprised how free I felt in shedding many things I had thought necessary. I tried to express my joy in letters to friends and in a blog called Finding the Treasure, where I recalled Jesus' parable of one who finds a hidden treasure in a field, then uses all his resources to buy the field and possess the treasure. For much of my life I had been praying that God's Reign or Kingdom would come, in the future. I began to see more clearly that most of Jesus' stories tell about the Reign of God now. The leaven is already working in the dough; the seed is planted and sprouting in darkness; the salt and the light are already at work; the pearl and the treasure have been found. On most days I would recall this, and spent many moments being supremely grateful that in this moment I was alive.

The tropical climate in the Solomons was debilitating – more than 30°C every day, with high humidity. On the small island of Loga, where I spent the first two years, we had no fridge, and only after dark used a generator for fans and light, but such inconveniences were trivial beside the awareness that the Transcendent was within me, the 'one thing necessary'[128]. My ageing body was constantly telling me that my days were, quite literally, numbered. Barring accidents, with luck I would last perhaps past eighty: another ten years, or 3,650 days. Even if I were to last longer, the next stage of the journey was not far off and would bring the greatest adventure of my life: the journey through the gateway into Infinite Love.

This was no exaggeration: I was absolutely certain. I felt this, even as I recalled that Tillich had claimed: 'Doubt is not the opposite of faith; it is an element of faith' (Systematic Theology, Volume 2)[129]. In that part of faith involving the will's assent, as distinct from our wondering about the stories, I found myself agreeing with the much-maligned Bishop Geoffrey Robinson, who wrote: 'There is an absolute certainty of faith … that comes before words … faith in the person of Jesus Christ and in the love that fills his story'[130]. This certainty was soon to be tested more than I could imagine.

It has been in times of crisis that I have learned most about assenting to faith's invitation. When I was seriously ill with peritonitis soon after returning from the Solomons, and might soon have died, I became conscious that the one whom Martin Buber called Thou was not only real but was very near. I was left in no doubt that this Being was Personal, intimate and compassionate, more than I had ever known.

In Calvary hospital Canberra where I had sought refuge during this crisis, I was surprised to find that when challenged to step further out into darkness I was not surrendering my independence to an opponent, but was making deeper contact with the compassionate Force which was and is the origin of my own being. My attempts to trust seemed to ground me more strongly, making me more aware than before of the intimate relationship that must have begun at a primitive level when I uttered my first cry.

Early in our 'religious life', I had understood that the reason behind its monastic and penitential structures was to challenge and strengthen our faith. But this does not work automatically. It looked easy to live selflessly in close community with men who call each other 'brother', but it was a delusion to think that I had given up my independence. There *is* a true independence of conscience at the heart of our being which we must never be asked to surrender, but we can deceive ourselves endlessly that we are 'dying to ourselves' in serving the community, when we are mostly only seeking to be noticed and praised.

Even more difficult to let go, I found, were the mass of principles which we imagine are essential to our 'image' or identity. The strongest among these convictions may be religious ones: practices or words that are precious to us because we imagine they are essential links to the Transcendent. We fear to let go of them lest in doing so we might diminish our self or even 'betray God'. From these convictions fanatics are made, who cannot see validity in any other than their own chosen path. Such persons can be found among Christians and Buddhists, Muslims, Jews, and Atheists, when their mental convictions have hardened into a kind of misdirected faith, not far from idolatry. My own upbringing in the fundamentalist Catholicism of the pre-Vatican II era had caused me to cling to many apparent absolutes which later I found painful to abandon, or allow evolve into convictions modified and strengthened, I hope, by reason, humanity and mercy.

‿

Now, not far off eighty years old, I am dealing with another cancer, a lymphatic leukaemia which seems to have developed after several severe infections in recent years. This new challenge has not lessened the deep joy and peace that I feel. Like the love of a human person, there is the delight of being close to one who accepts and welcomes us despite our limits and faults. Thanking the other for their gifts deepens the beauty of our experience. I find it a sheer delight to know that the Absolute accepts me totally, even with my self-centredness and blunders, my ageing body, its sexuality, its several unpleasant ailments. Even to begin to think of the encounter that awaits beyond my death fills me with a joy deeper than any temporary discomfort or pain.

Like millions of others, I was helped to this discovery by the stories of the Judaic tradition and the Christian belief in Jesus' resurrection, but I have seen it also in people of other faith traditions. In itself, the joy is powerful evidence that there is a Transcendent dimension which can be described by analogy as a Person with whom we are in intimate relationship. Could countless multitudes, over centuries, be deluded by this? For those who struggle to see any further than the physical world, this joy challenges them: a phenomenon that takes us beyond the power of the senses and whose cause must lie well beyond what physical science can explain.

Mystics assure us that this Transcendent One is Love. I felt I was seeing another peep through to Infinity when I first heard the *First Letter of John* bluntly telling congregations: God *is* love (1 John 4:8). If it were otherwise, where did human love come from? It hardly matters how it evolved from attraction among amoebae, or desire among dinosaurs, dogs or birds. I was compelled by the conclusion that if there is not a greater Love behind it, we might as well claim that two plus two can produce five, or eight, or anything we like.[131] More than that, I was overwhelmed by the thought that all the loves known to us must be merely pale copies of that Love that is their source. When we discover that this Lover knows us fully and yet loves us without any conditions, what else could we feel but limitless joy?

Day follows day in the long wait for some progress in curing my chronic lymphatic leukaemia. I ponder more that this love cannot depend on what I am, or anything that I achieve, so I can shed, bit by bit, all fear of bodily difficulties yet to come, or of what people might think or say about me. In the abundant reflection time available, past follies sometimes flash back to haunt me: the harm I have done to others; the times when I neglected to give help when needed; but it is a total relief to know that no mistakes of mine can impede this Love in the least. To use Isaiah's picturesque metaphor, these burdens of our wrongs are tossed 'behind God's back'[132]. Although I have about twenty percent of the energy I had a few years back, this transcendent Love renews me.

In earlier years I used to scoff inwardly, just a little, at those love songs that followed Robbie Burns in claiming that human love will last beyond time.[133] Now I see that they are probably right, but there is no doubt that this Infinite Love will be eternal. This dissolves the fear that lurks behind every happiness: that it will soon come to an end, at least with our death. But when we are promised that at death we will be alive in another dimension, together with those who have gone before, who could not be seized by indescribable delight? St Thomas Aquinas called it beatitude – or eternity – and succinctly described it as 'the total, simultaneous and perfect possession of endless life'[134]. Many others have tried to put it into words, with varying degrees of success. The repentant slave ship captain John Newton, in his 1779 hymn 'Amazing Grace', famously expressed his delight in the hope of living forever in the presence of God:

> When we've been there ten thousand years,
> bright shining as the sun.
> We've no less days to sing God's praise,
> than when we first begun.

Within my own lifetime, Arthur Stace acted on this discovery in a remarkable way. In 1930 he heard a sermon that attempted to describe eternity. It so moved him that he mastered his addiction to alcohol and for the next 35 years, on several mornings each week, walked the streets of Sydney secretly writing the word Eternity in chalk. He could hardly write his own name legibly but was surprised that Eternity came out in beautiful copperplate script, an estimated 500,000 times. 'I couldn't understand it, and I still can't,' he admitted.

I treasured the statement of an early Christian writer that God became human so that human beings might become God.[135] This astonishing conclusion, straight from John's gospel[136], challenges those Christians who picture the Divine Being as remote, in a place apart. These people think that we must speak to or about God in a special language; they seem not to have found the archway that opens up when we discover the astonishing truth that God is in us, and that we become God. It seems to them like pantheism.

This is not to say that we are coextensive with God. I am not yet eight decades old; and our humanoid ancestors were first exploring African valleys just a few hundred thousand years ago. The One who caused the cosmos in which we came to birth can have had no beginning, but as these chapters have tried to show, all through our lives we are offered abundant archways leading to glimpses into this ageless One. In ways beyond our comprehension we will have access to that realm.

On most days I spend a little time hearing, reading or watching current news. It is always crammed with the suffering of many, and the gross manipulation of events in favour of a greedy few. The millions who flee as refugees or live out their lives in shanty-towns seem to have no hope, but this unfortunate majority – broken by natural disasters or the deliberate destruction brought on by the weapons of war – are not the only ones whose future is insecure. *All* future generations, even of our wealthy nations, cannot avoid the scarcely imaginable crises that are coming. We can no longer deny the science showing the melting of land-ice; retreating glaciers; gradually rising sea levels and usable water becoming scarcer. It is difficult to comprehend the damage being done to the oceans by our junk. Even the main cultural stay of my youth, the Church itself, cracks apart in many of the forms it had mistakenly devised for itself, while we wait to emerge from its broken chrysalis something more like what Jesus intended.

Do these things make me sad or afraid? Yes, in so far as they will bring suffering to countless individual people. I hope I do not turn away from any person's pain, or from weeping for the grief of anyone, or in doing what I can to help. For all are my sisters and brothers. But does such massive human brokenness and the threat of far more to come overwhelm the deep joy I feel? Not at all. The ocean's wildest surface waves scarcely disturb the water beneath. At greater depths, storms cannot even be felt. When many other peoples' enormous sufferings would churn my feelings into turmoil, or my own body feels wretchedly ill, I put this calmly beside the deep, transcendent Thou.

But how can the desperate ones find their way to this? What do they know of archways?

The wonder is that we do not have to find Infinity. With ultimate care for all that it has made, it will find us. Our metaphors of the pursuing hound, or the loving parent are trivial beside its Infinite desire. When I reflect that the Transcendent Thou that has found me is present to the most abandoned sufferer in the most extreme situation, I have no fear for their final destiny.

It is sufficient for each of us to explore the archways of our own lives. In the vistas they offer we will find that something in this earthy nature of ours promises not to come to an end, for the endpoint of all our striving, as must have been its starting point, is limitless Love.

BIBLIOGRAPHY

Some of the books that have influenced this narrative:
Aquinas, Saint Thomas, *Summa Theologiae*, [Trans. Fathers of the English Dominican Province] Benziger Brothers, New York, 1947.

Arraj, J, *The Mystery of Matter; Nonlocality, Morphic Resonance, Synchronicity and the Philosophy of Nature of Thomas Aquinas*, Inner Growth Books, Chiloquin, Oregon, 1996.

Ashkar Matta, Y, *No Stone Unturned: a Lebanese-Australian Family Memoir*, Brisbane, Yvonne Ashkar Matta, 2016.

Baxter, A, *We Will Not Cease; The Autobiography of a Conscientious Objector*. Cape Catley, Whatamongo Bay, Queen Charlotte Sound, NZ, 1980. [First published, 1939.]

Blomfield, G, *Baal Belbora: The End of the Dancing. The Massacre of a Peaceful People; The Agony of the British Invasion of the Ancient People of the Three Rivers; The Hastings, the Manning and the Macleay, in New South Wales*, Sydney Alternative Publishing Co-operative, 1988.

Blum, W, *Killing Hope: U.S. Military and C.I.A. Interventions Since World War II*, Common Courage Press, Monroe, Maine, 2008.

Boros, L, *The Moment of Truth*, Burns & Oates, London, 1965.

Buber, M, *I and Thou*, Scribners, New York, 1971 (1923).

Burrows, R, *Before the Living God*, Continuum, London, 1975.

Clark, I D, *Scars in The Landscape, A Register of Massacre Sites in Western Victoria, 1803-1859*, Australian Institute of Aboriginal and Torres Strait Islander Studies, 1995.

Chossudovsky, M, *America's War on Terrorism*, Global Research, Montreal, 2005.

Conlon, G, *In the Name of the Father*, 1993. Motion picture directed by Jim Sheridan, screenplay adapted by Terry George and Jim Sheridan from Conlon's autobiography: *Proved Innocent: The Story of Gerry Conlon of the Guildford Four.*

De Bono, E, *I'm Right, You're Wrong*, Viking, New York, 1991.

Delacour, J-B. *Glimpses of the Beyond: The Extraordinary Experiences of People Who Have Crossed the Brink of Death and Returned*, Harwood-Smart, London, 1975.

Douglass, J, *Resistance and Contemplation*, Delta, New York, 1973.

Earl Grey Surgeon's Log.

See: https://jenwilletts.com/convict_ship_earl_grey_1836.htm (accessed 27th November 2017).

Elder, B, *Blood on The Wattle; Massacres and Maltreatment of Aboriginal Australians since 1788*, New Holland Publishers, Chatswood, 1999.

Green, C, *Out-of-the-Body Experiences*, Hamish Hamilton, London, 1977.

Green, N, *Forrest River Massacres*, Arts Centre Press, Fremantle, 1995.

Greenberg, K J & J L Dratel, eds, *The Torture Papers: The Road to Abu Ghraib*, Cambridge University Press, 2005.

Grof, S, *The Adventure of Self-Discovery. Dimensions of Consciousness and New Perspectives in Psychotherapy and Inner Exploration*, SUNY Press, 1988.

Hager, N, *Secret Power, New Zealand's role in the international spy network*, Nelson, Craig Potton, 1996.

Halse, C, *A Terribly Wild Man*, Allen & Unwin, Crows Nest, 2002.

Haraldsson, E & Osis, K, *At the Hour of Death: A New Look at Evidence for Life After Death*, White Crow Books, 1977, 2012.

Hick, J, *Evil and The God of Love*, Macmillan/Palgrave, London, 1966.

Holden, JM, B Greyson, B & D James, *The Handbook of Near-death Experiences: Thirty Years of Investigation*, Praeger, Santa Barbara, 2009.

Hornadge, B, *The Hidden History of Australia*, ETT Imprint, Watsons Bay, 1997.

James, H, *Stories of the Supernatural*, Barrie and Jenkins. London, 1971.

James, W, *The Varieties of Religious Experience*, (Gifford Lectures, 1901-2), *Collins-Fontana*, London 1960.

Joyce, J, *Portrait of the Artist as a Young Man*, in *The Portable James Joyce*, Penguin Books, Harmondsworth, 1946.

Koestler, A, *The Sleepwalkers: A History of Man's Changing Vision of the Universe*, Penguin, London, 1959.

Kühl, S, *The Nazi Connection: Eugenics, American* [sic] *Racism and German National Socialism*, Oxford University Press, 2002.

Kuhn, T, *The Structure of Scientific Revolutions*, University of Chicago Press, 1962.

Lakoff, G & Johnson, M, *Metaphors We Live By*, University of Chicago Press, 1980.

Lewis, C S, *The Great Divorce*, Geoffrey Bles, London, 1945.

Loos, N, *White Christ Black Cross: The Emergence of a Black Church*, Aboriginal Studies Press, Canberra, 2007.

McInerny, R, *Aquinas and Analogy*, Catholic University of America Press, Washington DC, 1996.

McKenna, B, OSC, with H Liberset, *Miracles do Happen: The Inspiring True Story of the World-Famous Healer and the Reality of Miracles*, Veritas, Dublin, 1987.

Maloney, J, *By Wendouree: Memories 1951-1963*, Ballan: Connor Court, 2010.

Moody, R, *Life after Life*, Bantam Books, New York, 1975.

Moorhead, A, *Gallipoli*, Hamish Hamilton, London, 1956.

Mott, M, *The Seven Mountains of Thomas Merton*, Sheldon, London, 1984.

Murif, JJ, *From Ocean to Ocean: across a continent on a bicycle, an account of a solitary ride from Adelaide to Port Darwin*, George Robertson, Melbourne, 1897.

Murnane, G, *Invisible but Enduring Lilacs*, Giramondo, Melbourne, 2005.

Murnane, G, *Tamarisk Row*, Giramondo, Melbourne, 2008.

Murnane, G, *Something for the Pain*, Text, Melbourne, 2017.

Nichols, P, *The Pope's Divisions; The Roman Catholic Church Today*, Faber, London, 1981.

Northrup, S, *Twelve Years a Slave*. Motion picture [2013] directed by Steve McQueen, screenplay by John Ridley. Adapted from Northrop's memoir: *Twelve Years a Slave*, 1853.

Ortiz, Sr. D, with P Davis, *The Blindfold's Eyes, My Journey from Torture to Truth*, Orbis, Marynoll, 2002.

Ring, K, *Life at Death*. William Morrow and Company, New York, 1980.

Robinson, Bishop G, *Confronting Power and Sex in the Catholic Church; Reclaiming the Spirit of Jesus*, John Garratt, Mulgrave, 2007.

Roy, A, *The Cost of Living*, Modern Library, New York, 1999.

Russell, E F L [Lord Russell of Liverpool], *The Scourge of the Swastika: A History of Nazi War Crimes during World War II*, Cassell, 1954.

Sabom, M B, M.D, *Recollections of Death: A Medical Investigation*, 1981.

Sassoon, S, *Memoirs of an Infantry Officer*. 2nd edition, 1945.

Savage, J, *Fenian Heroes and Martyrs*, Boston, Patrick Donahoe, 1869.

Schumacher, E F, *A Guide to the Perplexed*, Jonathan Cape, London, 1977.

Tacey, D, *Beyond Literal Belief: Religion as Metaphor*, Melbourne, Garratt Publishing, 2015.

Tarnas, R, *The Passion of the Western Mind*, Ballentine, New York, 1991.

Tarnas, Richard, *Cosmos and Psyche: Intimations of a New World View*, Viking, New York, 2006.

Vltchek, A, *Exposing Lies of The Empire*, Badak Merah, Jakarta, 2015.

Von Balthasar, H U, *Dare We hope?* Ignatius Press, San Francisco, 1988.

Wilde, O, *The Picture of Dorian Gray*, . Project Gutenberg Ebook.

Wills, G, *Papal Sin*, Doubleday, New York, 2000.

Wolff, L, *In Flanders Field: The 1917 Campaign*, Viking, New York, 1958.

Zaleski, C, *Otherworld Journeys: Accounts of Near-Death Experiences in Medieval and Modern Times*, http://www.near-death.com/experiences/medieval.html#ref02, (accessed 4/10/2017).

Zinn, H, *A People's History of the United States*, The New Press, New York, 2003.

… and others too numerous to count.

ENDNOTES

Chapter 1
1. Piano Sonata No 11, K 331, *Rondo alla turca*.
2. Eliot, TS, *Burnt Norton*, 1935.

Chapter 2
3. I thank William Golding for explaining the origin of this well-worn metaphor.
4. Leon, E (ed), *Henry James: Stories of the Supernatural*, Barrie and Jenkins, London, 1971, p. 741.
5. Tacey, D, *Beyond Literal Belief*, Mulgrave, Garratt Publishing, 2015, p. xxii.
6. David Tacey argues that religious stories, indeed all religious language, *must* be metaphorical, for it tries to tell of things that transcend the senses and so can never be put directly into words.

Chapter 3
7. F Thompson (1859-1907) *The Mistress of Vision*.
8. Y Ashkar Matta, *No Stone Unturned: a Lebanese-Australian Family Memoir*, Brisbane, Yvonne Ashkar Matta, 2016
9. A translation from the German *apophänie*, which describes a psychiatric disorder.
10. *PGS: Intuition Is Your Personal Guidance System*. pgsthemovie.com
11. From the diary of Fr Peter Lucas, who died in 2016.
12. See Chapter 17, Pilgrimage of Reconciliation.
13. G Murnane, *Invisible but Enduring Lilacs*, Giramondo, Melbourne 2005.

Chapter 4
14. Hopkins, GM (*1844 – 1889*), *God's Grandeur*.
15. Father Gratry in *Souvenirs de ma Jeunesse, 1897*, quoted in W James, *The Varieties of Religious Experience*, Lecture XIX, p. 255.
16. *...formae substantiales, quae secundum se sunt nobis ignotae, innotescunt per accidentia ... Summa Theologiae* I q. 77 a.1 ad 7. See also *Super Sent.*, lib. 1 d. 25 q. 1 a. 1 ad 8, *De Veritate*, q. 10 a. 1 co. and other places.

Chapter 5

17. Matthew 27:55, 61; 28:1; Mark 15:40, 47; 16:1,9; Luke 8:2; 24:10; John 19:25, 20:1-2, 11-18.
18. See Chapter 14, *The Narrow Gate*.
19. Preface to his poem: *The Holocaust*.
20. Unless otherwise stated, all quotes from the Bible are from the New Revised Standard Version.
21. For example see: Gollaher, DL, From Ritual to Science: The Medical Transformation of Circumcision in America, *Journal of Social History*, Volume 28, Number 1: Pages 5-36, Fall 1994, at http://www.cirp.org/library/history/gollaher/ (accessed February 2018)
22. R Tarnas, *The Passion of The Western Mind*, Ballantine, New York, 1991, pp. 425ff. & S Grof, *The Adventure of Self-Discovery; Dimensions of Consciousness and New Perspectives in Psychotherapy and Inner Exploration*, SUNY Press, Albany, 1988.
23. See Ch.14: *The Narrow Gate*.
24. Luke has the identical passage (Luke 9:24) and Matthew (Matt 10:39) uses 'find' rather than 'save'.
25. I first saw this apt phrase in Charles Davis' book *Temptations of Religion*, Hodder & Stoughton, London, 1973.

Chapter 6

26. De Bono, Edward, *I'm Right, You're Wrong*, Penguin Harmondsworth, 2009. Chapter 6 from 27.
27. Frost, Robert (1874-1963) *The Road Less Taken*.
28. Many decades later, when Plenty Rd had become a six-lane highway and Latrobe University had been built, the brick cottage became its creche. The cottage has since been demolished.

Chapter 7

29. Murnane, G, *Tamarisk Row*, Giramondo, Melbourne, 1974.

Chapter 9

30. Some would limit this to 600 – 550 BCE; others would see it as extending through several centuries.
31. Tarnas, R, *Cosmos and Psyche*, Viking, New York, 2006, p. 415.
32. Tarnas, R, *Cosmos and Psyche*, p. 411.
33. Russell, EFL, (Lord Russell of Liverpool), *The Scourge of the Swastika: A History of Nazi War Crimes During World War II*, Cassell, London, 1954.

34 Later published as *The Varieties of Religious Experience*.
35 This and the two following quotes from J Joyce, *Portrait of The Artist as a Young Man*, in *The Portable James Joyce*, Penguin Books, Harmondsworth, 1946. pp. 373 ff.

Chapter 10
36 Wolff, L, *In Flanders Field: The 1917 Campaign*, New York, Viking Press, 1958.
37 Moorhead, A, *Gallipoli*, Hamish Hamilton, London, 1956.
38 Sassoon, S, *Memoirs of an Infantry Officer*, 2nd edition 1945, p. 179.
39 Chapter 7.
40 In *The Great Divorce*.
41 An Ancient Homily for Holy Saturday: *The Divine Office*, E J Dwyer, Sydney, 1974, Vol II, p. 320.
42 Hick, J, *Evil and the God of Love*, Macmillan/Palgrave, Basingstoke, 1966.
43 Boros, l, *The Moment of Truth*, Burns & Oates, London, 1965.
44 Von Balthasar, HU, *Dare We hope?* Ignatius Press, San Francisco, 1988.
45 2 Kgs 23:10, Jer 7:31, 32:35.
46 Luke 15:11-32, as discussed in Ch.8.
47 Chapter 19.

Chapter 11
48 Chapter 7.
49 *The Sacrament of The Present Moment*, attributed to Jean Pierre De Caussade. His authorship of the work has since been questioned.
50 Curiously, St Thomas Aquinas anticipated Murphy by seven centuries, with his *quae deficere possunt, quandoque deficiant.* (Whatever can break down – or fail – will eventually do so.) He expressed this several times, e.g. in *Contra Gentiles*, lib. 3 cap. 71 n. 3 ... *quia quod potest deficere, quandoque deficit* (... for what can fail, at some moment will fail) and in *Summa Theologiae* I, q. 48 a. 2 ad 3 ... *ipsa autem natura rerum hoc habet, ut quae deficere possunt, quandoque deficiant.* It is in the very nature of things that whatever can fail, at some time will fail.
51 Chapter 3.
52 This might not have involved any *predictive* vision, but 'merely' a kind of vision, almost as puzzling – by which the child could 'see' through or around the intervening houses, and know where the bicycle was at the instant he described it.

Chapter 12
53 *Othello, I,1*.

54 Pronounced *a-nít-sha*.
55 'God created humankind in his image, in the image of God he created them; male and female he created them', Genesis 1:27.
56 James, W, *Varieties of Religious Experience*, Lecture VIII.
57 Stevenson, RL, *The Strange Case of Dr. Jekyll and Mr. Hyde*, Thomas Nelson, London, 1886, p. 123.
58 Stevenson, p.126.
59 Wilde, O, *The Picture of Dorian Gray*, Project Gutenberg E-book, p. 128.
60 Baily, L, *Because We Are Bad*, Allen & Unwin, Crows Nest, 2017.
61 Genesis 2:9 and 3:22; Revelation 22:1, 14, 18.
62 See Chapter 18.
63 See Chapter 17.
64 Quoted in Tarnas, R, *Cosmos and Psyche*.
65 Unpublished fragment, reprinted from *The Common Good*, Magazine of The Catholic Worker community, Christchurch, New Zealand, no. 27, Easter 2003.

Chapter 13

66 The name has been changed. The priest in question died when several accusations against him were being investigated. The Dominicans paid this survivor substantial compensation.
67 Ortiz, D and P Davis, *The Blindfold's Eyes; My Journey from Torture to Truth*, Orbis, Marynoll, 2002.
68 Chapter 18.
69 Greenberg KJ and JL Dratel (eds), *The Torture Papers: The Road to Abu Ghraib*, Cambridge University Press, 2005.
70 *KUBARK Manual*, PDF version, p. 51 of 71.
71 *KUBARK Manual*, PDF version, p. 51 of 71.
72 'The Real Terrorist Was Me', Speech by a War Veteran (not named), https://www.youtube.com/watch?v=4Aev7OzSVmI. Downloaded 1st May 2017.
73 Griffin, B, *The Making of a Modern British Soldier*, https://www.youtube.com/watch?v=6tHvtFibhic Accessed 24 May 2017.
74 Reed, F, *I Am A Soldier. I Am Dirt. I Kill* http://wariscrime.com/new/i-am-a-soldier-i-am-dirt/ Accessed 10th May 2017.

Chapter 14

75 Buber, M, *I and Thou*, Scribners, New York, 1971 (1923).
76 Chapter 21.

77 See Chapter 2: Myths are not false stories, as Post-Enlightenment 'scientific' minds tended to think, but are deeply true.
78 See Ch.19.
79 Jones, C, *The Search for Meaning*, ABC-Collins Dove, North Blackburn, 1989.
80 i.e. pounds, in the old Australian currency '… for all the money in the world.'

Chapter 15

81 Thanks to the New Zealand monthly magazine *Tui Motu* for permission to reprint the substance of this story, which appeared as *Reality Wedding*, in Issue no. 102, February 2007, pp. 17-18.

Chapter 16

82 According to Edmund Burke, the Penal Laws were: *a machine of wise and elaborate contrivance, as well fitted for the oppression, impoverishment and degradation of a people, and the debasement in them of human nature itself, as ever proceeded from the perverted ingenuity of man.* John Savage, *Fenian Heroes and Martyrs*, Boston, Patrick Donahoe, 1869, p. 16.
83 Under the command of James Talbert (surgeon William Evans), *Earl Grey* left Cork, Ireland on 27 August 1836, with 297 male convicts. Nine had died *en route* before she arrived in Sydney on 31 December 1836. *Earl Grey, Surgeon's Log: Medical Journal of William Evans,* Ancestry.com. UK, Royal Navy Medical Journals, 1817-1857, The National Archives, Kew.
84 See W Blum's extensive study: *Killing Hope: U.S. Military and C.I.A. Interventions Since World War II.*
85 Chossudovsky, M, Chapter XI: War Propaganda: Fabricating an Outside Enemy, *America's War On Terrorism*, 2nd Edition, Global Research 2005.
86 The massacre occurred at Murdering Gully, on Mt Emu Creek, near Camperdown, Clark, Ian D, *Scars In The Landscape, A Register of Massacre Sites in Western Victoria, 1803-1859,* Australian Institute of Aboriginal and Torres Strait Islander Studies, Canberra, 1995.
87 Kühl, S, *The Nazi Connection: Eugenics, American* [sic] *Racism and German National Socialism,* Oxford University Press, 2002. p. 86.
88 *12 Years a Slave* [2013], adapted from the 1853 memoir *Twelve Years a Slave* by Solomon Northrup, directed by Steve McQueen, screenplay by John Ridley. *In the Name of the Father* [1993]. Directed by Jim Sheridan, screenplay adapted by Terry George and Jim Sheridan from Gerry Conlon's autobiography: *Proved Innocent: The Story of Gerry Conlon of the Guildford Four.*

89   A Roy, *The Cost of Living*, Modern Library, New York, 1999.

Chapter 17

90   Kuhn, T, *The Structure of Scientific Revolutions*, University of Chicago Press, 1962.
91   Attributed to Thich Nhat Hanh.
92   On 26th October 1985, by the Governor-General Sir Ninian Stephen.
93   B Elder, *Blood On The Wattle; Massacres and Maltreatment of Aboriginal Australians since 1788*, New Holland Publishers, London, 1999.
94   Established in front of [old] Parliament House, Canberra on 26 January 1972. Despite several interruptions, it has been there almost continuously since 1992.
95   Murif, JJ, *From Ocean to Ocean*, George Robertson & Co., Melbourne, 1897.
96   Hornadge, B, *The Hidden History Of Australia*, ETT Imprint, Watsons Bay, 1997.
97   Wyndham had had a telegraph link to Perth since 1889, and a radio link since 1914.
98   Halse, C, *A Terribly Wild Man*, Allen and Unwin, Crows Nest, N.S.W., 2002.

Chapter 18

99   More than 2,300 architects and engineers have united to demand a credible explanation for the catastrophic event. The committee investigating 9/11 failed to address the mysterious explosions that firemen and other witnesses heard before the collapse of the buildings; nor the fact that these fell precisely in the manner of planned demolitions. Nor did the committee explain the presence – in all three buildings – of much molten steel, which melts at around 1370 C, whereas burning aircraft fuel and building materials cannot produce temperatures beyond 980 C. See: https://en.wikipedia.org/wiki/Architects_26_Engineers_for_9/11_Truth (accessed 4th April 2017).
100   The half-life of depleted uranium is 4.4 billion years. The rate of infant deformity in Iraq has increased six-fold since the recent wars, and of leukemia threefold. For abundant scientifically backed information on DU, see http://www.cadu.org.uk/cadu/index.html . Accessed 10th March 2018.
101   From the Statement read to the US Consul: '… your country's invasion of Iraq [is] … an immoral and criminal act. The crimes [of] your government … dwarf the many serious crimes of Saddam Hussein. … In 1991 your government specifically targeted basic infrastructure: hospitals, water treatment plants, and electricity stations. Sanctions have denied food and medicine to civilians. By 1997 [they] had claimed around 2 million Iraqi lives.

Your government … is again using Depleted Uranium munitions which are causing an epidemic of cancer and birth defects, and will continue to kill for thousands of years. ... we cannot stand by as your government once more unleashes weapons of mass destruction upon the people of Iraq, and prepares to take direct control of a sovereign state.

Mr Young, by continuing to work for the U.S. government, you are actively supporting imperialism and genocide. We urge you ... to resign in protest at your government's actions.

We have family in Iraq: Dominican sisters and friars communicate with us... In solidarity with those people whose blood you are shedding, and to make present to you the consequences of the USA's war, ... we now make the sign of the cross with our blood on your floor.'

102 Chapter 13.
103 Maloney, John, *By Wendouree: Memories 1951-1963*, Connor Court, Ballan, 2010. p. 139.
104 Mark 11:17, Matthew 21:12-13, Luke 19:45, John 2:14-15.
105 Douglass, James, *Resistance and Contemplation*, Delta, New York, 1973.
106 Nicky Hager, *Secret Power, New Zealand's role in the international spy network*, Nelson, Craig Potton, 1996.
107 Camus, A, The Unbeliever and Christians, *Resistance, Rebellion and Death*, Modern Library, New York, 1960, p. 55.

Chapter 19

108 Keats, J, *Ode to a Nightingale*, 1819.
109 Hamlet III, 1.
110 Sabom, MB M.D, *Recollections of Death: A Medical Investigation*, Corgi, London, 1981.
111 Ring, K and S Cooper, *Mindsight; Near-Death and Out-Of-Body Experiences in the Blind*, iUniverse.com, 2nd ed., 2008.
112 Acts 14:19
113 *Dialogues* 4:37.
114 Book XII, Chapter V.
115 Zaleski, Dr C, *Otherworld Journeys: Accounts of Near-Death Experiences in Medieval and Modern Times*, Ch 2. http://www.near-death.com/experiences/medieval.html#ref02, accessed 4/10/2017.
116 J Brown, *Mediumistic Experiences of John Brown, the Medium of the Rockies*, 1897. Forgotten Books, London, 2018, p. 87-91.
117 J-B Delacour, *Glimpses of the Beyond: The Extraordinary Experiences of People Who Have Crossed the Brink of Death and Returned*, Mass Market Paperback, 1975;

Raymond Moody, *Life After Life*, Bantam Books, New York, 1975.
118 Ring, K, *Life at Death*, William Morrow, New York, 1980.
119 Ring, K, *Life at Death*, p. 83.
120 Haraldsson, E and K Osis, *At the Hour of Death: A New Look at Evidence for Life after Death*, White Crow Books, 1977. Chapter 20 from 121.
121 Murnane, G, *Invisible but Enduring Lilacs*, Giramondo, Melbourne, 2005.
122 October 1962 - December 1965.

Chapter 20

123 e.g. B McKenna OSC, with H Liberset, *Miracles do Happen: The Inspiring True Story of the World-Famous Healer and the Reality of Miracles*, Veritas, Dublin, 1987, p.54. Among many other creditable books and websites on this topic, see, for example, http://documentedhealings.com and http://www.seangeorge.com.au/mystory.php
124 e.g. Matt 13:58
125 Possibly as late as 90CE, although some opt for as early as 70CE.
126 John 4:26; 6:35,42,48,51; 8:12,24, 28; 9:5; 10:7, 9, 11, 14; 11:25; 13:19; 14:6; 15:1, 5; 18:5, 6,8.
127 Quoted in *Cosmic Consciousness*, by RM Bucke and EP Dutton, New York, 1901, p. 293.
128 As Jesus described Mary's choice to listen to him, rather than worry about domestic tasks, in Luke 10:42.
129 Systematic Theology, Volume 2
130 Robinson, Bishop G, *Confronting Power and Sex in the Catholic Church: Reclaiming The Spirit of Jesus*. John Garratt Publishing, Mulgrave, 2007, p. 261.
131 Schumacher, EF, *A Guide to the Perplexed*, Jonathan Cape, London, 1977, p. 28.
132 '... *you have cast all my sins behind your back*'. Isaiah 38:17
133 See Robbie Burns': *Till a' the seas gang dry, my dear, And the rocks melt wi' the sun ...* from *A Red, Red Rose*, 1794.
134 Super Sent., lib. 1 d. 8 q. 2 a. 1 arg. 1. He was borrowing the definition by Boethius (c. 480–524): *aeternitas est interminabilis vitae tota simul et perfecta possessio. Eternity is the endless, total, simultaneous and perfect possession of life.* [*De Consolatione Philosophiae*, Book 5]. Also *Summa Theologiae* I-II, q. 5 a. 2 ad 2. *beatitudo dicitur ... summi boni perfecta possessio sive fruitio. Beatitude is called ... the perfect possession or enjoyment of the highest good.*
135 St Irenaeus, *Adversus Haereses*, book 4:20, 5-7.
136 [The Spirit of truth] *abides with you, and he will be in you* (John 14:17), and: *On that day you will know that I am in my Father, and you in me, and I in you* (John 14:20).

www.ingramcontent.com/pod-product-compliance
Lightning Source LLC
Chambersburg PA
CBHW021850230426
43671CB00006B/331